ENGLISH THOUGHT IN THE NINETEENTH CENTURY

BY THE SAME AUTHOR

A SHORT HISTORY OF OUR RELIGION
DISRAELI AND GLADSTONE
ETC.

ENGLISH THOUGHT IN THE NINETEENTH CENTURY

BY

D. C. SOMERVELL

NEW YORK
LONGMANS, GREEN AND CO.
55 FIFTH AVENUE
1929

PRINTED IN GREAT BRITAIN

PREFACE

THE subject indicated by the title of this book is a large one. The nineteenth century was no longer than any of its predecessors, but it left vastly longer records, and it is hard to deal adequately with an age of which we know so much and might easily, with a little diligence, know so much more. None the less, it seems that an elementary survey of the currents of thought or opinion that stirred English society this way and that in the course of the nineteenth century, might prove useful. Every year thousands of people are making their first serious attempt to study either the history or the literature of that century, or both. Yet 'History' can easily find itself confined to a record of merely political events, disconnected with the everyday life of the nation, and 'Literature' is apt to be treated as a study of isolated works by isolated masters. This book may be regarded indifferently as a 'Companion' to nineteenth-century British history or to nineteenth-century English literature; for its purpose is to supply something of the background, or (to use another metaphor) the connective tissue, of both studies.

It is hardly necessary to say that such a book makes no claim to be either complete or original. Completeness is obviously excluded by its size, but it may be well to indicate at once a class of topics which are excluded by my conception of the subject.

By 'English Thought' I mean thought which exercised a direct influence upon some considerable body of English people, and became an appreciable element in what we call public opinion. Between thought and opinion there is no clear line of division. A current of opinion has its source in the thought of one or more original thinkers, and often the best and easiest way of describing a current of opinion is to go straight to the 'thought' of its original or, at any rate, its best exponents. But such thought, when traced to its source, is often of a highly specialized and technical character, and its specialized and technical aspects never become, in the form of 'opinion', the property of a wide public. For this reason, though I shall often be concerned with the work of technical experts, I shall not attempt to elucidate the technical and specialized aspects of their work Thus, though I shall touch upon the work of specialists in the fields of economics, biological evolution, and theology (for example), my object will be only to expound those simplified and generalized ideas in which their thought penetrated to those sections of the general public which actively supported or opposed them. Again, the work of the very greatest thinkers in certain fields such as metaphysics or mathematical physics, F. H. Bradley and Clerk Maxwell for example, is excluded from my survey, since such thought was too abstruse to make any perceptible mark upon the general public.

As for originality, the number of entirely novel ideas to be found in this book must be very small indeed. My indebtedness to other writers could be traced on almost every page. Of some of these debts I have been conscious as I wrote, and some I have acknowledged; but a complete inventory of my indebtedness, while advertising my modesty, would serve no useful purpose and irritate the reader with unprofitable footnotes. Of some of my debts I am no doubt unconscious, for what one has read becomes part of the furniture of one's own mind.

One debt I will acknowledge at once, that to the late Professor Dicey's *Law and Opinion*; I have, for example, adopted his threefold division of the century, and have followed his guidance on many points. My subject, however, is wider than his; indeed, I know of no book

PREFACE

which attempts as a whole the particular task I have set myself, and that must be the excuse for the book's existence.

I have quoted fairly frequently and at length. Where the quotations are taken from exponents of nineteenth-century opinion, their appearance in the text needs no more apology than the use of illustrations in a book on the history of painting. When, as much more occasionally happens, I have quoted from a modern writer, I have done so because, since the writer in question has said exactly what I wanted, the best course seemed to be to borrow, and to acknowledge the loan of, his own words.

The dates of all the more important characters introduced in the text of the book will be found in the index. They are always significant, for the opinions of a man born in, say, 1780, rest upon one set of data, while the opinions of a man born in 1800 or 1820 or 1850 rest upon quite another.

D. C. S.

January 1929

CONTENTS

CONTENTS

ENGLISH THOUGHT IN THE
NINETEENTH CENTURY

ENGLISH THOUGHT IN THE NINETEENTH CENTURY

CHAPTER I

THE FIRST THIRD OF THE CENTURY

THE progress of opinion is fluid and indefinite; it does not easily lend itself to any system of dates and clear-cut chronological divisions. None the less, some such divisions must be made, and for our purpose the century may be divided into three periods of more or less equal length. The first may be taken to end with the enactment of the Great Reform Bill in 1832, an event almost coincident with the deaths of some of the leading exponents of English thought—Bentham, Scott, Wilberforce, Coleridge, Cobbett. The second period will end somewhere between 1865 and 1874, and a variety of events falling within these nine years might be taken to mark its close—the death of Lord Palmerston, the Second Reform Bill, the establishment of the Trade Union Congress, the discovery of diamonds at Kimberley, the Franco-German War, the Conservative victory of 1874.

Such are the divisions within our century, but where does the century itself begin and end? for the dates 1800 and 1900 are nothing but accidents of our decimal system of numeration. 1800 is a poor date, signifying nothing, and if we are to have an initial date at all it must obviously be 1789, the date of the French Revolution. 1900, on the other hand, is a better date; it marks the conquest of the Boer Republics, which proved to be the climax of the imperialist movement, and it fails by only a few weeks to include the death of Queen Victoria. The death of the Queen was no trifle even in the history of opinion; it brought home to the popular mind the fact that we could no longer regard ourselves as 'Victorians', and were in process of becoming something else: and this realization of the process hastened the process itself. The years between the death of the Queen and the outbreak of the Great War have been called 'the death-agony of the nineteenth century'; but they might equally be called the birth-pangs of the twentieth. The thought of those years, the years dominated by Lloyd George in politics and Shaw and Wells in literature is closely related to the thought of the present day, for the Great War made less of a breach with the past than is sometimes supposed. We shall find ourselves compelled to pursue certain topics beyond the formal end of the nineteenth century, but in general 1789–1901 may be taken as the 'nineteenth century' for the purposes of this book.

I

THE OLD TORY ORTHODOXY

THE Tory party came into power, with the vigorous assistance of George III, in 1783, under the leadership of the younger Pitt. It remained in power, with one interval so brief that it can be ignored, until 1830. As a rule the essentials of public opinion can hardly be deduced from the political label of the party that happens to be enjoying a brief spell of office, but here we have a Tory domination of such abnormal length, so utterly unlike anything that has followed it, that we may quite confidently attribute to it some deep significance. It was, in fact, the political response of the governing classes of England to the French Revolution.

Ever since the English Revolution, the 'Glorious Revolution' of 1688 which overthrew James II, ordinary Englishmen of all classes had been proud of their constitution and their national way of life. The French Revolution quickened their pride in what they possessed, for it added a feeling of genuine alarm lest what they possessed should be taken away from them. For a whole generation the word Jacobin came to hold in the public mind the place occupied between the Armada and the Popish Plot by the word Jesuit, the place occupied to-day in many minds by the word Bolshevik. It symbolized the political and spiritual enemies of England, a class of continental mischief-makers, with disciples—alas!—in our very midst, who would, if they could, defeat us in war, destroy us by revolution, or transform us into their own likeness by propaganda. For over twenty years Pitt and his disciples had fought

3

revolutionary France; for the first fifteen years of the peace they continued to rule England in face of a hopelessly divided opposition.

Pitt himself had been a man with many enlightened ideas of reform, ideas which he rigorously postponed until the war should be over. Some of Pitt's disciples in the last ten years of the period of Tory domination showed themselves ready to accept, without abandoning their essential Toryism, a variety of reforms dictated by proved practical expediency. But such measures were to be taken as exceptions. The fundamental 'Die-hardism' (to use modern jargon) of the rank and file was hardly affected, and its representative was Lord Eldon, who was Lord Chancellor in a succession of Tory Governments from 1801 to 1827. He was, we are told, a very great lawyer, though he was certainly a very slow one. He made the Court of Chancery a byword for the interminable delays of its procedure, and as such it was long afterwards satirized by Dickens in *Bleak House*. Here we are concerned not with his law but his politics. We may look at him through mid-Victorian eyes. Only thirty years after his death such political ideals as those of Lord Eldon had become quite inconceivable. Walter Bagehot, a mid-Victorian Liberal, wrote in 1855: 'As for Lord Eldon, it is the most difficult thing in the world to believe that there ever was such a man. He believed in everything that it is impossible to believe in,—in the danger of Parliamentary reform, in the danger of Catholic emancipation, in the danger of altering the Court of Chancery, in the danger of abolishing capital punishment for trivial thefts, in the danger of making landowners pay their debts.'[1] The Jacobins had altered everything, from God down to the calendar, and had sought to make a clean slate and a fresh start; the response of Lord Eldon and the section of the public he genuinely represented was to hold fast to everything and alter nothing.

It is easy to present Eldonism as something simply absurd,

[1] Bagehot, *Literary Studies*, Vol. I, p. 5.

but to do so is not, perhaps, very helpful. For if there is one thing which, more than another, we must always bear in mind when studying the history of opinion, it is that no opinion ever enjoys prolonged authority over the minds of men outside a lunatic asylum unless there is a certain amount of real good sense behind it. To understand the mind of the old Tory orthodoxy of the first thirty years of the century, we must go behind Eldon and behind Pitt to the great philosopher and prophet of the old Toryism, Edmund Burke. He died in 1797, but his thought dominated the rulers of England for a generation after his death. It is very English thought and its influence is by no means entirely exhausted to-day.

The leading principle of all Burke's thought seems to be distrust of political theory. 'Talk not to me', he seems to say (these are not his own words), 'of schemes which prove by infallible logic how happy man would be if only his affairs were organized on an entirely new pattern. Man is not a logical animal. The present social and political system is no doubt very much open to criticism, but it is the product of past experience. It *works*; who can guarantee as much for any other system that has not yet been tried? Old institutions, like old boots, are more comfortable than new ones, even of the cleverest workmanship, can possibly be, for they have been shaped not by artifice but by use; and, unlike old boots, they can, if properly looked after, be made to last for ever.'

The French Revolution has exalted 'Reason'; Burke rejects 'Reason' as Voltaire and his disciples had understood it, in favour of Tradition, or, as he calls it sometimes, Prescription. 'Truth', he says, 'may be far better than prescription; but as we have scarcely ever that certainty in the one that we have in the other, I would, unless the truth were very evident indeed, hold fast to peace.' Better, in fact, endure those ills we have than fly to others that we know not of. It is more surprising to find Burke exalting against 'Reason' not merely Tradition but Prejudice.

Wise men, he says, 'instead of exploding general prejudices will employ their sagacity to discover the latent wisdom that prevails in them. If they find what they seek, and they seldom fail, they will think it more wise to continue the prejudice, with the reason involved, than to cast away the coat of prejudice and to leave nothing but the naked reason'. Prejudice, in fact, is not necessarily mistaken; it is simply opinion held, for which the holder cannot himself find the reasons; it comes near to what we call instinct, the common sense of the plain man. And Burke always had his eye on the plain man, for whose benefit, after all, laws and constitutions exist. 'Burke was essentially a thinker,' writes a modern Tory, Sir John Fortescue, 'and, moreover, one of those rare thinkers who cannot contemplate human institutions apart from human nature. A political constitution, for instance, was not a code of articles, nor a carefully devised machine. It was rather something alive—a concourse of bustling men with more prejudices than principles and more passion than prejudice; fallible men with their pageantries and pedantries, their intrigues and their jobbery, and all the strange appliances that go to the government of mankind. Vast historical knowledge, with long pondering thereupon, wide sympathy and vivid imagination——'[1] Burke, in fact, was grounded in history. Some people, such as Voltaire and Rousseau, learn from history to despise the past for its crimes and blunders: others, like Burke, learn to respect it for its achievements and to thank it for its heritage.

Such a heritage of the past, such an embodiment of the wholesome prejudices of human nature, Burke found in the old unreformed English constitution, rotten-boroughs and all. He speaks of it in terms of almost superstitious respect. 'Great critics', he says, 'have taught us that if ever we should feel ourselves disposed not to admire those writers and artists whom all the learned had admired, not to follow our own fancies but to study them until we know

[1] Fortescue, *British Statesmen of the Great War*, p. 155.

6

how and what to admire. It is as good a rule, at least, with regard to this admired constitution. We ought to understand it according to our measure; and to venerate where we are not able presently to comprehend.' Let us, at least, refrain from laying rash reforming hands upon it. 'Our constitution stands on a nice equipoise, with steep precipices and deep waters upon all sides of it. In removing it from a dangerous leaning towards one side there may be a risk of oversetting it upon the other.'

A great man is seldom, perhaps never, faithfully represented by those of the next generation who most fervently proclaim themselves his disciples. The living thought of the living man is ossified into a scheme of barren dogmas. We cannot tell what Burke would have been if he had lived through the fifteen years after Waterloo, but we may be fairly certain that he would not have contemplated Lord Eldon with unmixed approval. None the less, he more than any other man was responsible for the Old Tory orthodoxy. The governing class up to 1830 were, it has been said, a surviving fragment of the eighteenth century. In 1830 the Duke of Wellington, the last of the Old Tory Prime Ministers, made a famous statement which ensured his immediate defeat. 'The English (unreformed) Parliament', he said, 'answers all the good purposes of legislation, and this to a greater degree than any legislature has ever answered in any country whatever: *it possesses the full and entire confidence of the people.* I will go further. If at the present moment I had imposed upon me the duty of forming a legislature for any country, and particularly for a country like this, in possession of great property of various descriptions, I do not mean to assert that I could form such a legislature as we possess now, for the nature of man is incapable of reaching such excellence at once, but my great endeavour would be to form some description of legislature which would produce the same results.' This statement is pure Burke, except for one clause which I have placed in italics. That clause might have been spoken by Burke in 1790, for it would

7

have been approximately true; it was notoriously untrue in 1830 and Burke, unlike the Duke, would have refrained from asserting it. The whole speech from which the words are taken is a last defiance from the generation soaked in anti-Jacobinism to a new generation which had forgotten the Jacobins and was pressing forward into new paths.

Thirty thousand copies of Burke's *Reflections on the French Revolution* are said to have been sold between 1790 and 1797, but it is probable that Burke's works were not widely read by ordinary people during the first thirty years of the nineteenth century. But people who did not read Burke certainly read the Waverley Novels. *Waverley* was published in 1814 and took the reading public by storm. From that year onward until Scott's death in the year of the Reform Bill, every year saw the publication of at least one new novel by 'the Great Unknown'. Taken in bulk the publication of the 'Waverleys' was a literary event of enormous magnitude. It would hardly be an exaggeration to say that, for writers and readers alike, Scott raised the novel to its modern position as the biggest department of the literary industry.[1] And Scott transposed into the key of fiction the fundamental doctrines of Burke. It would be interesting to know if he realized the relation of his work to Burke's. He certainly admired Burke, and in a letter written in the last years of his life refers to the 'almost prophetic power' by which Burke awoke the British peoples to the value of their ancient heritage, and the dangers of the doctrines of the French Revolution. But the references to Burke in Scott's Letters and Journals as published in Lockhart's *Life of Scott* are few, and there are none, so far as I know, in the novels themselves. Scott does not force Burke upon his readers; but he expounds

---

[1] Leslie Stephen, writing in about 1880, says that statistics recently published had shown that the Waverley Novels were 'still among the books most frequently bought at railway stations'. We have moved a long way since then.

him none the less effectively though the reader and possibly the writer also was unconscious of the fact.

Before we pursue the subject of the Waverley Novels, we must face a problem that will confront us again and again in the course of this book. How far can novelists and poets, whose object is primarily to delight rather than to instruct, be regarded as creators of public opinion? For example, in the last fifteen years of the nineteenth century there was a marked development of pride in the British Empire and also a continuous output of stories by Rudyard Kipling; in the first fourteen years of the twentieth century there was a marked increase of socialistic opinion and a continuous output of stories by H. G. Wells. There can be no doubt, of course, that the imperialist movement contributed to the formation of the mind of Kipling, and the socialist movement to the formation of the mind of Wells. Both are products and exponents of phases of public opinion. How far, if at all, can they also be regarded as creators of opinion? To put the matter to a crude issue, how many people, if any, voted for the Conservative Imperialist party in 1895 and 1901 because they had read Kipling, and how many, if any, for the Labour party in 1906 and 1910 because they had read Wells? Such questions cannot be very confidently answered, but he would be a bold man who would deny to these popular novelists an influence on the results of general elections. And so also with Scott in the days of the Old Tory supremacy. Lockhart, Scott's biographer, had no doubts upon the subject. 'His services,' he says, 'direct and indirect, towards repressing the revolutionary propensities of his age were vast—far beyond the comprehension of vulgar politicians.' 'Direct and indirect'—we must remember, of course, that Scott (and the same is true of Wells and to some extent of Kipling) had other activities besides those of a purveyor of fiction. He wrote voluminously on history and politics. None the less, it was through his fiction that he gained the attention of the public for his other writings. Many years later

9

Ruskin said that he learnt his Toryism from Scott and Homer, and, since Homer is bracketed with Scott, we may be sure that Ruskin was thinking of Scott's novels and the poems and not of his histories and his journalism.

The Waverley Novels may be roughly divided into two classes. All are historical; but in some, such as *Ivanhoe* and *The Talisman*, the author is seeking to recreate a past that has altogether disappeared; in others, such as *Old Mortality* and *Waverley*, he is reconstructing the recent past of his own country from surviving fragments of that past which had come under his daily personal observation; for Scotland in Scott's boyhood was still full of potential Covenanters and potential Jacobites. There is, I believe, a general agreement to-day that the second group of novels is greatly superior to the first.

The first or mediaeval group belong to a department of nineteenth-century thought of which something will be said on later pages of this book—the renewal of respect for the Middle Ages. Scott's mediaevalism belongs to the crude beginnings of that movement. It is a fancy-dress mediaevalism, and has much in common with the architecture of the 'Gothic' mansion Scott built himself at Abbotsford. The roofs of Abbotsford 'were, in appearance at least, of carved oak, relieved by coats of arms duly blazoned at the intersection of beams, and resting on cornices, to the eye, of the same material, but composed of casts in plaster of Paris, after the foliage, the flowers, the grotesque monsters and dwarfs, and sometimes the beautiful heads of nuns and confessors, on which he had doted from infancy among the cloisters of Melrose Abbey'. This is a long way from Burke, whose 'Tradition' was not that of the Middle Ages but of the Revolution of 1688.

In the second group of novels Scott gives us something much better than fancy dress. The Victorian essayist and biographer, Leslie Stephen, seems to have been the first to indicate the relation between Scott and Burke. 'Burke', he says, 'denounced abstract reasonings in the name of prescription. A traditional order and belief were essential, as he urged, to the well-being of every human society. What Scott did afterwards was precisely to show by concrete instances, most vividly depicted, the value and interest of a natural body of traditions. Take the beggar, for example, Edie Ochiltree, the old "blue gown." Beggars, you say, are a nuisance, and would be sentenced to starvation by Mr. Malthus in the name of an abstract principle of population. But look, says Scott, at the old-fashioned beggar as he really was. He had his place in society; he was the depositary of the legends of the whole country-side: chatting with the lairds, the confidential friend of fishermen, peasants, and farmers: the oracle of all sports and ruler of village feasts; repaying in friendly offices far more than the value of the alms which he took as a right; a respecter of old privileges because he had privileges himself; and ready when the French came to take his part in fighting for the old country. There can be no fear for a country, says Scott, where even the beggar is as ready to take up arms as the noble. Scott was really the first imaginative observer who saw distinctly how the national type of character is the product of past history.'[1]

Such was the Old Toryism in its best and most romantic mood; and to understand anything we must see it at its best. It was not the creed of a callous and cynical oligarchy intent on claiming all the good things of life for the rich and pushing the poor to the wall. It was a faith in a social ideal, an ideal which had perhaps never existed quite as its devotees conceived it, and which was in any case rapidly passing away; a conception of a society in which all might find satisfaction. Burke and Scott rejected with scorn the new doctrines of Equality. A society in which all men

---

[1] Leslie Stephen, *Hours in a Library*, Vol. I, pp. 163–5. I have some-what condensed the passage quoted. The allusion to Malthus will be explained on a later page. Wordsworth's poem *The Old Cumberland Beggar* expresses the same line of thought.

were equal was, they held, a sheer impossibility, and those who preached it were merely making mischief; the upshot would be not equality but merely discontent—envy, hatred, malice, and all uncharitableness in the relationship of the classes. Inequality was destiny. How much better, then, to accept it as such, in the spirit of the old hymn.

> The rich man in his castle,
>   The poor man at his gate,
> God made them high and lowly
>   And ordered their estate.

We are all, in some sense, democrats to-day, and we can all discover and expound the imperfections of the social philosophy of Burke and Scott. But has their criticism of our own philosophy as yet altogether lost its sting?

I have called this book 'English Thought', and most of its first twenty pages have been given to an Irishman and a Scotsman! Though it lies off the main line of our subject, I am tempted to say something about Scott as a Scotsman, for in this capacity also he made an important contribution to both English and Scottish thought.

The typical Englishman of the eighteenth century was, by general consent, Dr. Johnson, and he never tired of pouring ridicule upon the Scots. It is true that much of this ridicule was a device for pulling the leg of Johnson's Scottish friend Boswell, but we cannot doubt that there lay behind it a genuine feeling of dislike for the Scottish people. The most unpopular Prime Minister of the eighteenth century was Lord Bute, and a principal count against him was the fact that he was a Scot. When Wilkes started a newspaper for the purpose of blackguarding George III's favourite, he called it *The North Briton*. Cobbett was a contemporary of Scott, but in many respects he belonged to the eighteenth century: he was certainly a typical Englishman, John Bull incarnate, and he too, if any of his numerous *bêtes noires* came from Scotland, makes the most of it. He disliked the steam-engine, and duly noted, not once nor twice, that James Watt was a Scotsman. He disagreed on most subjects with Henry Brougham; accordingly he mocked him not merely as a man but as a Scotsman. 'Scotch Feelosophers', he tells the members of the London Mechanics Institute, 'are, sometimes, varey cleever men; but, etc.' All this is entirely gone to-day. You may dislike Mr. Gladstone, Lord Balfour, Mr. Ramsay MacDonald, or Sir James Barrie, but it would never occur to you to reproach them with being Scotsmen, though it is still just possible to use Mr. Lloyd George's Welsh nationality for purposes of opprobrium. What has changed the Englishman's idea of the Scotsman? Many things perhaps, but one of them Sir Walter Scott.

We might go further and say that, for Scotsmen themselves Scott created the modern conception of Scotland. Until well on in the eighteenth century the Highlanders and the Lowlanders had been two different and hostile communities. They had taken opposite sides in the great quarrels of the seventeenth century, the Highlanders supporting the King and the Lowland Kirk the parliament. The Highlanders long continued partly Catholic and more largely pagan. One of the most terrible incidents in the history of the Covenant had been when the English viceroy Lauderdale in 1678 let loose 8,000 Highlanders upon the Covenanting rebels of the southwest. When the Highland Jacobites entered Edinburgh in 1745 they entered it as a foreign capital. In the same year an eminent Lowland writer remarked that the Highlanders had not advanced in civilization beyond the stage of the Germans described by Julius Caesar, in that robbery among them was no reproach if committed beyond the border of their own clan. It was only after the Jacobite rebellions that the conquest and civilizing of the Highlands was taken in hand. Boswell's *Journal* of his Tour with Dr. Johnson in the Hebrides gives an interesting description of a society in a state of rapid transformation, with the old clan system already far gone in decay.

Scott was a Lowlander, but he was the first Scotsman to take all Scotland as his province, and by taking it as such he made it spiritually one in the minds of his countrymen. Highland Jacobites and Lowland Covenanters are all fellow-countrymen to him. One of his best novels, *Rob Roy*, tells the story of Robert Macgregor, who was, in fact, one of the last great Highland brigands, carrying on his business on the very frontier of the Lowlands, only thirty miles from Glasgow, and dying in his bed at the age of eighty, in 1736. How he was regarded by his contemporaries in Glasgow we need not pause to inquire. Yet for Scott he is simply a Scottish hero, in whom all Scotsmen, bygones being bygones, may now delight.

And this united Scotland he presented to his English readers. They forgot what little Scottish history they had ever known before they read his novels, and fell in love with the Scotland he presented to them. Scott himself became one of the most popular figures in London. Among his admirers was the Prince Regent himself, and when the Prince became George IV one of his first acts was to confer a knighthood on his friend. It was Scott who arranged George IV's visit to Edinburgh, when the King paid his hosts the compliment of assuming the kilt. It was supposed to be the Scottish national dress! Yet a hundred years before the Highland kilt was, in Lowland estimation, the dress of savages and brigands; its wearer would hardly have been safe in the streets of Edinburgh.

Scott's effusive adulation of the most contemptible of our kings may be set down as an amiable weakness. Biographers regretfully record that he begged to be allowed to keep the glass in which George IV had drunk his health; and are glad to find a happy ending to the sad story; for after he had brought his trophy home, Sir Walter placed it on a chair and then inadvertently sat upon it.

Some twenty years after this royal visit a very different sovereign began to establish her holiday home in the Highlands. It is not a long step in thought from Abbotsford to Balmoral. In uniting the sympathies of the English and Scottish peoples Queen Victoria carried on the good work of Sir Walter.

II

RELIGION AND PHILANTHROPY

THE most conspicuous fact about the state of religion in England in the first third of the nineteenth century was the entire insignificance of the official heads of the Established Church as leaders of religious opinion. That Church was still, as it had been since the Reformation, a heavily privileged institution, and a privileged Church will always be tempted to think more of its privileges than its mission. The State, it was said, paid lipservice to the Church, and the Church in return paid lifeservice to the State. The Church was described as the praying section of the Tory party. This was too sweeping, for there were, even at the end of the eighteenth century, many devoutly religious men in the Church of England, and we shall have something to say of them later, but they were not its official leaders; they were not found upon the episcopal bench. Most of the bishops were politicallyminded Tories for the same reason as the judges in the Ship-money case were royalists; Charles I selected the judges, and since 1783 a long succession of Tory Prime Ministers had selected the bishops. Some of them had served the party by political activity, some had been the college tutors of eminent statesmen, some were the near relations of noblemen who owned rotten boroughs. In 1815 eleven of the bishops were of noble family, and ten had been the tutors or schoolmasters of a prince, a duke, or a Cabinet minister.

It has been said that those who rise to leadership within the sheepfold generally exhibit some of the qualities of the wolf; but the metaphor is too harsh to describe the mild and decorous rapacity of such a one as Manners-Sutton, Archbishop of Canterbury from 1805 to 1828, who distributed sixteen livings as well as a variety of cathedral appointments among seven members of his family. Another notable bishop of the age was Watson of Llandaff, whose long life extended to the year after the battle of Waterloo. As a very young man he became Professor of Chemistry at Cambridge, and subsequently Professor of Divinity. His knowledge of both subjects was slight, but his services to chemistry were the greater, for he secured an endowment for the professorial chair. In 1782 the Whigs made him Bishop of Llandaff for his political services in opposing the American war. Shortly afterwards he appointed a deputy to undertake the duties of his professorship, and withdrew to a country house on the shores of Windermere. He visited his diocese once in the thirty-four years of his episcopate; he held sixteen livings; he was deservedly popular among his north-country neighbours, and desired to be remembered as an improver of land and a planter of trees. The possibility of such a career throws a flood of light on one department of English thought at the beginning of the nineteenth century.

Among the rank and file of the parish clergy it would be easy to select examples of notorious impropriety, but such examples would not be typical. The ordinary parish clergymen were entirely respectable, and, as such, respected; they were kindly men who, though they did not do much, did all that was expected of them. Like the House of Lords in *Iolanthe* they 'did nothing in particular and did it very well'. They have left no mark, unless a negative one, on history, but their type is embalmed in current fiction. Jane Austen's novels were written in the first twenty years of the century, and contain a variety of parsons; some of these young men are amiable and some ridiculous, but none of them has anything to do with religion, nor does the novelist ever notice this deficiency in them. The poet Crabbe describes exactly the same type in a more critical spirit:

> Fiddling and fishing were his arts; at times
> He altered sermons and he aimed at rhymes;
> And his fair friends, not yet intent on cards,
> Oft he amused with riddles and charades.

The Church and the Army were the obvious alternatives for young men of good social position and no particular gifts or inclinations. During the French wars the army naturally took first place; after 1815 there was a marked increase of candidates for ordination, but its causes were economic rather than religious. Too many of the new ordinands were of the type of the half-pay officer who figures in an old forgotten book of reminiscences; he secured a substantial benefice 'by which he was enabled to launch again into the gay world'.

This half-pay officer presumably did not reside in the parish from which he drew his stipend. Many others, who drew stipends from several parishes, obviously could not reside in all of them, and sometimes found it less invidious and more convenient to reside in none. Porteus, Bishop of London, in his charge to his clergy in 1790 deals earnestly, if gently, with these evils. 'There are, indeed,' he writes, 'two impediments to constant residence which cannot easily be surmounted; the first is (what unfortunately prevails in some parts of this diocese) unwholesomeness of situation; the other is the possession of a second benefice. Yet even these will not justify a *total and perpetual* absence from your cures. The unhealthiness of many places is of late years by various improvements greatly abated, and there are now few so circumstanced as not to admit of residence there in *some* part of the year without any danger to the constitution.'

Such was the old 'High Church' at the beginning of the nineteenth century. It had nothing in common with the ardent and Anglo-Catholic High Church party which has long since supplanted it. It has been called the 'high and dry' Church; it detested nothing so much as 'enthusiasm', a term used to include all Methodists and nearly all missionaries. The most notable exponent of its religious philosophy was Archdeacon Paley, whose *Evidences of Christianity* were published in 1794, and continued to be set as a compulsory subject to all candidates for admission to Cambridge University down to 1921. It is an admirable text-book, a model of lucidity, logic, and well-marshalled evidence, proving the truth of the dogmas of the Church with the quiet efficiency of a mathematical demonstration. 'To take it to pieces and put it together again, noting how each part fits into the whole, is an education in reasoning and in the art of advocacy.' In fact, it assumes that the truths of religion are akin to scientific truths and defensible by the same methods. Long afterwards, Charles Darwin, the evolutionist, found it the one item of his Cambridge curriculum that was of the least use to him. 'I did not at that time', he says, 'trouble myself about Paley's premises; and, taking these on trust, I was charmed and convinced by the long line of argumentation.'

Paley defines virtue as 'doing good to mankind in obedience to the will of God, and for the sake of everlasting salvation'. An old hymn at once suggests itself:

> Whatever, Lord, we lend to Thee
> Repaid a thousandfold will be;
> Then gladly will we give to Thee . . .

Christ, says Paley, was quite unlike the Methodists; he was *not* marked by 'impassioned devotion'; there was no enthusiasm, no 'heat in his piety'; on the contrary, he was a person of 'moderation and soundness of judgement'. Paley was a good writer and a good man; his work is much less absurd than a brief description, spiced with comical quotations, would suggest; but it is not, in the modern sense, a religious work at all.

Typical in a very different way of the old Church was
Sydney Smith, a man of the generation after Paley's; he
lived till 1845. Sydney Smith was a man of exuberant
energy, intelligence and humour, who went into the Church
because his father would not support him while he read
for the Bar. He was one of the founders of that great
Whig journal, *The Edinburgh Review*, and contributed
to it regularly for a quarter of a century, so that, when
the Whigs came into power in 1830, most people expected
that he would be made a bishop. He also did his duty
manfully for many years as the rector of a remote Yorkshire village. There are many worse parish priests to-day
than this vigorous journalist who, finding himself saddled
with parochial duties, proceeded to constitute himself
'village parson, village doctor, village comforter, village
magistrate'. In London he was reckoned an attractive
preacher, for in fact the man himself was attractive, but
his published sermons are the weakest part of his writings.
And the reason is plain. 'The Methodists', he says somewhere, 'are always desirous of making men more religious
than it is possible, from the constitution of human nature,
to make them.' True perhaps; but all real leaders of
real religions have been such because they have devoted
their lives to this impossibility. Sydney Smith's sermons,
says Bagehot, 'are sensible and well-intentioned, but they
have the defect of his school. With misdirected energy
these divines have laboured after a plain religion: they
have forgotten that religion has its essence in awe, its charm
in infinity, its sanction in dread; that its dominion is an
inexplicable dominion; that mystery is its power'.[1]

There was indeed abroad in England a religion very
different from that of Archbishop Manners-Sutton, Bishop
Watson, Archdeacon Paley, and Sydney Smith, a religion
which they all condemned as 'enthusiastic', a religion
which, among the poor, had established the new sects of
the Methodists, and within the Church had created the

[1] Bagehot, *Literary Studies*, Vol. I, p. 39.

already powerful party of the Evangelicals. It had many roots far back in the middle of the eighteenth century, but its most powerful apostle had been John Wesley, who died in extreme old age, after half a century of incredible activity, in the first years of the French Revolution.

The eighteenth century was, in the main, an age of clear and limited views, an age of placid optimism. Yet that quiet century was disturbed by two prophets, two experts in the arts of rousing violent and sustained emotions, two men who exercised an influence upon thought which long survived their deaths and is not exhausted to-day—Wesley and Rousseau. It is impossible to imagine two men more unalike—Rousseau, the disreputable dreamer of dreams, writing in a garret books which kindled strange fancies of human perfectibility; Wesley, respectable to the point of unattractiveness, one of the few major prophets of religion who was also a consummate man of business, yet gifted so markedly with the power of kindling in his hearers the sense of sin and the awfulness of divine judgement, that, when he preached, the days of the early Church seemed come again, and sinners exhibited contrition by foaming at the mouth, speaking with tongues, and falling down in convulsions. Rousseau came as near as any literary man can come to being the author of a political and social revolution; Wesley, by his influence on the religious revival in which his was the most important single figure, did more than anything or anyone else to inoculate the English people against the virus of revolutionism. Rousseau impelled a whole society to seek to establish by violence a Kingdom of heaven upon earth; Methodism and Evangelicalism set men's hearts upon a Kingdom which was not of this world, and certainly could not be established by violence.

When the nineteenth century opens, the grosser transports of religious ecstasy, which signalized the early triumphs of the new preachers, were happily over and done with.

The new movement had firmly established itself both in the Church and in the world of Nonconformity. The new emotional Nonconformity of the Methodist chapel gave a colour of idealism and romance to the lives of thousands of the victims of the power loom and the steam engine in the new industrial slums of the north. Within the Church of England Evangelicalism was not yet the party in power, but it was already a formidable and active opposition. Its leaders were not clergy, for it was a type of religion which did not exalt its priesthood. The leaders of Evangelicalism were wealthy laymen. Some of the most conspicuous, William Wilberforce for example, lived in pleasant mansions upon the edge of Clapham Common, and Sydney Smith gave them the nickname of 'the Clapham Sect'.

Wilberforce was a man of considerable wealth and remarkable charm of personality. His election to parliament for the County of Yorkshire in 1784 was a singular personal triumph in a constituency normally reserved for members of great county families. As the ablest of the intimate friends of Pitt he had before him, if he had chosen to avail himself of it, a political career of assured brilliance. But accident brought him into contact with Isaac Milner, an Evangelical divine, and immediately afterwards with Thomas Clarkson, a Quaker who was about to devote himself to the cause of the abolition of the Slave trade. From 1787 onwards Wilberforce abandoned the ambitions of an ordinary politician; he remained in parliament as an independent member, devoted to the advocacy of great causes outside party politics. He wrote religious books, promoted religious education and foreign missions, and was one of the founders of an Association for the Better Observance of Sunday. From the beginning of the century until his death in 1833 he was certainly one of the most influential men in the country.

Associated with Wilberforce in many of his activities was Hannah More. In the early part of her long life she made a reputation as a witty and charming young lady in the circle of Johnson, Garrick, and Reynolds, but she too, like Wilberforce, and at about the same date, was claimed by the Evangelical movement. Henceforth she devoted herself to the religious education of destitute children and to the writing of enormous quantities of religious tales and tracts. These had a very large circulation. One of the best known, *The Shepherd of Salisbury Plain*, was translated into several foreign languages, and was sufficiently familiar in the middle of the nineteenth century to be satirized by Thackeray as *The Washerwoman of Hampstead Heath*. Cobbett, who included the Evangelicals among the many objects of his detestation, calls her an 'Old Bishop in petticoats', and offers as a sample of her tracts 'Hannah More's account of the celestial death of an Evangelical mouse who, *though starving*, would not touch the master's cheese and bacon'.

Another important figure in the movement was Charles Simeon, Fellow of King's College, Cambridge. He made his university a nursing mother of the Evangelicals of the next generation, and it is said that, far on into the nineteenth century, undergraduates of marked piety were known in Cambridge as 'Sims'. One of Gladstone's earliest recollections was being taken as a child of five to Cambridge to see Mr. Simeon. Gladstone's father was a wealthy Evangelical merchant in Liverpool; he had paid for the building of a new church, and went to Cambridge to get Simeon's advice as to the choice of its minister. It would be easy, but unnecessary, to mention many more conspicuous Evangelicals. A characteristic example would be Thomas Bowdler, who produced an edition of Shakespeare in which 'those words and expressions are omitted which cannot with propriety be read aloud in a family'. His name has contributed a verb to the English Dictionary, a verb now generally used with contemptuous intentions; yet there seems to be no doubt that Bowdler did more than many of the subtlest critics to promote the popular reading of Shakespeare.

He also produced an expurgated edition of Gibbon's *Decline and Fall of the Roman Empire,* which strikes one as a less useful enterprise.

The Evangelicals accounted nothing of importance in comparison with the human soul and its eternal welfare, yet they were eminently practical, and their energies were poured into all kinds of constructive organizations. Among these was the Bible Society, founded in 1804 'to encourage a wider dispersion of the Holy Scriptures'. It was notable as a completely undenominational society; indeed, the new religious movement, developing simultaneously within and without the Church, was a powerful solvent of the barriers between the Establishment and the Nonconformists. Wesley, in fact, had virtually founded a Nonconformist sect without ever ceasing to be himself a clergyman of the Church of England. The immediate occasion of the foundation of the Bible Society was a shortage of Bibles in the Welsh language, for the Society for the Promotion of Christian Knowledge, whose duty it was to produce Welsh Bibles, had fallen into a comatose condition. From Welsh the Bible Society proceeded to all the languages of the world, and became an indispensable ally of the various Missionary Societies. It need hardly be said that the Bible Society is still very much alive to-day. It so happens that I am writing these words on the day after its hundred and twenty-fourth annual meeting, presided over and addressed by Mr. Baldwin. No Cabinet minister attended the first meeting, though the Bishop of London 'after reasonable delay' gave his approval to the scheme and suggested Lord Teignmouth as its President. Lord Teignmouth is described as 'a fervent Christian and an excellent man of business'; as such he was a typical leader of the Evangelicals.

The Bible Society accidentally inspired one of the minor classics of English literature, George Borrow's *The Bible in Spain,* recording the adventures of the author as a travelling agent of the Society in that country during the years 1835–39. Nothing illustrates the wide ramifications of the

Evangelical movement more pointedly than the fact that Borrow, the Bohemian eccentric and associate of gipsies and bruisers, should for a time have taken service in its ranks.

Borrow's principal motive as a distributor of Bibles seems to have been hostility to Popery. 'No popery' had been a potent watchword ever since the Reformation. The Gordon riots of 1780 witnessed its hold on the lowest classes of the London population, and Evangelicalism had strengthened the prejudice. When Louis XVIII left England on a Sunday to resume his throne in France, Wilberforce recorded in his Diary: 'What ingratitude, and without temptation! What folly! Is this the Roman Catholic religion? O shame, shame.' Catholic Emancipation was carried through parliament, it is true, in 1829, but solely to avert a rebellion in Ireland, and the text of the Act reveals the popular prejudice against the persons who were to benefit by it in a curious clause (never enforced) banishing all Jesuits from the British Isles. Walter Scott was not an Evangelical; his religion was entirely conventional, and he might have been expected to sympathize with those who still cherished the Church of the Middle Ages. He did indeed support the Emancipation Act, but for the most singular of reasons. He held that, since we had repealed or ceased to enforce all the rest of the anti-Roman statutes, it was mere pedantry to retain the exclusion from the franchise. He wished that the old statutes had been maintained and enforced with rigour; if they had, he thought we should have long since succeeded in 'smothering the Old Lady of Babylon'.

This age of Tory domination was marked by a number of humanitarian reforms, the abolition of the slave trade in 1806, the partial abolition of the pillory in 1816, the abolition of flogging as a punishment for women in 1820, the first attempt to illegalize various forms of cruelty to animals, e.g., bull-baiting and cock-fighting, in 1822, the prohibition of the use of spring-guns and man-traps to protect property against poachers in 1827. Evangelicals supported all these movements, but it would be a mistake to suppose that they were their only supporters, or that the new religion produced the new philanthropy and humanitarianism. Humanitarianism was a distinctive feature of the age that produced the French Revolution as well as the Evangelical movement. Voltaire was, in his different way, as great a philanthropist as Wilberforce, and the Evangelicals found themselves working as allies with the followers of Bentham and James Mill, who set reason above emotion and regarded religious revelation as moonshine.

Yet it would be true to say that in England the whole movement towards philanthropy was coloured with religious sentiment. The first Factory Act of 1802, a very modest and practically inoperative measure, contained a clause enacting that all pauper apprentices should every Sunday for the space of one hour 'be instructed and examined in the principles of the Christian religion by a qualified person'. After securing the abolition of the slave trade, the energies of Wilberforce and his friends were directed towards the abolition of slavery itself throughout the British colonies. Their first small success was to secure the enactment of an experimental code restricting slavery in the island of Trinidad, and one of its features was that slaves were not to be employed by their owners on Sunday.

The establishment of what came to be called 'the English Sunday' was one of the features of the generation we are concerned with. 'The red skies of Paris', wrote Mr. and Mrs. Hammond in *The Town Labourer*, 'sobered the English Sunday and filled the English churches. *The Annual Register* for 1798 remarks: "It was a wonder to the lower orders throughout all parts of England to see the avenues of the churches filled with carriages. This novel appearance prompted the simple country people to inquire what was the matter." In the merry days of Archbishop Cornwallis (1768–83) the Church had set the fashion in Sunday parties. After the Revolution these dissipations ceased and Sunday became much stricter. Wilberforce, in whose mind the most tremendous problems the nation had ever faced did not over-shadow the danger that Parliament reassembling on a Monday might cause many members to travel to London on a Sunday, persuaded Perceval, who spent a good deal of his time in tracing parallels between Napoleon and the Antichrist of the Book of Revelation, to alter the day of meeting to a Tuesday. "House nobly put off by Perceval," he records in his diary.' [1]

A quotation from Mr. and Mrs. Hammond is a reminder that the Evangelicals both in their own day and in ours, have been subjected to a great deal of bitterly ironical criticism by philanthropists of a different school of thought. In the days of the first steam factories and the last enclosures of the commons the rural and the urban poor of England were being driven wholesale, if not into greater poverty, at least into new, unfamiliar and consequently less endurable conditions of destitution; and the Evangelicals stood by with a tract or a Bible, or a request for a subscription to promote the emancipation of the negro in the tropical plantations. Wilberforce had been one of the most prominent advocates of the Combination Acts of 1799 and 1800 which made Trade Unions illegal conspiracies. Hardened men of the world who professed no philanthropy incurred much less hatred from the champions of the cause of the English working classes than these pious and active men who seemed to refuse to social evils at home the attention they lavished upon remote and exotic enterprises.

If we were to regard the Evangelicals as professional philanthropists who took all human suffering and social injustice as their province, we should be forced to convict them, as many writers have done, of inconsistency, or hypocrisy, or stupidity, or all three. But it is unfair so to regard them. Social problems were not their *métier*. They attacked the slave trade and slavery not as social evils but as abominations in the eye of God. The slave had an immortal soul, and that was their concern. It was monstrous that

[1] Hammond, *The Town Labourer*, p. 235.

the possessor of an immortal soul should be himself the property of one of his fellow creatures. As for poverty, they did not find it recorded in the Gospels that poverty was an evil to be cured; much the reverse, in fact. 'The poor are always with you . . . Blessed are the poor.' Oppression and injustice they would not have defended, but they were not acutely aware of the existence of oppression and injustice; nor should we be in haste to accuse them of wilful blindness, for the facts and statistics of social conditions were not easily accessible then as they are to-day. It was left to a later generation of Evangelicals, under the leadership of Lord Shaftesbury, to extend the championship of their philanthropy to the cause of 'wage-slaves' at home.

In his *Practical View of the System of Christianity* Wilberforce explains that 'the more lowly path of the poor has been allotted them by the hand of God; that it is their part faithfully to discharge its duties and contentedly to bear its inconveniences; that the present state of things is very short; that the objects about which worldly men conflict so eagerly are not worth the contest; that the peace of mind which Religion offers indiscriminately to all ranks affords more true satisfaction than all the expensive pleasures that are beyond the poor man's reach; that in this view the poor have the advantage; that if their superiors enjoy more abundant comforts, they are also exposed to many temptations from which the inferior classes are happily exempted,' etc.

This is more than Tory: it is mediaeval. One may say, if one likes, that it would have come with better grace from a St. Francis who himself adopted the poverty he praised, than from one who, like Wilberforce, retained enough, after all his extensive charities, to live very comfortably as an English gentleman. The question whether one can, without hypocrisy, remain a rich man and preach the valuelessness of riches is somewhat akin to the question, recently raised in *The Times*, whether one can, without hypocrisy, be a wealthy socialist. The answer to both questions is, I believe, in the affirmative.

Enough has been said to show that in treating of the Evangelical movement we have not yet gone outside the old Tory orthodoxy. That frontier, however, we must now proceed to cross.

VARIETIES OF RADICALISM

THE French Revolution, while giving an extra lease of life to our eighteenth-century Toryism, was not without its English admirers. There were indeed plenty of revolutionary Radicals in England before the fall of the Bastille. London mobs had shouted for 'Wilkes and Liberty' twenty years before Paris mobs shouted for 'Liberty, Equality, and Fraternity'. Burke's *Reflections on the French Revolution* (1790) is, in form, a reply to the published Discourse of Dr. Price, an eminent and elderly Nonconformist, who greeted the birth of a new world with an eloquent *Nunc Dimittis*. 'I have lived', says Dr. Price, 'to see thirty millions of people indignant and resolute, spurning at slavery and demanding liberty with an irresistible voice, their king led in triumph, and an arbitrary monarch surrendering himself to his subjects. And now, methinks, I see the ardour for liberty catching and spreading, a general amendment beginning in human affairs; the dominion of kings changed for the dominion of laws, and the dominion of priests giving way to the dominion of reason and conscience.' As Burke answered Price, so was he answered in turn by Thomas Paine's *Rights of Man*, which sold more copies than Burke's pamphlet, though it was banned by the government, and its sale and possession made criminal offences. Probably no single book did as much as Paine's *Rights of Man* to kindle the first sparks of what is now called class-consciousness in what is now called the proletariat.

'Tom' Paine—the familiarity was bred by a contempt which it has survived—was an admirable man. Born of poor Quaker parents, he ran away to sea; returned to land and earned his living by making stays; studied astronomy; became successively an exciseman, a schoolmaster, and a tobacconist; emigrated to America on the eve of the rebellion of the colonies; published a pamphlet called *Commonsense* which was far the most effective statement of the American case for a 'fight to the finish'; gave all his literary profits to the American war-chest, and held high office under the first Congress, only returning to England after the peace when American affairs seemed to be relapsing into an uninteresting quietude. When the Bastille fell, Lafayette sent its key to Paine for presentation to the American Republic which had blazed in advance of France the pathway to freedom.

The Rights of Man is, unlike Burke's *Reflections*, somewhat unreadable to-day. Burke, even when he is most desperately wrong, provokes trains of interesting reflection; Paine is often so desperately right that we tend to forget his date and to dismiss him as a dealer in platitudes. But the pamphlet contains a remarkable assemblage of twentieth-century political programmes. Government is conceived as the instrument of the social conscience. The naval Powers are to co-operate in a limitation of armaments and the revenue saved is to be expended on social reforms. There is to be free education, maternity benefit, old age pensions, and a graduated income tax. Mixed up with, and of course quite inconsistent with, this 'socialism' there is an anticipation of philosophic anarchism. Government is an evil, 'the badge of our lost innocence: the palaces of kings are built on the ruins of the bowers of paradise.'

The latter part of Paine's career was worthy of its beginnings. Crossing to France to escape prosecution, he was convicted of high treason in his absence. He became a member of the French Convention, supported the abolition of monarchy, became suspect on account of his chivalrous opposition to the execution of the King, escaped the guillotine by a mere accident, and ultimately returned to America. But while in France he had attacked the Christian religion in his *Age of Reason*, and he found himself an outcast in the Republic which, unlike that of France, had shown no inclination to serve its God as it had served its king. It is recorded that Paine was denied a place on an American stage-coach, lest an offended Deity should strike the coach with lightning. He died as he had lived, a rebel, and not the only rebel of the nineteenth century who spoiled the credit of a flourishing political unorthodoxy by adding religious unorthodoxy to his programme.

While Paine was skirting the guillotine, William Godwin, another English 'Jacobin', more ponderous and pretentious, published at the price of three guineas an extensive treatise on *Political Justice*. Pitt did not interfere with Godwin; he thought the price of the book sufficient for the security of the Government. Godwin is one of those philosophical gas-bags who has been so long pricked and deflated, that it has become extremely difficult to reconstruct him in the dimensions he assumed in the eyes of his contemporaries. Yet Hazlitt, who was a good judge, says: 'No one was more talked of, more looked up to, more sought after, and wherever liberty, truth, justice was the theme, his name was not far off.' Burke was 'a flashy sophist' compared with him. To-day he is remembered only as the source of the philosophic dreamland of Shelley, who married his daughter. Godwin's purpose was to prove that the perfectibility of human society is an achievement well within the reach of man, if only he will focus his 'will' upon it. Men's characters, he says, depend on their external circumstances, but their external circumstances depend upon their voluntary actions. Their voluntary actions depend upon their opinions. 'Opinion' is the crux of the matter. Change opinion by the application of 'reason', and everything else will follow of itself. Godwin speaks of 'reason' as if it were a rather recent invention, in which he himself had made the latest improvements.[1]

[1] Godwin's book has long been out of print, and is seldom found in ordinary libraries. Nearly all modern references to it have been contemptuous, but there is a careful and sympathetic analysis in Mr.

Godwin's book provoked a rejoinder much more interesting and enduringly important than itself, namely *An Essay on the Principle of Population as it affects the future improvement of society, with remarks on the speculations of Mr. Godwin, M. Condorcet and other writers*, by T. R. Malthus. Malthus was a thoughtful young man who suffered from the exuberant Godwinian radicalism of his father. Godwin had suggested that 'reason' could and would extinguish the passion of the sexes. Malthus turned his attention to the consideration of the physical bases of life, food and the mouths to be fed, and his *Essay* proved to be a douche of cold water sufficient to extinguish the 'Perfectibility' school of thought in England. Every species, he said, and man among them, tends to increase in a geometrical ratio; the production of food, though it may be increased, does not tend to increase with this rapidity. Population therefore is kept in check by scarcity. Actually, since man so mismanages his affairs, the maximum suppply of food is not secured, and the normal checks on population are 'vice and misery . . . famine, disease and war'. In a second edition of his *Essay* Malthus added that population could also be restricted by voluntary 'moral restraint'.

Widespread controversy arose over the argument of the *Essay*, and we shall come across the influence of Malthus again in a later part of this book. His name became an abomination to those who were trying to raise the lot of the poor, for he seemed to prove that the lot of the poor could not be raised; they would always increase their numbers until their economic condition reached the starvation level. True, Malthus had, in his second edition, maintained that this need not be so, but when a treatise becomes the subject of violent popular controversy it almost always happens the finer points at issue are forgotten. Cobbett, the champion of the poor, hated Malthus as much as he hated Wilberforce.

Brailsford's *Shelley, Godwin, and their Circle*. After reading the analysis the reader may judge for himself whether Godwin deserves as much sympathy as Mr. Brailsford gives him.

He even wrote a little anti-Malthusian stage-play which was to have been performed at Tonbridge; but it was forbidden by the magistrates. The following in dialogue occurs in the play:

Thimble. So, young woman, you are going to be married, I understand.
Betsy. Yes, sir.
Thimble. How old are you?
Betsy. Eighteen, sir.
Thimble. Eighteen ! No wonder the country is ruined. How many children had your mother?
Betsy. Seventeen, sir.
Thimble. Monstrous. Nothing can save the country but plague, pestilence, and famine, and sudden death. Government ought to import a shipload of arsenic. But, young woman, can't you impose on yourself *moral restraint* for ten or a dozen years?
Betsy. Pray, what is that, sir?
Thimble. Can't you keep single till you are about thirty years old?
Betsy. Thirty years old, sir! (*stifling a laugh.*) [1]

Pitt, on the other hand, was an early convert to the doctrines of the *Essay.* By suggesting to superficial readers the comfortable notion that all social reform was fundamentally futile because its benefits would be cancelled by the operation of the iron law of population, Malthus achieved a result he neither intended nor desired. The old Toryism which opposed reforms because it regarded them as 'the thin end of the wedge', or revolution by instalments, had now another line of argument. They could not only argue that the reforms would lead to too much; they could also argue that they would lead to nothing at all. The growing body of the doctrines of political economy, to which Malthus himself, in later works, made important contributions,

[1] Quoted from G. D. H. Cole's *William Cobbett.*

pointed in the same direction. Every price was settled, said the economists, by the laws of supply and demand, and wages were after all only prices of labour. The 'laws of political economy' were represented as ordinances of providence, with which the man-made laws of the statute book could no more interfere than Canute with the incoming tide. In fact the orthodoxy of the economists was ultimately to replace the orthodoxy of the old Toryism as the bugbear of the social reformers.

The later history of 'Malthusianism' does not belong to this chapter, but a word may be spared for it before passing on. The middle of the nineteenth century witnessed an unabated increase of population accompanied by a marked and steady rise in the general level of prosperity. Vast food-producing areas of distant continents were brought under cultivation, and the development of steam navigation brought their produce easily and abundantly to the ever-growing millions at home. The 'iron law' seemed to be disproved, and Malthus's work was discredited and well-nigh forgotten. In actual fact, his law was not disproved, though its operation had been postponed. As the new lands, e.g. the prairie of the United States, filled up and began to consume more and more of the food they produced, the possibility of the pressure of population upon the means of subsistence was again envisaged. The rate of increase of population in all highly civilized countries has markedly declined, and the name and theory of Malthus have once again, in our own age, become common topics of discussion.

William Cobbett, like Paine and Godwin, failed to found a stable and enduring school of thought in England, but that is the only feature he has in common with them. While they dreamed of an unrealized future, Cobbett fought the last battle of a vanishing past. He was a rebel, no doubt, but he began as a Tory, and in sense he never ceased to be one. The essence of all his writing is compressed into the words: 'We want nothing new; we want only what our forefathers enjoyed, what the stock-jobbers and the place-

hunters and the Pittites and the cotton lords have taken away.'
His life of seventy-three years (1762–1835) covered the
whole of the period conventionally assigned to the agrarian
revolution which enclosed the old common lands and abolished
the old communal agriculture, and the industrial revolution
which created the new industry of the power loom and the
steam engine. He saw a new society supplanting the
'Merrie England' of the past; he hated it; he fought everything and everybody associated with it. He failed, and in
a sense he marks an end, but he has, as will be seen, affinities
with the anti-commercial prophets of the Victorian age,
with Disraeli, Carlyle, Ruskin, and William Morris. He
left no great book, but it is generally agreed that he was almost
a great writer. 'With two or three qualities more', said Sir
Henry Bulwer, 'he would have been a great man; as it was
he made a great noise.'

Certainly few Englishmen who died a hundred years ago
stir as much affection to-day, and the reasons for this are fairly
obvious. He is a writer at once amusing and autobiograph-
ical; he survives not as the author of his works but as their
hero, a Johnson who was his own Boswell, and the cause
for which he fought and lost, the cause of the country against
the town, is one that does not become less attractive with the
lapse of time.

Cobbett was the son of Surrey peasants. He ran away
from home at the age of thirteen in order to see Kew Gar-
dens, and spent part of the scanty pocket-money intended
for his dinner on a copy of Swift's *Tale of a Tub*—this, he
says, was the beginning of his taste for good writing. Later
on he enlisted in the army, and, after a very creditable career
as a non-commissioned officer, left it in order to expose financial corruption among his senior officers. Failing in this
characteristically disinterested and difficult undertaking, he
emigrated to the United States. Here he found what was
to be his life's work, the career of a fighting journalist. The
French Revolution had begun, and the newly united States
were carried away with a sentimental enthusiasm for the

Revolution, which readily expressed itself in hatred and contempt for England. Cobbett, always a patriot, took up the cudgels for King George and all his works and trounced the theory and practice of democracy in the style, at once good-humoured and uncompromising, which made him in time the greatest popular journalist who ever wielded the resources of the English language. When he returned to England in 1800, he received and accepted flattering offers of journalistic activity in support of the Tory Government. But from the first he lacked docility; at present he was too Tory for the Tories, and he had his windows broken for refusing to illuminate them in celebration of the faint-hearted Treaty of Amiens. He was often in later years to bring himself within measurable distance of imprisonment for seditious libel, but it is eminently characteristic that the only occasion on which he was actually convicted and sent to prison was for a ferocious attack on the Government for employing German mercenaries to flog English militiamen.

In 1802 Cobbett started his *Weekly Political Register*, which continued to be the principal repository of his message until the day of his death. But by 1804 the character of that message had begun to change. Hitherto Cobbett had stood for a personified and abstract England against her foreign enemies; now that he had an opportunity of looking more closely into the matter, he began to discriminate between the English people and their official and unofficial rulers. The most formidable enemy was in fact the enemy within the gate. For the last thirty years of his life he is driving home with ever-increasing emphasis his lesson that the people of England were letting themselves be made the victims of a combination of politicians, borough-owners, fund-holders,[1] squire-magistrates, canting parsons, profiteering manufacturers, and pseudo-scientific Malthusians.

Thus his enemies were many, and he fought them all at once. In 1817 after the suspension of the Habeas Corpus

[1] I.e. investors in the Napoleonic war loans, which seemed as crushing a burden to our ancestors as our own war debt seems to us.

Act he executed a temporary retreat to America, and it is amusing to find how his impressions of that country had been transformed. 'And then,' he writes in his message to the *Register*, 'to see a free country for once, and to see every labourer with plenty to eat and drink! Think of *that*! And never to see the hang-dog face of a tax-gatherer. Think of *that*! No Alien Acts here. No long-sworded and whiskered Captains. No judges escorted from town to town and sitting under a guard of dragoons. No packed juries of tenants. No Crosses. No Bolton Fletchers. No hangings and rippings up. No Castleses and Olivers. No Stewarts and Perries. No Cannings, Liverpools, Castlereaghs, Eldons, Ellenboroughs, and Sidmouths. No Bankers. No Squeaking Wynnes. No Wilberforces. Think of *that*! No Wilberforces!' Cobbett was nothing if not personal, and the climax is well managed. We begin with magistrates, and proceed, through discredited police-spies, Cabinet ministers, and others to the great philanthropist who stood in Cobbett's mind for the very quintessence of pharisaism and hypocrisy.

Yet Cobbett was never a revolutionist. While Godwin preached the transformation of everything into its opposite in the monotone of a second-rate university don, Cobbett employed the manners of a literary pugilist in the cause of moderation. In this, once again, he is utterly English—and the term English may here be taken to exclude the Irish, the Scotch and the Welsh. It has been said that there might have been an English Revolution in the years after Waterloo but for the fact that the one Englishman who could have led a revolution threw the whole of his weight into the alternative scale of Reform. Cobbett rebukes the Luddites, for example, and explains to them the usefulness of machinery in terms that might have satisfied an economist. Of all the authors of the movement that drove the Whig party into the enactment of the Reform Bill of 1832 Cobbett was by far the most influential.

After the Bill was carried, Cobbett was elected for Oldham,

and the polite society of Westminster gazed with curiosity at the vigorous old countryman whose 'stuff' they had read for as long as many of them could remember, but whose face most of them had never seen.   In his dust-coloured coat and drab breeches with gaiters he looked the very embodiment of John Bull; and what he looked he was.   He was quite at his ease, and enjoyed a certain popularity, but when invited by the Speaker to an official dinner he refused, saying that 'he was not accustomed to the society of gentlemen'. The Speaker 'took this for a sign of humility', we are told; it was a sign of pride.   Cobbett was in a very real sense the first Labour member; but the Labour he stood for was the age-long labour of the countryside, whereas modern Labour represents something quite different.

Among Cobbett's books are a *History of the Protestant Reformation*.   It was written in support of Catholic Emancipation, which Cobbett somewhat unexpectedly championed —perhaps because it was the religious opposite of Evangelicalism.   The book is a popularized and exaggerated version of the story as told by the great Roman Catholic historian, Lingard, but it gives Cobbett a place with Scott among the pioneers of that revival of appreciation of the Middle Ages which was to be one of the features of the nineteenth century. Cobbett realized a fact which we associate with post-Victorian historians, Mr. Belloc, Mr. Chesterton, and Mr. Tawney, that the Reformation, by its transference of wealth from public corporations to private individuals, was the beginning of modern capitalism in the most general sense of that term.

But it is as the author of the travel-journals collected under the title of *Rural Rides* that Cobbett has secured his place in literature.   He belongs to the school of naturelovers, but not to the school of Wordsworth and the romantic poets.   They love wild nature as a means of escape from civilized society.   Cobbett is depressed even by such moderate exhibitions of the wild as Hindhead and Bagshot Heath; his 'Nature' is the paradise of honest and wholesome work, a Nature not outside society, but its proper basis, the 'chief nourisher of life's feast'. Its population is for him the real England; they are 'the commons'. He protests against the new habit of calling them 'the lower orders', a vile phrase he was wont to hear from the lips of 'tax-devourers, bankers, brewers, monopolists of every sort, but also from their clerks, from the very shopkeepers and waiters, and from the very fribbles stuck up behind the counter to do the business that ought to be done by a girl'. Brewers figure in this list. Cobbett was a doughty champion of beer, and defended it against 'tea-slops', but the beer should be brewed by the peasant from his own barley, as was done of yore. He is for everything old. We find him trying to revive the old country sports and country dancing.

Such was Cobbett. In his own day he was, as it were, a monster unto many, though a hero to many more, and thirty years after his death an able man, Sir Henry Bulwer,[1] who had sat with him in Parliament, wrote an interesting and in some ways a friendly biographical sketch of his career, which none the less misses the whole point of it. Bulwer can discover in Cobbett's career no 'cause' at all; he regards it as an entirely undirected exhibition of pugnacity and self-assertion; its motive he finds to be partly mischief, partly vanity, and partly mere 'sport'. No doubt Cobbett was pre-eminently a sportsman in every sense of that Protean term, but the fact that Bulwer saw no more in him is a significant measure of the failure of Cobbett's cause; the cause of anti-industrialism had failed so completely as to have become incredible as the mainspring of the activities of anyone more practical than a poet or an art-critic.

Yet Bulwer makes one very good point. Cobbett, he says, 'represented journalism, and fought the fight of journalism, against authority when it was still a doubt which would gain the day. Let us not forget the blind and uncalculating intolerance with which the law struggled against opinion from 1809 to 1822. Writers during this period

[1] Brother of the novelist Bulwer Lytton.

were transported, imprisoned, and fined, without limit or conscience. The contest was one of life and death. Amidst the general din of the battle, but high above all shouts more confused, was heard Cobbett's bold, bitter, scornful voice, cheering on the small but determined band which defied tyranny without employing force. The failure of the last prosecution against the *Register* was the general failure of prosecutions against the Press, and may be said to have closed a contest in which government lost power every time that it made victims.' [1]

The same writer has a striking account of the impression produced in the polite world by Cobbett's death. 'His death struck people with surprise, for few could remember the commencement of his course, and there had seemed in it no middle and no decline. He left a gap in the public mind which no one else could fill or attempt to fill, for his loss was not merely that of a man but that of a habit—of a dose of strong drink which all of us had been taking for years, and which it was impossible for anyone again to concoct so strongly, so strangely, and with so much spice and flavour, or with such a variety of ingredients. And there was this peculiarity in the general regret—it extended to all persons. Whatever a man's talents, whatever a man's opinions, he sought the *Register* on the day of its appearance with eagerness, read it with amusement, partly, perhaps, if De la Rochefoucault is right, because, whatever his party, he was sure to see his friends abused, but partly also because he was certain to find, amidst a great many fictions and an abundance of impudence, some felicitous nickname, some excellent piece of practical-looking argument, some capital expressions, and very often some marvellously fine writing.' [2] Cobbett, in fact, had failed as a prophet; he had succeeded as a public entertainment.

The intellectual leadership of the rising generation fell neither to Godwin with his sky-scraping audacities, nor to

[1] Bulwer, *Historical Characters*, Vol. II, p. 192.
[2] *Ibid.*, Vol. II, p. 178.

Cobbett with his immense journalistic vogue, but to an industrious and pedestrian writer who, despising alike abstract rights and historic traditions, set himself to devise practical legal remedies for concrete wrongs. The future lay with Benthamism.

Jeremy Bentham was born in 1748, the son of a wealthy London solicitor, and died in 1832. His father early detected his remarkable abilities and hoped that he had begotten a future Lord Chancellor, but before young Bentham was out of his 'teens' he was so much impressed by the defects of the legal system he was set to study, that he determined to devote his life to the alteration rather than the administration of the law. Long afterwards he related how a single phrase inspired his whole career. In a pamphlet by the scientist and radical Priestley, he came across the words 'the greatest happiness of the greatest number'. 'It was by that pamphlet and that phrase of it', he wrote, 'that my principles on the subject of morality, public and private, were determined. At the sight of it, I cried out as it were in an inward ecstasy, like Archimedes on the discovery of the fundamental principle of hydrostatics, *Eureka*.' Again: '"Have I", he asked, "a *genius* for anything? What can I produce?" That was the first inquiry he made of himself. Then came another. "What of all earthly pursuits is the most important?" "Legislation" was the answer Helvetius gave. "Have I a genius for legislation?" Again and again was the question put to himself. He turned it over in his thoughts; he sought every symptom he could discover in his natural disposition or acquired habits. "And have I indeed a genius for legislation?" I gave myself the answer, fearfully and tremblingly, "Yes." ' [1]

Once his course was chosen Bentham set to work, and methodically he worked away for sixty years, issuing the gospel of Benthamism in a long succession of pamphlets and

[1] Quoted by Dicey, *Law and Opinion*, p. 132, from Sir R. K. Wilson's *History of Modern English Law*. Helvetius was a French philosopher of the age of Voltaire and Rousseau.

treatises. Ample wealth set him free from all cares except that for 'the greatest happiness of the greatest number'. His first publication (1776) [1] was a *Fragment on Government* which was an attack on Blackstone, whose eulogy of English Law in his *Commentaries on the Laws of England* was the orthodoxy of the day. But Bentham was never content merely to criticize. He had compared himself with Archimedes, and he was first and foremost an inventor. He set himself to devise improvements in the clumsy machine of English law much as James Watt set himself to improve the rudimentary steam-engine. One of the oddest of his notions was a design for a model prison. In his enthusiasm for this device his habitual common sense deserted him. He foresaw 'morals reformed, health preserved, industry invigorated, instruction diffused, public burdens lightened, economy seated as it were upon a rock, the Gordian knot of the Poor Law not cut but untied—all by a simple idea in architecture'. The Panopticon, as the prison was called, must not be taken as typical either of the wisdom or of the fruitfulness of Bentham's ideas; but it illustrates an important aspect of them all. Its virtue resides in a commonplace material expedient, an 'idea in architecture'. What a reassuring alternative to the proposals of the French and English 'Jacobins'! Bentham among the 'Jacobins' is like an engineer in a community smitten by an epidemic, who, while one agitator recommends the overthrow of the government and another advocates a reform of the religion, quietly suggests a repair of the drains. Bentham's message was in a sense uninspiring, but for that very reason it secured the confidence of a generation which had observed in France the appalling results of an overdose of political inspiration.

[1] The early date of the beginning of Bentham's activities should be observed; long before the French Revolution, or the first publications of Paine, Godwin, or Cobbett. His movement was the first as well as ultimately the most successful of the 'oppositions' to the Old Tory 'Orthodoxy'. John Stuart Mill writes, 'Who, before Bentham, dared to speak disrespectfully of the British Constitution and English Law?'

Bentham held that the aim of life is happiness. Here he was not far from Paley, who held that virtue is 'doing good . . . for the sake of everlasting happiness'. The moral philosophy of the Archdeacon was in fact 'other-worldly Benthamism', and conversely Benthamism has been defined as 'Paley minus Hell-fire'. This happiness-philosophy, utilitarianism as it was called, makes an immediate appeal to the superficial kind of thinking that is called common-sense; if our aim in life is not 'happiness', what is it? As a matter of fact utilitarianism is not only objectionable on moral grounds but also unsound as an intellectual system. If happiness, or 'pleasure', is the sole ultimate object of life, then one sort of happiness is as good as another. Bentham, who was fond of deriding what modern jargon calls 'high-brows', once said that if the amount of pleasure secured was equal, then push-pin [1] was as good as poetry. We all know that many people get more pleasure from 'push-pin' than from poetry, and we also firmly believe that it is not *good* to do so. We know that the happiness of a thoroughly selfish life is often equal in quantity and intensity to the happiness of an unselfish life, and we justify the latter by saying that it is a superior quality of happiness. But if there are 'higher' and 'lower' *kinds* of happiness, then there is a standard involved which is not happiness at all, i.e. goodness; in fact, goodness cannot be explained simply as that which produces happiness. Thus to the sphere of pure thought Benthamism contributed nothing of any value. But Bentham was not primarily a philosopher, he was an exponent of practical legislative reforms, and in the sphere of practical legislation 'happiness' is a good rough-and-ready test. We are often told that people cannot be made good by Act of Parliament. That may or may not be true. There are also limits to the extent to which good laws can make them happy. But there are hardly any limits to the extent to which bad laws can make them unhappy, and here Bentham found the sphere of his

---

[1] A form of gambling then popular in taverns.

labours. He emphatically disagreed with the sentiment of Dr. Johnson's couplet:

> Of all the ills that human hearts endure
> How small the part that laws can cause or cure.

To the principle that legislation ought to aim at the greatest happiness of the greatest number Bentham added a second principle, much more disputable, that every man is the best judge of his own interests. Hence the policy that came to be called *laissez-faire*, i.e., leave people free to act for themselves and they will act for the best. In the latter part of the nineteenth century, after the Benthamite movement had done its work and spent its force, *laissez-faire* became a term of abuse in the vocabulary of socialism. It indicated the refusal of government, from indifference or timidity, to intervene, in the cause of social justice, to protect the weak against the strong. *Laissez-faire* in fact came to be equivalent to the policy attributed to Lord Melbourne: 'Why not let it alone?' But for the early Benthamites *laissez-faire* was a war-cry—a call to strenuous political action. At every turn the laws of England placed obstacles in the way of the individual's reasonable and profitable freedom of action. To Burke and Blackstone the laws of England were a garment which must be presumed to fit because it had so long and so becomingly been worn; to Bentham they were a 'strait-waistcoat' which hampered at every turn the free development of a growing society. He was uninterested in their past history; he asked only, what is their use to-day?

In a real sense Benthamism had begun before Bentham, when Adam Smith published his *Wealth of Nations* (1776), and dismissed as injurious almost the whole of the system of elaborate regulation that centuries of commercial policy had built up for the supposed benefit of trade. Bentham held that every man was the best judge of his own happiness just as Smith held that every trader was the best judge of his own profit. He attacked all laws interfering with the free expression of religious belief, or political opinion; he attacked all laws that maintained the privileges of privileged classes, whether the privileges of the Church of England, or the political sinecures (stoutly defended by Burke) which constituted in fact a system of unemployment doles and old-age pensions for the rich and influential. He advocated the legalizing of trade unions, the abolition of the savage punishments of the criminal law, the reform of the parliamentary franchise and—most important of all, perhaps, though the subject is a technical one—the reform of the actual procedure and methods of the courts of law. No one now reads his books, but he was one of those to whom might be applied the Latin tag, *Si monumentum quaeris, circumspice*. Practically all the legislative reforms of the middle period of the nineteenth century, a period of unprecedented activity in legislation, can be traced to his influence. Those reforms which ran counter to Benthamite doctrine, such as the Factory Acts, encountered a strenuous opposition, which would be inexplicable but for the fact that Bentham had convinced a whole generation of politicians that men ought to be left alone to pursue their own interests according to their own lights.

The man himself was an amiable, unworldly, and unimpressive recluse. Though he despised poetry, which played tricks with the plain sense of words and substituted sentiment for argument, he delighted in music, in flowers, and in animal pets. Tame mice fed out of his hand, and a tame cat followed him about the roads of his country home;—indeed it is odd that the co-existence of cats and mice in the same establishment did not suggest to him one of the important limitations of the doctrine of *laissez-faire*. He knew little of the world of men, and imagined them to be much more reasonable than they really were; the maxim that every society has the government it deserves was no part of his optimistic philosophy. He is described as 'boyish' to the end of his days, and his philosophy, if unsweetened by sentiment, was richly seasoned with humour. His most notable joke was the clause in his will directing that his body should be dissected in the presence of his friends and his skeleton presented to London University, where (I hope) it is still to be seen, 'seated in a chair, with a wax mask, and wearing Bentham's wonted dress'. Bentham rejected with scorn the doctrine of the immortality of the soul, but he could at least illustrate the utility of the skeleton.

For long he worked with but little recognition, quietly convinced that his labours would not ultimately be wasted. It was only after the nineteenth century had opened that disciples, the first generation of the Benthamites, began to gather round him. The first and principal link between Bentham and the Benthamites was James Mill.

James Mill was the son of a Scottish shoemaker. He availed himself to the full of the admirable 'educational ladder' of his native country and, having reached the top of it, found, like other able and ambitious Scots, that the best thing in Scotland was the road to England.[1] He wrote a remarkable *History of India*, which brought him employment in the office of the East India Company. In character he was as unlike Bentham as possible. He was one of those Scots (Carlyle was another) who, while abandoning the religious doctrines of the Kirk, retained all its austere and narrow Puritanism. He regarded the production of pleasure as the exclusive test of right and wrong, but pleasure itself, said his son, 'he had scarcely any belief in. He was not insensible to pleasures, but he deemed very few of them worth the price which, at least in the present state of society, must be paid for them. He thought human life a poor thing at best, after the freshness of youth and of unsatisfied curiosity had gone by.' He combined in fact the Epicurean philosophy with the Stoic character—not an impossible nor

---

[1] 'Mr. Ogilvie observed that Scotland had a great many noble wild prospects. *Johnson.* I believe, sir, you have a great many. But, sir, let me tell you, the noblest prospect which a Scotchman ever sees is the high road that leads him to England!' (Boswell's *Life of Johnson*, Everyman ed., Vol. I, p. 264.)

an uncommon combination. Epicurus himself, the Greek exponent of the pleasure-philosophy, whose very name has given us, in 'epicure', an alternative term for *gourmet*, was by some accounts a teetotaller and a vegetarian who regarded cheese as one of the principal luxuries of diet.

Political theorists who devote their lives to books, and rub shoulders but little with ordinary people, are very apt to imagine that ordinary people are more like political theorists than is in fact the case. James Mill seems to have fallen a victim to this error, and in a greater or less degree it is characteristic of all the early Benthamites. They believed that a wide extension of the suffrage, coupled with complete freedom of political discussion, would almost automatically produce legislative wisdom. Long afterwards James Mill's son, John Stuart Mill, wrote : 'So complete was my father's reliance on the influence of reason over the minds of mankind, whenever it is allowed to reach them, that he felt as if all would be gained if the whole population were to be taught to read, if all sorts of opinions were allowed to be addressed to them by word and in writing, and if by means of the suffrage they could nominate a legislature to give effect to the opinions they adopted. Accordingly a democratic suffrage was the principal article of his political creed, not on the grounds of liberty, rights of man, or any of the phrases, more or less significant, by which, up to that time, democracy had usually been defended, but as the most essential of securities for good government.' [1]

To-day we find it very easy to criticize optimism of this kind. John Stuart Mill himself was, as we shall see in the next chapter, one of the most formidable critics of this faith in the wisdom of the majority. Again, in a generation later than John Stuart Mill's, modern psychology has taught us that reason plays but a small part in forming most people's opinions and a still smaller part in deciding their conduct. To-day it is less necessary to criticize the faith of the early Benthamites in popular wisdom than to remind ourselves

[1] J. S. Mill, *Autobiography*, p. 105.

that it was, after all, up to a point, entirely justified. The extension of the franchise and the development of free discussion, through education and cheap newspapers and books, did in fact promote an immense amount of indisputable legislative improvement.

Among the Benthamites who were engaged in practical politics during the first third of the nineteenth century far the most conspicuous and many-sided was Henry Brougham, Cobbett's 'Scotch feelosopher'. He was not of the inner circle of the disciples, but for that reason he illustrates all the better the widely ramifying character of the Benthamite movement; for though the central core of Benthamism was the teaching of Bentham, there was a wider Benthamism which was rapidly becoming, as the Tory domination drew to a close, the spirit of the new age.

Brougham was born in Edinburgh in 1778 and from the age of twenty-four onwards contributed voluminously to the *Edinburgh Review*, founded by Sydney Smith and Jeffrey as an organ of political liberalism in the most general sense of the term. He wrote fluently on science, politics, literature, and the fine arts. Restless ambition carried him to London and he was called to the Bar in 1808. He entered the House of Commons in 1810, and rapidly became the most talkative as well as the most formidable member of the Opposition. He secured the abolition of the Orders in Council which, intended to injure Napoleon, more obviously injured British trade. He thrust himself to the forefront of the agitation which secured the abolition of the Income Tax on the close of the war. We will not pursue in detail his parliamentary activities; suffice it to say that he took all law-reform as his province, delivering in 1828, to a somewhat empty House of Commons, a speech of six hours duration on the subject. Canning once said of him: 'The honourable and learned gentleman having in the course of his parliamentary life supported or proposed almost every species of innovation which could be practised on the constitution, it was not very easy for members to do anything without seeming to borrow from him. Break away in what direction they would, whether to the right or to the left, it was all alike. "Oh," said the honourable gentleman, "I was there before you: you would not have thought of that if I had not given you the hint." '

Brougham had all the qualifications of a political agitator—a ready sympathy with every kind of grievance, unflagging industry, and an almost unparalleled capacity for the rapid assimilation and lucid exposition of complicated subjects. He had also another quality, for an account of which I will rely on the evidence of one who had often seen him in the flesh. 'There is a last quality', said Bagehot, 'which is difficult to describe in the language of books, but which Lord Brougham excels in, and which perhaps has been of more value to him than all his other qualities put together. In the speech of ordinary men it is called "devil". What it is one can hardly express in a single sentence. It is most easily explained by physiognomy. There is a glare in some men's eyes which seems to say, "Beware, I am dangerous; *noli me tangere*." Lord Brougham's face has this. A mischievous excitability is the most obvious expression of it. If he were a horse, nobody would buy him; with that eye, no one could answer for his temper. Such men are often not really resolute, but they are not pleasant to be near in a difficulty. They have an aggressive eagerness which is formidable. They would kick against the pricks sooner than not kick at all. A little of the demon is excellent for an agitator.' [1]

It was characteristically Benthamic in Brougham that he made a speciality of education. He was one of the leading spirits in the movement which established the unsectarian or 'godless' University College in London. He promoted Mechanics' Institutes for working men, and founded the Society for the Diffusion of Useful Knowledge, writing its first pamphlet on *The Pleasures and Advantages of Science*. It was here most particularly that Cobbett fell foul of him.

[1] Bagehot, *Biographical Studies*, p. 69.

Brougham believed intensely in all that the Industrial Revolution stood for. He thought that working men only needed to be intellectually convinced of its benefits and they would become the docile agents of the new capitalism. They would learn the truths of political economy, and cease to kick against the iron pricks of the laws of supply and demand. Cobbett warned the members of the London Mechanics' Institute—'If you suffer yourselves to be put into the crucibles of Scotch "feelosophers", you will make but a poor figure when you come out.' But Brougham expected from popular education even greater things than industrial docility. He expected what Americans now call the out-lawry of war. 'Let the soldier be abroad if he will,' said Brougham in 1828; 'he can do nothing in this age. There is another personage, a personage less imposing in the eyes of some, perhaps insignificant. The schoolmaster is abroad, and I trust him, armed with his primer, against the soldier in full military array.' Exactly a hundred years have passed since these words were spoken, and now that we know the schoolmaster better we have moderated our expectations of him. We have discovered that the teaching of schoolmasters is likely to reflect rather than to correct the shortcomings of the society to which they belong. After all, they are but men.

By 1830, when the Whigs took office, Brougham had secured an extraordinary reputation. He was absolutely indispensable to the new Government, but they distrusted him. Lord Althorp, who was to lead the Commons, refused to have him as a fellow-minister in the same House, so he was sent to the Lords as Lord Chancellor. 'If only he knew a little law,' said some one, 'he would know a little of everything.' His fame was that of an agitator; men doubted, said Bagehot, 'if he would sit *still* on the Woolsack.' [1] In fact the fruitful part of his career was nearly over. Lord

[1] In actual fact, he used to *spit* from the Woolsack upon the carpet of the House of Lords. This was, no doubt, a less remarkable performance in 1830 than it would be to-day: but it was not altogether liked.

Brougham and Vaux, to give him his new title, played an active part in pushing his colleagues through the prolonged crises of the Reform Bill, but after that it was, as a wit said, 'Vaux *et praeterea nihil*'. Melbourne got rid of him in 1834, and the long remainder of his career was an anti-climax marred by deplorable eccentricities. One of his eccentricities was to announce his own death in order to read his own obituary notices. But the later career of Lord Brougham, whether we regard it as a tragedy or a farce, has nothing to do with the development of the Benthamite movement.

The Benthamites were ardent reformers, but their philo-sophy of reform, if judged by any modern standard, was confined within somewhat narrow limits. It excluded practically everything which passes under the title of social reform to-day. Indeed, on social questions the Benthamites were generally found, as the century advanced, to be the allies of the old propertied classes, and as such they became the butt of the social reformers of the Victorian epoch, as will appear in the next chapter. If the Tories believed in the defence of property the Benthamites believed in the freedom of competition, and from the standpoint of the reformer who desired the State to step in and improve the position of the poor, if necessary at the expense of the rich, the Benthamite was as bad as the Tory. Perhaps he was worse, for he defended his opposition to social reform with more plausible arguments.

The negative aspects of Benthamism are imposingly dis-played in the work of the 'classical school' of political econo-mists. British political economy had its roots in Adam Smith and not in Bentham, for Bentham was no economist. But James Mill was an economist as well as a Benthamite, and the classical economic doctrines may be regarded as a specialized and technical application of the Benthamite principle of individualism or *laissez-faire*. Specialized and technical studies are necessarily outside the scope of this book, and it is impossible to give more than a brief and very inadequate idea of the work of the economists. What follows will, however, suffice to demonstrate the limitations of *laissez-faire* as a principle of reform.

Adam Smith was a professor of moral philosophy in the University of Glasgow, who was attracted to economic studies by his intercourse with the merchants of that rapidly developing city. When the Act of Union with Scotland first threw open to Scotsmen the trade of the English colonies Glasgow was no more than a village; by the end of the century it was on its way to becoming what it now is, the second largest city in Great Britain. Smith's *Wealth of Nations* (1776) is a very great, but also a very miscellaneous book. Much of it is exceedingly practical and concrete, the work of an observer of facts, a student of history. But if Smith enjoyed the talk of merchants he was also, by profession, a philosopher. His work is a mixture of induction and deduction. He is inductive when he is basing conclusions upon the facts of his observation; he is deductive when his conclusions come to him from the axioms of his philosophy. Of these axioms the most important is that Nature has made provision for social well-being by arranging that every man shall seek to better his own condition. The individual aims only at his private gain, but is 'led by an invisible hand' to promote the public good. State-made laws, by interfering with this principle in the name of public interest, defeat their own end; when restraints of trade are taken away 'the obvious and simple system of natural liberty establishes itself of its own accord'. Smith was the author, so far as British thought is concerned, of the theory of free trade. The practical side of his mind suggested many objections and limitations to the application of the theory, and if he had returned to life in the middle of the nineteenth century, he would have viewed the completeness of the triumph of his theory with astonishment and possibly with disapproval.

Economic science, however, was to develop, for the next seventy years, along abstract and deductive rather than along practical and inductive lines. That was the golden age of the now discredited, perhaps unduly discredited, 'classical' economists. Seventy years after the publication of *The Wealth of Nations*, John Stuart Mill published (1847) his *Principles of Political Economy*.[1] That book, though professedly a treatise of the classical school, marks the beginning of a return to the concrete and the practical. Henceforth economists would not be content to simplify their problems by assuming the existence of a society of 'economic men' led by 'invisible hands'; they would attempt to grapple with the complexities of human society as it exists. They would no longer seek to achieve the neat finality of mathematical demonstrations. They would realize that their studies were a department of politics rather than an abstract science.

At the same time, it would be a great mistake to suppose that the ingenious analyses of the classical economists were so much labour wasted. They were, along their own lines, genuine men of science, and the history of all the sciences shows that research is not wasted even when it has led a particular researcher to a wrong conclusion. All the economic schools of a later day have made use of the work of the classical school.

Of the many acute and pertinacious theorists who devoted their energies to economic theory in the first thirty years of the nineteenth century, the best remembered to-day is David Ricardo. He was a Jew by birth and a stockbroker by profession. His best work was done in connexion with problems of currency, banking, and taxation, where an understanding of social conditions is not, perhaps, of primary importance. His principal contribution, however, to the general thought of his age was his theory of wages. Wages, he seemed to have proved, were determined mechanically and inevitably by laws of supply and demand. All attempts, by philanthropic or revolutionary agitation, to raise the standard of wages were bound to fail, and, by dislocating trade, to leave things worse than before. There is a 'wages

---

[1] Discussed in the next chapter, p. 95.

fund'. Nothing can add to it. It can only be divided, and the more the competitors for it, the smaller will be the shares.

The 'wages fund' theory was not abandoned by a professional and accepted economist until 1869, by John Stuart Mill in a revised edition of his *Principles*. The actual fact, of course, is that there is no such limited 'fund'. Human ingenuity and industry can increase the production of wealth, and its distribution is governed by no such iron laws as those formulated by the deductive reasoning of the classical economists.

The reputation of the classical economists has suffered from the fact that their works were extremely hard to understand, and few made much effort to understand them. Biblical texts have been quoted, out of their context, to justify all kinds of absurd or immoral purposes. In the same way, fragments of economic argument from Smith, Ricardo, and others were taken out of their context by hasty and prejudiced politicians, and used to justify, in the House of Commons, policies which the economists themselves would have derided and condemned. A notion arose that the economists were worshippers of Mammon, and hired scribes of the rich. On the contrary, many of them were humane and kindly persons who supported, in their non-professional capacity, the very reforms which their writings were supposed to condemn. The Scotsman McCulloch seems to have been popularly regarded as a particularly pitiless economist, on the strength of his professional works, yet he was very ready to support Lord Shaftesbury in his agitation to secure a legal interference with 'economic laws' in the interests of women and children in factories. None the less the fact remains that the work of the classical economists reached the general public and the ordinary politician in the form of a gospel of economic fatalism. It discouraged social reform, for social reform could always be represented as interference with economic liberty; and to a generation which was achieving religious liberty by the abolition of tests, and political liberty by the extension of the suffrage, economic liberty appeared to be equally desirable.

It would be hard to say whether public opinion is more influenced by books or by newspapers. Indeed the question is an unprofitable one, for much of the influence of books upon public opinion is indirect and comes through the channel of newspapers. For journalists have little time to think, and are therefore the retailers of the thought of others.

The foundation of our modern Press was the discovery that newspapers could sell their space for purposes of advertisement. Newspaper advertising began in about 1770, and from that date onwards the future of newspapers was assured. The French Revolution and Napoleon furnished, for over twenty years, a continuous supply of interesting news. Interesting news multiplies readers, and increased circulation means increased power and independence. In 1795 the editor of *The Times* agreed to support the Government in return for a pension of £600. His successor in 1815 would have laughed at such a proposal, not because he was more virtuous but because he had acquired larger ideas. The Prime Minister, Lord Liverpool, discussed the changed conditions somewhat peevishly with his colleague, Lord Castlereagh. 'No paper of any character, and consequently an established sale', he writes, 'will accept money from Government; and indeed their profits are so enormous in all critical times, when their support is the most necessary, that no pecuniary assistance that Government can offer would really be worth their acceptance. The truth is they look only to their sale. They make their way like sycophants with the public, by finding out the prejudices and prepossessions of the moment and flattering them; and the number of *soi-disant* Government or Opposition papers abound just as the Government is generally popular or unpopular.' It is not difficult to construct from these sentences the old Tory idea of the functions and duties of the Press.

The Press, in fact, was in general more liberal than the Government, and for obvious reasons. The Government depended on the votes of the House of Commons, and nearly half the members of that House were nominated by controllers of rotten-boroughs. The Press depended on its circulation. Moreover it is always easier to make effective popular journalism on the Opposition side. John Morley, who edited a daily paper in mid-Victorian days, once asked a young journalist what was his speciality, and he replied, 'Invective'. There are many such journalists, and their talents rust unused if they are employed in defending the established order and the established government.

Newspapers had been taxed since Queen Anne's reign, and in 1815 the tax stood at fourpence a copy, the normal price of a newspaper being sevenpence. The original purpose of the tax was revenue, but there is no doubt that the Tory Government regarded the tax also as a measure of self-protection. It helped to keep newspapers accounted seditious out of the hands of the working classes. Cobbett's *Political Register* evaded the tax in 1816, by producing an edition which escaped the tax because it was not technically a newspaper. 'Twopenny Trash', as the untaxed edition was called, was a commentary on news no longer new, like our present-day political 'weeklies'. Others carried on a subterraneous and illegal existence.

In the panic that followed the Peterloo meeting the Government carried an Act, one of the so-called Six Acts, imposing a small tax on political pamphlets. 'Twopenny Trash' came within the ambit of the new tax, and paid it, though the full story of the relations between Cobbett's cheap edition and the revenue officers is too complicated to be followed out here. The newspaper tax, and the Government's imperfect success in enforcing the payment of it, form part of the warfare between Government and Press to which we have referred in connexion with Cobbett. The Press was bound to win. Among the factors on its side was the progress of mechanical invention. Steam printing began just at the very time when Lord Liverpool was lamenting that the Press was the reflexion of public opinion.

The musketry of the quick-firing Dailies was supported by the heavy artillery of the Quarterlies, whose establishment is a feature of this period, the *Edinburgh* founded in 1802, the *Quarterly* in 1809, and the *Westminster* in 1824. The *Edinburgh* claimed to stand for progressive ideas, but it was not at all advanced or revolutionary. It derided Bentham even though it popularized many of his policies. Of the early *Edinburgh Reviewers* two, Sydney Smith and Brougham, have already been described. The editor from almost the beginning until 1829 was Francis Jeffrey, a lawyer and a very amiable man who took literature as his especial province. Unfortunately he is remembered now only for the superficiality of his judgements. He opened a review of Wordsworth's *Excursion* with the words 'This will never do', and declared that of all the poets of his day only Campbell and Rogers were secure of immortality. When the Whigs took office in 1830 they made him Lord Advocate of Scotland. The fourth member of the group was Francis Horner, a specialist in a very important department, namely economics. He was the author of the scheme for restoring the gold currency after the war, which Peel adopted in 1817. He seems to have been an earnest young Scot, and Sydney Smith said that the Ten Commandments were written on his face;—Bagehot adds, characteristically, that he was a very ugly man. Sir Walter Scott was not impressed by him. 'I cannot', he said, 'admire your Horner; he always reminds me of Obadiah's bull, who, though he certainly never did produce a calf, nevertheless went about his business with so much gravity, that he commanded the respect of the whole parish.'

Scott contributed to early numbers of the *Edinburgh*, but, being offended by its lukewarm attitude to the Peninsular War, promoted the establishment of the Tory *Quarterly* in 1809, and contributed freely to it. The *Quarterly* played the part of candid friend to the party it supported, and readers of Disraeli's *Coningsby* will remember that the vulgar herd of Toryism in the 'thirties always took their cue from the 'slashing articles' of Mr. Rigby. 'Rigby' was John Wilson Croker, a great factotum of 'Die-hard' Toryism and the founder of the Athenæum Club. In 1824 the Utilitarians, as the Benthamites at about this date began to call themselves, founded a Quarterly of their own, entitled *The Westminster Review*; James Mill was its most powerful contributor and it preached pure Benthamism, scorning the *Edinburgh* as an organ of a timid and compromising Whiggery.

It is perhaps a mark of the speeding-up of modern life that, by the middle of the century, the Quarterlies found that much of the influence they had enjoyed was passing to the Monthly magazines, of which the Tory *Blackwood's* (1817) was one of the earliest. Long before the end of the century Weeklies such as *The Spectator* and *The Saturday Review* were passing the Monthlies as the Monthlies had passed the Quarterlies.

IV

FIVE POETS

THE brief period that began in 1798 with the publication of *Lyrical Ballads* by Wordsworth and Coleridge, and ended with the deaths, in rapid succession, of Keats, Shelley, and Byron (1821–24), produced more, far more, great lyrical and reflective poetry than any other period of equal length in the history of English literature. Poetry, for poetry's sake, is not the subject of this book, and of one of these poets, Keats, we shall have nothing to say; for Keats's quest was beauty in itself and for its own sake, and his poetry was not concerned with thought or opinion. But three of them, Wordsworth, Byron and Shelley, had a message to the world, and their poetry is the vehicle of that message, though it is also, of course, being poetry, something more than that. Coleridge conveyed but little message in his poetry, but after he had ceased to be a poet he became a preacher or prophet, and the burden of his preaching had a quality at once visionary and inspiring, such as only one who had been a poet would have achieved. And it will be convenient to add another poet who was not a great poet, though a Poet Laureate, Robert Southey. He also had something to say, and it is perhaps well that he said it in prose.

All these poets, together with other poets and prose-writers, English, French, German, and Italian, not to mention artists, architects and musicians, have been grouped together in the tradition of criticism and treated as exponents of the Romantic Movement. The Romantic Movement is a topic on which so much has been written that one hesitates to add even a paragraph to the vast literature of the subject. None the less it is necessary to do so.

I believe that the fundamental impulse of the Romantic Movement can be found in a very simple phrase—'the Call of the Wild'. Throughout by far the greater part of the history of the human race life was rough, casual, disorderly, and adventurous, 'near to Nature' as we say. In very recent times, comparatively speaking, law and order were achieved. Now law and order, even if ideally organized (as they never have been), impose tiresome fetters upon the spontaneous impulses of the individual. Moreover, what our ancestors have achieved we take for granted. We forget how great an achievement it was, what an improvement it marked on what had gone before it. Rousseau was the first great prophet of the Romantic Movement, and his books (which were written in the middle of the eighteenth century) are continually contrasting civilization with 'Nature', to the great disadvantage of the former. Rousseau was, incidentally, very keenly alive to the beauty of wild scenery, to Nature in the visual sense, but the 'Nature' of his political treatises is a kind of Garden of Eden, out of which Man has mistakenly strayed, and to which he must at all costs find his way back. The reason why the French Revolution was something more than a mere ephemeral political storm in a French tea-cup was that it was an exposition in political terms of the Romantic Movement, a quest after some mysterious Rights of the Natural Man, out of which he had been tricked by the cunning schemers who entrapped him into civilization. Of course Rousseau and his disciples did not want to return to barbarism; they wanted, one may say, both to eat their cake and to have it. If Rousseau could have seen the result of the French Revolution he would certainly have condemned it. In fact the Romantic movement was bound to miss its ideal in politics, however valuable its political by-products. So it passed over into poetry, art, and music, and inspired the wild dreams of

Shelley, the sunsets of Turner and the solemn splendours of the later works of Beethoven.

Wordsworth was born and grew up in the English Lake country, the most sensationally beautiful region of England, its beauty then unravaged by the amenities of holiday tourists. In those early days, he tells us,

> the sounding cataract
> Haunted me like a passion; the tall rock,
> The mountain, and the deep and gloomy wood,
> Their colours and their forms, were then to me
> An appetite; a feeling and a love,
> That had no need of a remoter charm.

Visiting France in 1791 in order to learn French, he was intoxicated by the French Revolution, and only financial pressure exerted from home prevented him from throwing in his lot with the Girondin party. He returned to England, and the later course of the Revolution, culminating in the aggressive military tyranny of Napoleon, completely disillusioned him. He had worshipped Nature as a source of almost sensual intoxication: he had worshipped her as a symbol of political revolution. The first was inadequate, the second utterly mistaken. Nature was neither a picture book nor a political will-of-the-wisp. She was the mother of Man and his true home. She was around him and within him. The secret of life was to live in communion with Nature. From Nature alone can Man win for himself

> that blessed mood,
> In which the burthen of the mystery,
> In which the heavy and the weary weight
> Of all this unintelligible world
> Is lightened.

It was only after reaching this third stage of his development that Wordsworth began to write great poetry. There is danger of paradox and absurdity in comparing Wordsworth and Cobbett, in comparing the quietest of the greater poets with the noisiest and most pugnacious of journalists. But Wordsworth's philosophy is at this point the spiritual equivalent of Cobbettism. Cobbett stood for the country against the town as the sound and wholesome basis of workaday life. Wordsworth stood for the country against the town because, as some one said, God made the country and man made the town. Cobbett's country, it is true, is the cultivated farm land; Wordsworth's is the waste and the mountain. But both were utterly out of sympathy with the 'progress' of the new industrialism. Leslie Stephen offers an ingenious explanation of the fact that 'love of the sublimest scenery should be associated with a profound conviction that all things are out of joint. After all, it is not surprising that those who are most sick of man as he is should love the regions where man seems smallest. When Swift wanted to express his disgust for his race, he showed how absurd our passions appear in a creature six inches high: and the mountains make us all Lilliputians.'[1]

Love of Nature—love of home—love of country. In the series of political sonnets, begun in 1802 in conscious revival of the Miltonic tradition, Wordsworth gave the noblest poetic expression to English patriotism. In a prose pamphlet entitled *Tract on the Convention of Cintra* (an incident of the Peninsular War) he looks further afield and argues that Napoleon can only be beaten by arousing the dormant national spirit of the conquered peoples of his empire. He asserts the moral basis of nationalism as in accord with Nature, and in fact anticipates the doctrines associated with Mazzini, the prophet of Italian unity.[2]

Wordsworth lived to a great age, and when he died, in the middle year of the nineteenth century, he had long survived his own genius. But from the nature of his genius it was inevitable that he should grow more and more conservative as he grew older. He ends in mere negation, deploring the Reform Bill as heartily as Scott, and doubting, like a Tory extremist, whether popular education will

[1] Stephen, *Hours in a Library*, Vol. II, p. 221.
[2] I owe this point, and some others in this section, to Mr. Claude Brinton's brilliant book, *The Political Ideas of the English Romanticists*.

not do more harm than good. 'Can it in a general view be good that the infant should learn much which its parents do not know?' He was one of those who, as Hazlitt said, missed the road to Utopia, and alighted upon it in Old Sarum. Having preached in the season of his genius the virtual identity of God and Nature, he withdrew within the fortress of the Church of England and dedicated to it a long series of Ecclesiastical Sonnets. He stopped short, however, of forming the habit of going to Church. He was of the school that have been called not pillars but flying buttresses of the edifice.

But the Wordsworth whose influence grew as the century advanced was the Wordsworth of the prime. That influence was far too profound to be summarized adequately by me in a few trivial sentences. He has been the favourite English poet of many of the best and most characteristic Englishmen of the last hundred years, from Matthew Arnold to Lord Grey of Fallodon. He gave not the first, but the deepest expression to that love of the wholesome quiet of the countryside which grows upon us more and more as life becomes more and more urbanized. A French critic of the English novelists has remarked on the pervasive influence of 'fresh air' in modern English poetry and fiction. He points out how many of the greatest scenes in our classic Victorian novels are staged out of doors, and finds no parallel to this in the literature of his own country. The peasants of Thomas Hardy's Wessex novels have their forerunners in Wordsworth's Michael and Matthew.

Samuel Taylor Coleridge was the son of a Devonshire clergyman, but he was educated at Christ's Hospital in London, and he was all his life, what Wordsworth never was, a man of books; Wordsworth learnt his wisdom on mountains, Coleridge in libraries. He is commonly classed with Wordsworth as a 'Lake poet', but he lived only a short time in the Lake country and did little important work there. His early manhood is tarred with the revolutionary brush, for he planned, with his brother-in-law Southey, to found an ideal Pantisocratic (all-equal) community in the United States. It need hardly be said that nothing came of this guileless aspiration. In 1798 he visited Germany and drank deep of the new German philosophy; as one of the first to introduce the conceptions of this philosophy to England he was a forerunner of the Oxford school of philosophy, which we shall meet in a later chapter. The season of his poetic genius was brilliant but brief and early over, and his poetry hardly comes within the sphere of our subject. His best poems belong to the realm of pure unfettered imagination, though it would be just possible, on the strength of its final stanzas, to connect *The Ancient Mariner* with the humanitarian movement. In the first years of the nineteenth century he became a slave to opium, emerging, after many years of indulgence and misery, under the care of Dr. Gilman, of Highgate, with whom he lived from 1817 onwards until his death in 1834. At Highgate the last phase of his life begins. He was no longer a poet but a sage, surrounded by a group of earnest disciples, eager to discover the secrets of his cloudy and incoherent philosophy.

Carlyle wrote a biography of John Sterling, one of these disciples, and it contains a chapter from which few writers on Coleridge have resisted the temptation to quote. The chapter, however, should be read in its entirety. The quotation that follows is made up of passages from various parts of the chapter.

'Coleridge sat on the brow of Highgate Hill in those years, looking down on London and its smoke-tumult, like a sage escaped from the inanity of life's battle; attracting towards him the thoughts of innumerable brave souls still engaged there. A sublime man; who, alone in those dark days, had saved his crown of spiritual manhood; escaping from the black materialisms and revolutionary deluges, with "God, Freedom, and Immortality" still his; a king of men.

'Nothing could be more copious than his talk. Besides, it was talk not flowing anywhither like a river, but spreading everywhither in inextricable currents and regurgitations like a lake or sea; terribly deficient in goal or aim, very often in logical intelligibility; *what* you were to believe or do, on any earthly or heavenly thing, obstinately refusing to appear from it. So that, most times, you felt logically lost; swamped near to drowning in this tide of ingenious vocables, spreading out boundless as if to submerge the world.

'The constant gist of his discourse was lamentation over the sunk condition of the world: which he recognized to be given up to Atheism and Materialism, full of sordid misbeliefs, mispursuits and misresults. The remedy, though Coleridge himself professed to see it as in sunbeams, could not, except by processes unspeakably difficult, be described to you at all. On the whole, those dead Churches, this dead English Church especially, must be brought to life again. Why not? It was not dead; the soul of it, in this parched-up body, was tragically asleep only. Atheistic philosophy was true on its own side; but lift the Church and it into a higher sphere of argument, *it* died into inanition, the Church revivified itself into its pristine florid vigour. But how, but how! By attending to the "reason" of man, said Coleridge, and duly chaining-up the "understanding" of man: the *Vernunft* (Reason) and *Verstand* (Understanding) of the Germans, it all turned upon these, if you could well understand them—which you couldn't.'

This is ironical and depreciatory, as is Carlyle's way. None the less, Coleridge's theory of the Church was one which, though fantastic in the form in which he stated it, had a real significance and a real influence upon the thought of the next generation. The National Church, he held, had been diverted from its proper function. In the Middle Ages it had been an endowment for the promotion of civilization in all its departments, education, art, literature—the whole spiritual life of man and not merely a particular variety of religion in the narrower sense. The Church must once again be made truly national, and its energies lifted above the sectarian channels into which they had narrowed since the Reformation. Here, be it observed, is the Romantic movement finding its goal not in the mountains, nor in Utopia, nor in Old Sarum, but in an idealized Middle Ages. The goals lie bewilderingly far apart, but they have this in common, that they are all remote from modern industrial society.

And what of the objection, frankly admitted by Coleridge, that much of what passed for the orthodox teaching of religion has been rendered incredible by anti-Christian critics of the school of Voltaire? His answer is that much which seems incredible to the mere 'understanding' will be justified by 'reason'. These terms proved a stumbling-block to Carlyle, and in fact do violence to the ordinary meanings of the words. By 'reason' Coleridge means very much what we call intuition, or faith, and by 'understanding' he means what we call reason. It is a common-place to anyone who has thought about the matter, that the fundamental assertions of religion, the existence of God, for example, are not capable of proof, as proof is understood in science. None the less many of the wisest and greatest are still convinced that God exists; they would say that their conviction of it is firmer and stronger than any merely 'rational' argument could make it. The strength of religion is not based on rational but on super-rational grounds.

Coleridge both claimed to be, and was, a Christian, but many of his contemporaries would not have admitted his claim, for his views were alarmingly liberal. He was, it appears, the first to use the word *bibliolatry* to denote a superstitious belief in the verbal infallibility of the Bible. Bibliolatry, he held, was the worst enemy of the Christian religion. The whole of the Broad Church school of the next generation, in all its varieties, is derivable from Coleridge.

A few years after Coleridge's death an interesting appreciation of him was written by John Stuart Mill. Mill was the son of James Mill and he had been brought up in accordance with the straitest sect of the atheistical Benthamites, who held that reason, and reason alone, sufficed. Yet Mill found as he grew older that Benthamism, though true as far as it went, was a painfully incomplete philosophy of life. He speaks of Bentham and Coleridge [1] as 'the two seminal minds of the age', and though he professes himself still a Benthamite, it is plain that he realized that Coleridge, however vague and unpractical his programme, reached a deeper stratum of truth than the triumphantly rational exponent of the 'greatest happiness' theory, whose legislative expedients were being added almost annually to the Statute book.

Robert Southey was the intimate associate of Wordsworth and Coleridge and he was also, as they assuredly were not, a somewhat ordinary man, an industrious and capable man of letters, a model of all the domestic virtues, the author of many long poems now unreadable, but also of a popular *Life of Nelson* which is recognized as an excellent specimen of its own type of composition. We find him starting life full of revolutionary ardour, like Wordsworth and Coleridge. While an undergraduate he wrote a play, *Wat Tyler*, glorifying rebellion, a play which was discovered and rather unkindly published by his enemies long afterwards. By 1809, however, he had so far passed over into the opposite camp as to be one of the founders of the *Quarterly Review*, and in 1813 he became Poet Laureate. His Ode on the Death of George III was the subject of a savage attack from Byron, who composed an alternative *Vision of Judgement* which is probably the most blasphemous poem of any real merit in our literature.

The outlook of the ageing Wordsworth was mere negation. He withdrew into his mountains and shook the

---

[1] It is curious how many of the principal writers described in this chapter died either in the year of the Reform Bill or very shortly after: Scott 1832, Bentham 1832, James Mill 1836, Wilberforce 1833, Coleridge 1834, Cobbett 1835.

dust of the progressive plains off his feet. One of his last sonnets is a protest against the building of the Kendal and Windermere railway. Coleridge developed an original philosophy which might be classed as Toryism since it was at the opposite pole to Benthamism, but was very far from being the Toryism of the Tory party. Coleridge in fact described the Tory party as 'a cyclops with one eye, and that in the back of the head'. Southey was neither a recluse nor a philosopher. He was a practical and public-spirited man, and he found his harbour in the Evangelical philanthropic party. He combined an entire disregard for liberty, applauding the suspension of the Habeas Corpus Act in 1817, with an active support of every movement for the relief of human suffering. He interested himself particularly in Lord Ashley's agitation on behalf of child labour in the factories, a subject which belongs to our next chapter.

Wordsworth, Coleridge, and Southey were born in the early 'seventies of the eighteenth century. They watched the French Revolution from start to finish and their early enthusiasm for it was extinguished by what they read in their newspapers. Byron and Shelley were born twenty years later. For them the Reign of Terror was an event in history, and they classed it among accidental events, discrediting not at all the essential gospel of the revolutionists. They died young, revolutionists of a sort to the last.

Byron was by far the most popular poet of his own day, and he enjoyed an immediate fame on the Continent such as has never before or since fallen to an English poet. Something of his vogue may have been due to extraneous circumstances, his noble birth, the notorious scandals of his private life, and his heroic and sensational death as a warrior in the earliest of the crusades of nineteenth-century nationalism. But in the main his poetry was popular because it had popular qualities; it was at once dashing and slipshod, easy and exciting, melodious and romantic. Byron holds, like all the revolutionists, that Man, that non-existent abstraction, is naturally good, and that Society and Civilization are the villains of the piece. His heroes are criminals, but their crimes are their misfortunes, for which Society must bear the guilt. Among these heroes are Cain, who first broke the Sixth Commandment, and Don Juan who held the record as a breaker of the Seventh. Byron has all the aristocrat's contempt for comfortable middle-class respectability. He must be one of the earliest writers to poke fun at the London suburbs. Don Juan approaches London

> Through Groves, so called from being void of trees,
> (Like *lucus* from *no* light); through prospects named
> Mount Pleasant, as containing nought to please,
> Nor much to climb; through little boxes framed
> Of bricks to let the dust in at your ease,
> With 'To be Let' upon their doors proclaimed;
> Through Rows most modestly called Paradise
> Which Eve might quit without much sacrifice.

Byron despised these things as an aristocrat despises them. But there is a large class below, as well as a small class above, the *bourgeoisie*, and Byron's romantic contempt for everything that could be called smug, struck a chord in the hearts of the men who read Tom Paine in garrets, planned the pitifully ineffective riots and demonstrations of the 1815–20 period, and looked forward to the English revolution which would be so much better than the French. It was known that Byron's first speech in the House of Lords had been a defiant defence of the Luddite rioters. Tory periodicals like *Blackwood's* talked of 'Benthamites and Byronites' as if they were much of a muchness. It is difficult to imagine two things more different than Benthamism and Byronism, yet both were unsettling the foundations of the Old Toryism, and Byron supplied an element that certainly could not have come from Bentham. He made discontent romantic. The mobs that frightened the politicians of both parties in the year of the Reform Bill certainly contained more readers of Byron than of Bentham.

Byron was a man very well acquainted with the world,

the flesh and the devil; he was a great satirist, but he was not a great poet. There is more petulance than programme about his revolutionary eloquence. He rails at kings, but after the death of George IV the sovereign ceased to be a bugbear of the dissatisfied Englishman. Byron's vogue rapidly declined. Shelley was, in the opinion of Matthew Arnold, who disliked his poetry, an 'angel' even though a 'beautiful and ineffectual angel'. Moreover, he was a really great poet, and a poet who has inspired enthusiasm even more than possibly greater poets. His vogue has steadily grown, and though it is easy to admire his poetry and ignore his philosophy, it is quite certain that his philosophy has coloured the outlook of life of many people, particularly young people, who have delighted in his poetry.

Shelley's philosophy is pure revolt, unqualified by a single saving clause of common-sense. He took up the dry bones of Godwinism and with them fashioned a figure of Man triumphant over God and over civilization as we know it.

> Kings, priests and statesmen blast the human flower
> Even in its tender bud.

Away with them! Religion is a 'prolific fiend'. The hero of his greatest work is Prometheus, the champion of Man against the Gods. In fact Shelley is an inspired child crying for the moon; or if this seems an unworthy metaphor, we may borrow one from Emerson and say that he 'hitched his waggon to a star'. In the last year of his life he beguiled himself with the hope that the Greek insurrection was the beginning of the New World.

> The world's Great Age begins anew,
> The mighty months return;
> The earth doth like a snake renew
> Its winter weeds outworn.

And yet he knew that it was not so:

> Oh cease! must hate and death return?
> Cease! must men kill and die?

In the striking paragraph which opens his little book on *Shelley, Godwin, and their Circle*, Mr. Brailsford writes: 'The history of the French Revolution in England begins with a sermon and ends with a poem. Between the famous discourse of Dr. Richard Price on the love of our country, delivered in the first excitement that followed the fall of the Bastille, and the publication of Shelley's *Hellas* there stretched a period of thirty-two years. It covered the dawn, the clouding, and the unearthly sunset of a hope. It begins with the grave but enthusiastic prose of a divine justly respected by earnest men who with a limited horizon fulfilled their daily duties in the City. It ends with the rapt vision, the magical music of a singer, who seemed as he sang to soar beyond the range of human ears. The hope passes from the confident expectation of instant change, through the sobrieties of disillusionment and the recantations of despair, to the iridescent dreams of a future which has taken wing and made its home in a fairy world.'

And yet not altogether in a fairy world, for Shelley has become one of the patron saints of Socialism. Socialism, like Shelley's dream, is based on a conviction of the natural goodness of man and the badness of the institutions with which he has none the less managed to provide himself.

CHAPTER II

THE MIDDLE THIRD OF THE CENTURY

I

THE BENTHAMITE-LIBERAL ORTHODOXY

WE took as our starting-point in the first chapter the fact that the Old Tory party controlled the government of the country almost without a break from before the French Revolution down to 1830. The verdicts of general elections and of votes in the House of Commons give no such clear indication in the period that lies before us, roughly definable as 1830–1874. Governments labelled Whig and Tory alternate, the Whig Governments lasting on the average three times as long as the Tory Governments. We might therefore conclude that English political opinion in the Early and Mid-Victorian periods was three-parts Whig and one-part Tory,—a simple and uninstructive conclusion, for what in the period was the meaning of Whiggery and what the meaning of Toryism?

The fact of the matter is that the old party labels had less significance in this period than in any period before or after. In 1832, no doubt, Whigs and Tories fought on the clear issue of the Reform Bill; should the historic and picturesque anomalies of the ancient 'rotten-borough' system be preserved, or should they be abolished in favour of a rigid middle-class franchise? But the Reform Bill, once passed, was recognized by its opponents as irrevocable. The Toryism of Burke and Eldon was dead. The party

73

delivered itself over to the leadership of the son of a Lancashire manufacturer, Sir Robert Peel, and Peel was so little enamoured of Tory traditions that he made a point of emphasizing the new name which some were applying to the Tory party. The name 'Conservative', originally borrowed (like its companion 'Liberal') from the political vocabulary of France, was used at the time of the Reform Bill struggle as a synonym for Tory. After the Reform Bill had become law, Peel was careful to draw a distinction. 'Conservatism' accepted the new franchise and would do its best to falsify the gloomy prediction of Old Toryism. It would conserve our institutions by submitting them to careful and judicious but, where necessary, thorough reform.

The classic criticism of Peel's Conservative policy was to come, in the 'forties, from Disraeli. It was, he says, 'an attempt to construct a party without principles. What will you conserve? The prerogatives of the Crown, provided they are not exercised; the independence of the House of Lords, provided it is not asserted; the Ecclesiastical estate, provided it is regulated by a commission of laymen.' In fact, 'an organized hypocrisy'. Or again, one may quote from *Coningsby*, published in 1844, a fragment of dialogue between characters who are meant to typify the political hacks of the party.

'"That we should ever live to see a Tory government again!" said Mr. Taper. "We have reason to be very thankful."

'"Hush!" said Mr. Tadpole. "The time has gone by for Tory governments; what the country requires is a sound Conservative government."

'"A sound Conservative government," said Taper, musingly. "I understand: Tory men and Whig measures."'

This seems very crushing, but it really only means that Peel was prepared to read and to follow the signs of the times; and that the Whig party were prepared to do exactly the same.

One man, and one man alone, enjoyed the personal authority which might have enabled him to reassert the principles of Old Toryism from their natural stronghold, the House of Lords. This was, of course, the Duke of Wellington whose personal opinions in 1830 have already been quoted (see p. 7). Had Wellington attempted to rally to his leadership the scattered but still formidable remnants of the Old Tory party it is impossible to say how our political history would have developed. He deliberately refrained from doing so. Henceforth his motto was: 'The King's (and subsequently, the Queen's) government must be carried on.' Again and again he threw the full weight of his authority on to the side of measures he personally detested and was known to detest. He remained at heart an Old Tory. He never became a Conservative, for he was, after 1832, a political pessimist, whereas the essence of Peel's creed was political optimism. He supported successive instalments of 'progress', not because he thought them 'progress' but because he preferred them to revolution. Finally he came to regard himself, with a certain reasonable arrogance, as a unique, non-party, institution. 'I am', he wrote in 1846, 'the servant of the Crown and the people. I have been paid and rewarded, and consider myself retained. . . . I might with consistency have declined to belong to Sir Robert Peel's Cabinet' (i.e., the Cabinet that introduced and carried the repeal of the Corn Law). 'But my opinion is, that if I had, Sir Robert Peel's Government would not have been framed; that we should have had —— and —— in office next morning.'

There were, of course, Old Tories who would have nothing to do with Conservatism. John Wilson Croker refused to tarnish the escutcheon of his political consistency by standing for election to the reformed House of Commons. 'I for one', he wrote, 'believe that this day twelve months I shall be either in my grave or in the workhouse, and hope it may be the former.' And there came a time when Peel's adaptability to new policies proved too much for his followers. The Tory party might change its name, but it was still the party of the country gentlemen, and it revolted when Peel, the manufacturer's son, adopted the manufacturer's policy of free trade in corn. In 1846 Peel and his personal following, the Peelites, were driven from the Tory-Conservative party. The Peelites, among whom was Gladstone, drifted across to the Whigs, and strengthened the Liberal element in that party. For Liberalism, after all, meant much the same as Conservatism. The Tory party, purged of Peelism, reluctantly accepted the leadership of Disraeli; but it is to be noted that this party never enjoyed a majority in the House of Commons during the period covered by this chapter. Between 1846 and 1874 the Tory-Conservative party (distinction of terms again becoming meaningless) enjoyed three brief spells of office, but on each occasion it was a minority government, like the Labour Government of 1924. It could enact only such measures as secured support outside the party ranks. Moreover, it early abandoned the policy of agricultural protection which had been the original excuse for its existence. Disraelian Toryism did not enjoy power as well as office until 1874.

Thus throughout our period the Tory party had ceased to be recognizably Tory. It may also be maintained that the Whig party ceased to be recognizably Whig. The Tory party was, by origin, the party dedicated to the maintenance of the authority of the Crown and the Church. The Whig party had been, essentially, the party of the great landed aristocracy, and Whig governments down to the middle of the nineteenth century were much less ready than Tory governments to find room in high office for men of ability who lacked both rank and inherited wealth. The Whig party had originated as the opposition to the Stuarts; it had been mainly responsible for transferring the crown first to William III and afterwards to George I; and its palmiest days had been the age of Walpole and the Duke of Newcastle, when, under foreign puppet-kings, the great nobles had ruled England through a House of Commons in which about half the members sat for rotten boroughs. The Whig faith in the rotten-borough system began to waver when George III showed that it could be used to advance the control of the king as easily as the control of the aristocracy over the nominally elected House. But the French Revolution nipped in the bud the democratic tendencies which the party had manifested in the days of 'Wilkes and Liberty'. A large section of the party had followed Burke into the Tory camp, for Burke, the oracle of the Old Toryism in its fight with the French Revolution, had been the oracle of the Whigs when the enemy was the rebel colonists in America.[1] The Whig party was reduced to a mere shadow of its former self throughout the Napoleonic wars. It was an aristocratic coterie cherishing democrat and even republican sentiments, but its sentiments often seemed more of a pose than a policy. It revered the memory of that most erratic and inconsequent of political gamblers, Charles James Fox, but it was impossible to discover an aristocrat of Fox's vital energy and brilliant gifts among the generation of Whig statesmen that grew to maturity during the French wars.

None the less, as the years passed after Waterloo, as peace failed to entail prosperity, and the Tory Government revealed its inability to discover any remedies for the notorious evils of that age of social and economic revolution, the prospects of the Whig party brightened almost in spite of the performances of the Whig leaders. These leaders still adhered, many of them somewhat half-heartedly, to Fox's policy of Parliamentary Reform. Cobbett and the demo-

---

[1] It is curious that the greatest exponents of party principles have often been converts from the opposite party. Besides Burke we have Gladstone, the hero of mid-Victorian Liberalism, who began his career as a Peelite Conservative; and Chamberlain, the most vigorous of late Victorian Tory-imperialists, who began his career as a member of the Radical wing of the Gladstonian Liberal party.

cratic Radicals also stood for Parliamentary Reform, and though the scheme they would have advocated was far more drastic than anything likely to come from the Whigs, the Whigs were the only group that could possibly beat the Tories in the political field. Some of the Whigs, following the lead of Lord Shelburne, a very able though unpopular statesman of the previous generation, had established contact with Bentham. Others were in close touch with the Edinburgh Reviewers. At last the death of George IV gave occasion for a general election at a moment uniquely favourable to the Whigs. The Tories were divided, and the July Revolution which overthrew Charles X of France, proved the danger of resisting the popular will. Many of the Whig candidates at that election inserted Parliamentary Reform into their programmes as an afterthought, born of the results of the Revolution in France. With but little premeditation and beyond their deserts, the Whig leaders found themselves launched upon the undertaking which, after the Revolution of 1688, will always rank as their most notable achievement.

The Whig Government that carried the Reform Bill was, in truth, a motley coalition. At one end of the scale was the Benthamite Brougham; at the other Melbourne and Palmerston, recent recruits from the Tory party, who regarded the Reform Bill as nothing but a disagreeable necessity, both of them much less inclined towards legislative reform in general than Sir Robert Peel. And it is to be noted that Brougham was, in four years' time, expelled from the inner counsels of the party, whereas Melbourne and Palmerston were both of them for long periods Whig Prime Ministers. Two other prominent members of the Cabinet, Stanley and Graham, passed over into Peel's Conservative party without perceptibly changing their politics. Graham, as a Peelite, passed back again into the Liberal fold. Stanley, subsequently Lord Derby, became the ally and titular leader of Disraeli in the new Tory party. Charles Greville, Clerk of the Privy Council and writer of a Diary which is a mine of information about the unofficial opinions of politicians, records that many of the great Whig lords who figured as heroes of the Reform Bill were 'heartily ashamed of the whole business'.

Enough has been said to suggest that between the Whigs and the Tories of the middle period of the nineteenth century there was very little to choose. Each group of leaders was ready, at the last moment, to enact the repeal of the Corn Law, though, for party reasons, each was reluctant to do so. As Disraeli said, the Whig leaders 'returned the poisoned chalice' to Sir Robert Peel. Twenty years later each competed for the privilege of carrying the second Reform Bill. Only after 1868, with the emergence of Gladstone and Disraeli as indisputable leaders of their respective parties, does the strife of parties become once again a strife of policies and of principles.

It has often been remarked with truth, that continuous and abundant legislative activity is a distinctive feature of modern political life. The Old Whigs of the first two Georges and the Old Tories of the reign of George III were not active in legislation. Innovation was not, for them, an essential feature of government. The characteristically modern abundance of legislation begins a few years before the Reform Bill. It still continues, but we are now concerned only with so much of it as belongs to the middle section of the nineteenth century. The great bulk of that legislation, whether enacted by Whigs or Tories, represents the influence of a single school of thought, the Liberal or Benthamite school. The characteristics of this thought have already been described. It was Liberal in the old and proper sense of that term, in that it stood for the liberation from legal restrictions of all individuals who were capable of intelligent and useful activity—all, let us say, who were neither children,[1] lunatics, paupers, or criminals. By this means it sought to secure the greatest happiness of the greatest number. It was a policy appro-

[1] Whether women were to be classed with children was left doubtful.

79

priate to an active and self-reliant nation of shopkeepers.
It was indifferent to tradition, despised sentiment, and
abhorred muddle and waste. A few illustrations must
suffice.

The Great Reform Bill of 1832 was essentially Benthamite. It was not a democratic measure, and its authors
did not appeal to democratic sentiments. Its purpose was
to enfranchise property and intelligence, to enfranchise not
'the greatest number' but those whose political power was
most likely to promote the greatest happiness of the greatest
number. Listen to Lord Chancellor Brougham as he
recommends the Bill to the House of Lords. 'If there
is a mob, there is the people also. I speak now of the
middle classes—of those hundreds of thousands of respectable persons—the most numerous and by far the most
wealthy order in the community: for if all your lordships'
castles, manors, rights of warren and rights of chase, with
all your broad acres, were brought to the hammer and sold
at fifty years' purchase, the price would fly up and kick the
beam when counterpoised by the vast and solid riches of
those middle classes, who are also the genuine depositaries
of sober, rational, intelligent, and honest English feeling.'
He prefaces his recommendation of the proposed new
electorate with an *Odi profanum vulgus*. He claims, it is
true, in his oratorical frenzy, that this mob is comparatively
small and his middle class the most numerous order in the
community, but that was doubtless not meant for cold
print. The new electorate was but a handful, a few hundred
thousands.

Thirty years later a second Reform Bill enlarging the
electorate had obviously become due. Why? Had the Whig
and Tory statesmen who competed to enact it become
democrats? Certainly not. The assumption underlying
and justifying the second Reform Bill was that 'sobriety,
rationality, intelligence and honest English feeling' had
spread further down the social scale.

There is no need to demonstrate that Acts extending

freedom of trade, and Acts extending religious equality, such as Catholic Emancipation, the admission of Jews to parliament and the abolition of University tests, are illustrations of Benthamite Liberalism. The same is true of a series of Acts giving individuals greater freedom in the disposal of their property, and of the Divorce Act of 1857, facilitating divorce.

At first sight the Poor Law Amendment Act of 1834 might seem to represent a revulsion from Benthamism. It was much the most important [1] as it was also much the most unpopular of the Acts of the first Reformed Parliament. More than anything else it provoked the Chartist movement. An Act which terminated a system of wholesale doles to the poor and substituted the workhouse, does not at first sight seem an Act for the promotion of the greatest happiness of the greatest number. But there were, it must be remembered, other elements in Benthamism besides philanthropy. Benthamism abhorred muddle and waste. It stood for business methods in administration. Its interest was in the self-supporting, self-reliant individual. The authors of the Act intended to relieve such individuals, namely the ratepayers, from an intolerable burden, and they believed that the hardships they were imposing upon the recipients of the dole would drive these unfortunates into self-reliance and self-help. The Act was also entirely in accord with the Population doctrines of Malthus, and those doctrines had from the first been accepted by the Benthamite school. The system of doles abolished by the Act had been graded in accordance with the size of the family. Some held that, as the doles were administered, it actually paid to have more children, even illegitimate children; and over-population, according to Malthus, was the prime cause of poverty. The abolition of the doles would check population, and the workhouses would check

---

[1] The most important for England; it may be claimed that the Act abolishing slavery was more important in the history of the world at large.

it still further, for an important feature of the workhouse in the eyes of all supporters of the Bill was the segregation of the sexes.[1] The Act was an astringent tonic, and a parliament elected by the 'mob' would not have dared to administer it.

More definitely on the fringe of Benthamism was the great Education Act of 1870, and one observes that it was postponed until the end of the Benthamite epoch. It followed the second Reform Bill, and carried out the advice of Robert Lowe, an opponent of that measure, when he said 'We must educate our masters'. State grants to voluntary educational societies had begun in 1833 and had steadily increased. The Act of 1870 created State schools to fill the gaps left by the voluntary societies. Though it did not in fact make education universally compulsory, it was clearly an advance towards that goal. The Act was anti-Benthamite in so far as it took the money of the self-reliant and spent it on the children of those who could not or would not educate their children at their own expense. But its aim, the promotion of intelligence, was in the earliest and most orthodox Benthamite tradition. James Mill, had he been alive and in parliament, would have opposed the clause ordaining religious teaching in State schools, but in all other respects would certainly have given the Act his whole-hearted support.

The Factory Acts, on the other hand, were carried in defiance of orthodox Liberalism, and the opposition they encountered from statesmen otherwise leaders in legislative reform, such as Peel, Gladstone, and Cobden, prove that they were against the spirit of the age. They were the work of laborious and obstinate philanthropists who insisted

[1] It was believed, not only in 1834 but until very recent times, that the unprecedented growth of population in the nineteenth century was largely due to these doles. Actually it cannot have been, as there was no increase in the birth-rate. The increase of population was due to the decrease in the death-rate, i.e. the same numbers were born but they lived longer.

upon dragging the horrors of the uncontrolled factories and mines into the light of day. The facts were eloquent and appalling, yet even so the cry of the children was drowned again and again by the clashing cymbals of the Benthamite orchestra. Shaftesbury was not a political theorist: he was an Evangelical philanthropist devoting himself to the factory slaves of England as Wilberforce and Buxton had devoted themselves to the plantation slaves of the tropics. Yet the Factory reformers had to make a concession to Liberalism. If they had asked parliament to infringe the 'liberty' of grown-up men to work fourteen hours a day, they would have achieved nothing at all. They concentrated on the women and children, who could not be expected to know how to use their liberty. Even so, of course, the liberty of the employer was infringed, and his champions put up a stout fight on his behalf.

It would, as anyone can now see, be very easy to defend the Factory Acts, like the Education Act, on Benthamite grounds. One need not press the argument that the best employers have found that sweated labour, like slave labour, does not pay; for the argument, though one would like to accept it, is not universally valid. But in the national interest it is surely plain that sweated labour could not promote rationality and sobriety, and it was on the spread of rationality and sobriety that prospects of an in-definite extension of individual liberty ultimately depended. Shaftesbury, however, did not argue along these lines. He was in all respects, in his strength and in his weakness, the complete anti-Benthamite. He disbelieved in liberty, and detested its application to what he recognized as the most important sphere of life, religion. He was scarcely more eager to shorten the hours of child labour than to prevent the opening of the Crystal Palace on Sunday.

Still there were occasions when the organizing zeal of those Benthamites who hated muddle more than they loved liberty brought them into alliance with the Evangelical philanthropist. A series of epidemics directed the attention of the Government to questions of drainage and water-supply. A Health of Towns Act was carried (1848) establishing a Board of Health, with powers to investigate local conditions and coerce local authorities. At its head was placed Edwin Chadwick, an ardent Benthamite who had accumulated a great store of unpopularity by the ruthless efficiency with which he had administered the New Poor Law, and Shaftesbury was one of his colleagues. The objects of the Board were admirable and its energies exemplary, but it only lasted six years and its abolition was enthusiastically applauded. The Benthamism of bureaucratic organization had overshot the mark and was defeated by the more popular Benthamism of *laissez-faire*. *The Times* was delighted. 'We prefer', says its leader-writer, 'to take our chance of cholera and the rest, rather than to be bullied into health. . . . It was a perpetual Saturday night, and Master John Bull was scrubbed and rubbed and small tooth-combed till the tears ran into his eyes, and his teeth chattered, and his fists clenched themselves with worry and pain.' In exactly the same spirit Macaulay, a few years earlier, dismissed some of the schemes of philanthropic organization suggested by the poet Southey, who combined, like Shaftesbury, an ardent humanity with a complete indifference to liberty. 'He conceives', says Macaulay, 'that the business of the magistrate is to be a jack-of-all-trades—architect, engineer, schoolmaster, merchant, theologian, a Lady Bountiful in every parish, a Paul Pry in every house, spying, eaves-dropping, relieving, admonishing, spending our money for us, and choosing our opinions for us.' Shaftesbury and Chadwick would gladly, for different reasons, have undertaken all or most of these duties. They were, in fact, well on the way to being State Socialists, and the age of Socialism was not yet.

Perhaps the most remarkable achievement of Benthamite Liberalism was that, for a whole generation, it secured the allegiance of the leaders of the industrial working-classes; the 'Scotch feelosopher's' policy was for the time being crowned with success. That generation begins not in 1832, but somewhere between 1840 and 1850, and its conversion was promoted by an event more convincing than any argument, the setting in of the great mid-Victorian prosperity, which followed close upon the 'hungry'—that is, the early—'forties, and lasted until the middle 'seventies. The causes of that prosperity, in itself one of the essential features of what we call Victorianism, were many. Free-traders attributed it to free trade, and it certainly killed protectionism. Perhaps the principal cause was the development of the railways and steamships, which enabled transport to keep pace with productivity.

Throughout the first half of the century Labour was in a state of smouldering revolt, not merely against the accidental hardships of the new conditions of industry, but against the new conditions themselves. The first generation of the factory workers was homesick for the green fields, and the immense vogue of Cobbett was based, at least in part, upon the fact that when he wrote for the townsman he remained at heart a countryman. The revolt expresses itself in its crudest form in the machine breaking of the Luddites in the closing years of the French war. The crude early socialisms of Spence and Owen [1] derived such attractions as they possessed from the fact that they were sketches of Utopia. The Chartist programme of the 'thirties with its parliamentary democracy defined in Six Points seems to be more substantial, but the famous Charter presented only the most superficial aspect of Chartism. The Chartist leaders were never agreed as to what they wanted nor as to how they should set about getting it. Chartism was simply an attempt, doomed to failure, to organize a general discontent.

The complete failure of the Chartist Movement has committed to a merciful oblivion the outpourings of the Chartist leaders. Some of these leaders were very far from confining themselves to the 'Six Points' and the repeal

[1] Described later, p. 203.

of the Poor Law. One of the most active in the industrial North was James Raynor Stephens, a Nonconformist minister who had quarrelled with the Wesleyans and founded a sect of his own. In 1838 he gave notice to the mill-owners in the following terms: 'If they do not reform, they shall have the revolution they so much dread. We shall destroy their abodes of guilt. . . . If they will not learn to act as law prescribes and as God ordains, so that every man shall by his labour find comfortable food and clothing . . . we have sworn by God, by heaven, and by hell, that we shall wrap in one awful sheet of devouring flame the manufactories of the cotton tyrants and the palaces of those who raised them by rapine and murder.' Stephens and his friends—they formed only one section among the Chartists —were the heralds of the revolution that did not occur. They were swayed by the passions of an age which, if not past, was rapidly passing. By the middle year of the century such language could nowhere have been heard in England.

The Chartist Movement was beaten off the field by the Anti-Corn Law League which, organized by manufacturers, sought to persuade the working man that the cause of his troubles was neither his exclusion from the franchise nor his inclusion in the factory, but the artificially created expensiveness of his daily bread. The successful co-operation of master and man in the work of the League may be taken as the beginning of conversion of the working classes to the new industrialism. At the same time the worst tyrannies of the factory system were being curtailed by the Factory Acts, and another group of Acts, less familiar to the general reader, were soon to make those tyrannies less necessary to the mill-owner.[1] Acts of Parliament of 1855 and 1862 legalized the Limited Liability Company,—

---

[1] I owe the point that follows, as well as much of the line of thought pursued in these paragraphs, to G. D. H. Cole's *Short History of the British Working Class Movement*.

the form of company, that is to say, in which the share-holders' liability is limited to the amount of his investment, however great may be the debts of the company in which he has invested his money. Before this type of company was legalized the manufacturer had been hard put to it to find capital for building up his business. Often his own savings were the only resource he could draw upon, and he was tempted to save at all costs, particularly at the cost of his employees. Henceforth the *entrepreneur* as economists called him, the enterpriser in business, could draw much more freely upon the savings of that great sleeping partner the general public, for the general public was much more ready to lend under the new safeguards. The workman began to be better paid and could now be encouraged to save and invest, and enjoy for himself what economists called 'the rewards of abstinence'; hitherto his abstinence had been enforced and unrewarded.

Henceforth the organization of thrift began to take the place of the organization of revolt. Two years before the final fiasco of Chartism on Kennington Common in 1848 there was founded in Rochdale the first successful Co-opera-tive Society, paying dividends on its members' purchases. Friendly Societies for working-class insurance were already developing, and the Government, cordially approving of such enterprises, established a Registry of Friendly Societies, which certified the businesslike management of such Societies as submitted their accounts for registration. There was also founded in 1846 the Permanent Building Society to advance money to working men for the purchase of their houses. Trade Unionism developed among skilled crafts-men—and the distinction both in work and in wages between skilled and unskilled labour was vastly greater in those days of comparatively primitive machinery than it is to-day. These trade unions of the 'new model', such as the Amal-gamated Society of Engineers, provided their members with unemployment, sickness, and superannuation benefits, and were consequently averse from strikes. In the 'sixties a group of able trade union secretaries established close contact with one another and with sympathetic professional men in the ranks of politics and journalism, among such being the barrister, Tom Hughes, the old pupil of Dr. Arnold of Rugby and author of *Tom Brown's Schooldays*. This group of trade union secretaries has been called the Junta. They were eminently moderate men, and as firmly convinced of the inevitability of the capitalist system as any employer could be. Their aim was to secure from all employers the conditions of labour already granted by the best. In fact a thoroughly Benthamized 'aristocracy of labour', imbued with 'middle-class ideals', had developed itself, and was ripe for enfranchisement by the second Reform Bill. The outlook of the Junta was as far removed from that of the Luddites of fifty years before as it is removed from the left-wing Socialists of fifty years afterwards.

Self-help was the ideal of the day, and in 1859 Samuel Smiles published the book which bears that title. It had an enormous success, twenty thousand copies being sold in the year of publication and 130,000 more in the next thirty years. Other volumes followed in the same vein from the same pen—*Thrift, Character, Duty*, and a series of *Lives* of successful inventors and industrialists. *Self-Help* is an amiable, if somewhat tedious work, a collection of lay sermons on industry and honesty, enlivened with innumerable anecdotes from the lives of the virtuous and successful. A sample from the Table of Contents gives an accurate notion of the book. Any of its thirteen chapters would do equally well, and I select at random:

CHAPTER IX. MONEY—USE AND ABUSE

'The right use of money a test of practical wisdom—Economy necessary to independence—The improvident classes helpless—Importance of frugality as a public question—Words of Richard Cobden and John Bright—Independence within reach of most working men—High purposes

of economy—Advice given to Francis Horner by his father
—Robert Burns—Living within the means—Wasters—
Running into debt—The debtor a slave—Haydon's debts—
Fichte—Dr. Johnson on Debt—The Duke of Wellington
on Debt—Washington—Earl St. Vincent—Beginning well
—Living too high, a vice in England—Napier's general
order to his officers in India—Hugh Miller's case—High
standard of living necessary—Secret of money-making
embodied in popular proverbs—Career of Thomas Wright
—All honest industry honourable—An illustrious sweep
—Mere money making—The "love of money"—Worldly
success—The power of money over-estimated—Joseph
Brotherton—Respectability, its highest standard.'

Matthew Arnold had a very pretty gift of parodying a
phase of public opinion by selecting a ludicrous example of
it. The Gospel according to Samuel Smiles he found
compressed into a nutshell in 'the beautiful sentence Sir
Daniel Gooch quoted to the Swindon workmen, which I
treasure as Mrs. Gooch's Golden Rule, or the Divine
Injunction "Be ye Perfect" done into British—the sentence
Sir Daniel Gooch's mother repeated to him every morning
when he was a boy going to work: *Ever remember, my dear
Dan, that you should look forward to being some day manager
of that concern.*'

Among the greater writers of books two have been accepted
as exponents of the Benthamite or Victorian-Liberal phase
of thought, Thomas Babington Macaulay and John Stuart
Mill. Both were sons of eminent and typical Scotsmen.
Zachary Macaulay was one of the principal allies of Wilberforce in his anti-slavery crusade, and was reckoned the
austerest member of the Clapham sect. James Mill we
have already met as the most rigid and indefatigable of the
Benthamites. Zachary Macaulay detested the atheism of
James Mill and James Mill despised the superstitious
enthusiasm of Zachary Macaulay, but they were really
very similar men, ardently industrious and public-spirited
Puritans. Both were extremely stern fathers. We may

carry the parallel further, though it becomes a parallel with an element of contrast. Macaulay wrote essays attacking the Utilitarian philosophy, yet he was in all essentials a fairly complete embodiment of Utilitarian or Benthamite thought. John Stuart Mill was carefully trained to be an apostle of Utilitarianism, and he never ceased to call himself a Utilitarian, but his creed developed so far from its starting-point that he became in effect one of the principal critics of the cruder doctrines of the school in which he was enrolled. John Morley, writing shortly after both had died, says that Macaulay and Mill were the two principal influences on the journalism of their day. He adds: 'It might perhaps be said of these two distinguished men that our public writers owe most of their virtues to the one, and most of their vices to the other. If Mill taught some of them to reason, Macaulay taught more of them to declaim; if Mill set an example of patience, tolerance, and fair examination of hostile opinions, Macaulay did much to encourage oracular arrogance, and a rather too thrasonical complacency; if Mill sowed ideas of the great economic, political, and moral bearings of the forces of society, Macaulay trained a taste for superficial particularities, trivial circumstances of local colour, and all the paraphernalia of the pseudo-picturesque.'[1] From all which it appears that Morley preferred Mill to Macaulay: he had been, in fact, Mill's devoted friend and disciple. It is amusing, then, to note that the style of this passage, with its smart antitheses and slapdash judgements, is very reminiscent of Macaulay's weaker moments.

Macaulay was one of the few who, with great achievements and brilliant prospects in politics, turned his back on public life and preferred to be a man of letters. He was consumed with a passion for history, particularly the history of England, and in his Essays, republished from the *Edinburgh Review*, and in his great unfinished History he did more than any Englishman has ever done to popularize, for his

[1] Morley, *Miscellanies*, Vol. I, p. 257.

own generation, the study of English history. The extent
of his success is half forgotten to-day. Morley was, as
we have seen, no great admirer of Macaulay, yet in 1881,
more than twenty years after Macaulay's death, he could
write: 'If we are to talk about "popular histories", the writer
who distances every competitor by an immeasurable distance
is Macaulay. . . . His *Essays* have done more than any
other writings of this generation to settle the direction of
men's historical interest and curiosity. From Eton and
Harrow down to an elementary school in St. Giles's or
Bethnal Green, Macaulay's *Essays* are a text-book. At
home and in the colonies they are on every shelf between
Shakespeare and the Bible.' We have, then, to ask how
he presented his subject.

He cared nothing for the Middle Ages, and wrote little
on any period before the Reformation. He detested Roman
Catholicism, distrusted kings, despised mobs, abhorred
Jacobins, and glorified parliaments. His heroes are Pym
and Hampden (but not Cromwell, whom he dismissed after
the fashion of his day as a hypocritical schemer and tyrant),
William of Orange, the Pitts, and Burke, though the Burke
of the *Reflections on the French Revolution* is a 'lost leader'
for him. His most popular Essays were devoted to Clive
and Warren Hastings; he is enthralled by the splendour of
their daring patriotism, but refuses to overlook or condone
(in fact he unintentionally exaggerates, in the case of Hastings) their high-handed improprieties. His great events
are the Reformation, though he despises the subtle and
scholarly Cranmer; the Long Parliament—he is brutally
contemptuous in his treatment of Charles I and Laud; the
Glorious Revolution; and the Great Reform Bill. In fact
'Rome' is Egypt; the Reformation is the Exodus; and the
passage of the Great Reform Bill is the entry into the
Promised Land. There is of course no single Moses,
though at a critical stage in the journey William III assumes
a stature worthy of that patriarch. But of the whole it
would be true to say that the British Israelites of Macaulay's

history need no monarch. The English People directs its own destinies, and 'People' in Macaulay must generally be understood to mean the parliamentary classes.

Macaulay in fact fixed firmly in the popular mind what some now call the 'Whig legend' of English history, and as such are seeking to demolish. Like most good legends it contains a great deal of truth, and the pulling down of Macaulay's legend has, in recent years, often meant no more than the setting up of another.[1]

Politically Macaulay was a Whig rather than a Benthamite. He was the kind of reformer who approved the reforms already enacted without demanding any more. But he was fascinated by the prospect of a future of unlimited social and industrial progress. In 'natural progress' he is an enthusiastic believer. 'If', he writes, 'we were to prophesy that in the year 1930 a population of fifty millions, better fed, clad, and lodged than the English of our time, will cover these islands, that cultivation, rich as that of a flower garden, will be carried up to the very tops of Ben Nevis and Helvellyn, that machines constructed on principles yet undiscovered will be in every house, that there will be no highways but railroads, no travelling but by steam, that our National Debt, vast as it appears to us, will appear to our great-grandchildren a trifling encumbrance, which might easily be paid off in a year or two, many people would think us insane. We prophesy nothing: but this we say: If any person had told the Parliament which met in perplexity and terror after the crash in 1720 [of the South Sea Bubble] that in 1830 the wealth of England. . . .' The drift of the argument is plain,

---

[1] Modern critics and journalists often assert that Macaulay always supports the Whigs against the Tories in his *History*. I cannot help thinking that these critics, though they have no doubt read each other's criticisms, have not read the *History* they criticize. The *History* is unsparing in its condemnation of numerous Whig politicians from Shaftesbury (of Charles II's reign) onwards, and often justifies the Tories against the Whigs on particular issues. Macaulay held a Whig philosophy, but he was anything but a dutiful henchman of the old Whig party.

and the rest of this admirably balanced sentence of a hundred and sixty words can be found near the end of the Essay on Southey's *Colloquies*.

Macaulay, though his literary career covered thirty-five years (1825–1859), remained all his life, as has been said, a man of 1832. His views were moderately 'advanced' in the 'twenties, and somewhat old-fashioned in the 'fifties, but they were the same views. The times had moved and he had not. John Stuart Mill, on the other hand, was a theorist whose theories would not stand still. His mind was not proof against the assaults of new ideas, and his works are a record of intellectual transition.

Autobiographies are proverbially interesting, and in the records of nineteenth-century thought there are few books more significant than the brief *Autobiography* of John Stuart Mill. If it were not a singularly conscientious record of fact one might suppose it was a biographical allegory designed to illustrate the mingled strength and weakness of the Utilitarian rule of life. At the conclusion one is left wondering how far James Mill had succeeded and how far he had failed in the task he set himself, of forming the perfect Benthamite. Certainly he set about his task in no half-hearted manner. John Mill began Greek at three years old; by the age of seven he had read most of the standard Greek and English historians. Thereafter he was introduced to Latin, algebra, chemistry, philosophy, economics, etc. At the age of sixteen his formal education was complete. He joined his father in the India House (the office of the East India Company), and became a regular contributor to Radical publications.

In many respects the education of John Mill had been a signal success; he had been braced by a training of extraordinary severity, to which the minds of most youths would certainly have succumbed. Yet it soon began to appear that for John Mill Benthamism was 'not enough'. At the age of twenty he found himself confronted with the following train of thought: ' "Suppose that all your objects in life were realized; that all the changes in institutions and opinions that you are looking forward to, could be completely effected at this very instant, would this be a great joy and happiness to you?" And an irrepressible self-consciousness distinctly answered, "No!" At this my heart sank within me: the whole foundation of which my life was constructed fell down. All my happiness was to have been found in a continual pursuit of this end. The end had ceased to charm, and how could there ever again be any interest in the means? I seemed to have nothing left to live for.'[1]

Mill found his salvation in the things that his education had omitted as of no account—in poetry, and particularly in the Nature poetry of Wordsworth. From the poetry of Wordsworth he passed to the philosophy of Coleridge, and we have already mentioned the celebrated essay in which Mill expounds Coleridge as the 'seminal mind' whose teaching was the necessary complement of that of Bentham. Published in the *Westminster Review*, such an essay had the daring and the paradox of a defence of Voltaire in the columns of the Evangelical *Record*. Mill never ceased to be a leader of the Benthamites, but he led them a very long way from the point at which he found them. Trained as a sworn foe of aristocracy and privilege, he concludes with an eloquent warning against the tyranny of democracy; trained as an individualist, upholding *laissez-faire* and freedom of contract in all departments of economics, he makes, as years pass on, many concessions to the school of thought which promoted the Factory Acts and prepared the way for Socialism; trained as an advocate of the orthodox Benthamite hedonism, i.e. 'pleasure' as the end of life, he transforms it into something not far removed from a philosophy of self-sacrifice; trained as a free thinker, he reaches at last a position which, though it is not dogmatic Christianity, is probably the position held by many who are prepared to call themselves Christians. Each of these four transformations must now be briefly illustrated.

(i) In 1859 Mill published the most popular and eloquent of his books, the *Essay on Liberty*. It occupies in our nine-

[1] *Autobiography,* p. 133.

teenth-century literature the place occupied by Milton's
Areopagitica in our seventeenth-century literature, as a plea
for freedom of thought and, within the utmost practicable
limits, of action. And the tyrant to be feared is no longer
a monarch or an aristocracy, but the tyranny of conventional
public opinion, which hates and fears originality and the
defiance of its prejudices as bitterly as any Inquisition or Star-
chamber of old. 'He who lets the world, or his own portion
of it, choose his plan of life for him, has no need of any other
faculty than the ape-like one of imitation.' Sometimes the
conventional majority will enforce its will by actual legislation, but it is equally dangerous when it exercises no other
pressure than that of social disapproval. He finds an obvious
example in the Puritanism of his day, which condemned
innocent and admirable recreations such as dancing or the
theatre. He finds another example in a tyranny which
we probably imagine to be peculiar to a later period, the
tyranny of trade unions. 'It is known that the bad workmen who form the majority of the operatives in many
branches of industry, are decidedly of opinion that bad workmen ought to receive the same wages as good, and that no
one ought to be allowed, through piecework or otherwise,
to earn by superior skill or industry more than others can
without it.' As an extreme example of the evil he glances
at the experiments in prohibihion already being made by
certain States of the American Union.

(ii) In 1847 Mill published his *Principles of Political
Economy*. It rapidly became the standard English treatise
upon the subject, and was still the one 'set book' on economics
in the Oxford History School twenty years ago. One of its
most significant chapters is the final one on 'The Grounds
and Limits of the *Laissez-faire* or Non-interference Principle'. *Laissez-faire*, says Mill, should be the rule, but he
proceeds to enumerate and defend a surprisingly long list
of exceptions. The State should supply free education and
compel parents to send their children to school. It should
control the authority of parents over their children and of men

over animals more completely than it does at present. It should be prepared to disannul certain types of contracts between individuals, when the contract is clearly undesirable and the result of the folly of one of the parties. It should control hours of labour, and assist emigration. It is a notable fact that the list of exceptions to *laissez-faire* grew in successive editions of the book from comparatively small dimensions in the 1847 edition. Indeed it has been said that the English Fabian Socialists of the 1880's, advocating 'socialism by instalments', should be regarded as disciples of Mill rather than of Karl Marx. But we shall return to this subject in the next chapter.

(iii) In a little book called *Utilitarianism* [1] Mill makes his famous distinction between 'higher' and 'lower' pleasures. The 'higher' pleasures are to be preferred and regarded in fact as more pleasurable pleasures; for in estimating pleasure, as in estimating anything else, the quality as well as the quantity of the articles must be taken into account. The higher pleasures may be called 'happiness', and happiness rather than pleasure is the end of life. This view, he tells us in the *Autobiography*, he never abandoned, but he found that happiness was only to be attained by those who set their hearts not on happiness but on something else,—'on the happiness of others, on the improvement of mankind, even on some art or pursuit, followed not as a means (to one's own happiness) but as an end in itself.' This is excellent but it is certainly not Benthamism! It is, in fact, as Richard Holt Hutton, the editor of *The Spectator*, remarked, 'a paradox which should suggest to utilitarians the deepest possible suspicion of the truth of the fundamental idea of their philosophy. That the true end of life should be always in the position of the old gentleman's macaroons, which he hid about amongst his papers and books, because he said that he enjoyed them so much more when he came upon them unawares,

---

[1] Mill claimed to have been the first to use this term as a name for the Benthamite philosophy at the age of sixteen!

than he did if he went to the cupboard avowedly to look for them, is surely a very odd compliment to the true end of life. The old gentleman did not regard the macaroons as the true end of life; and as a rule, unquestionably, what we do regard as the true end of life will bear contemplating and working for as such.' [1]

(iv) Immediately before his death Mill was engaged on writing *Three Essays on Religion*, and when they were posthumously published they met with much disapproval among most of those who had accounted themselves his disciples; and indeed it is not hard to imagine what Bentham and James Mill would have thought of them. Not only does the apostle of rationalism recognize the 'Utility of Religion' but he holds in the last essay (though not in its predecessor) that the best religion is one involving a Personal God. 'It cannot be questioned', he writes, 'that the un-doubting belief in the real existence of a Being who realizes our own best ideas of perfection, and of our being in the hands of that Being as ruler of the universe, gives an increase of power to these feelings (i.e. aspirations towards goodness) beyond what they can receive from reference to a merely ideal conception.' It is true that in the remainder of the essay he expounds the almost insuperable difficulties in the way of such a belief, but, like *Cleon* in one of the best of Browning's poems, he would fain believe it.

Mill was not a great thinker; his superstructure of thought was too ill-fitted to its foundations. But he was a very influential thinker, and a very admirable man. Gladstone, who detested rationalism, spoke of him as 'the saint of rationalism'. He did as much as any freethinker to persuade simple-minded religious people that it is possible to be both an atheist and a good man, and he did this more by his life than by his writings. It was characteristic of him that he published a cheap edition of his *Political Economy* without author's royalties, in order to bring the book as much as possible within reach of the purses of working men. That so dry a writer

[1] Hutton, *Contemporary Thought and Thinkers*, Vol. I, p. 185.

should have been so widely read is in itself a testimonial to the seriousness of his age. To-day the work of elucidating economic and political theory is in the hands of one set of people and the work, more highly remunerated, of serving it up with humorous sauce for popular consumption is in the hands of another set. Perhaps Mill's most distinctive contribution to national life was his advocacy of the rights of women. His little book *The Subjection of Woman* was the most important tract on the subject for a whole generation, and during his brief career as a member of parliament he introduced, as an amendment to the second Reform Bill, the first proposal of legislation in favour of Woman Suffrage to be debated in the House of Commons.

II

THE EVANGELICAL ORTHODOXY AND ITS RIVALS

WE have shown the Old Tory domination giving place, in the sphere of politics, to energetic optimism of the Utilitarian or Benthamite school of thought. In the same way and at about the same date the authority within the Church of the old High-and-dry school, with its complacent tolerance of worldliness and indolence, was effaced by the ardour of the Evangelicals. They never, perhaps, secured a majority on the episcopal bench, but they provided something more important than bishops; they provided religion. Benthamism was a European movement of thought; we could find its equivalent under other names in France and Germany. But Evangelicalism was peculiarly English, and it is therefore the more instructive to take foreign evidence upon it. Halévy, whose great *History of the English People in the Nineteenth Century* is already, though uncompleted, recognized as a standard authority, finds in Evangelicalism the principal ground of difference between our own modern history and that of other countries. He writes:

'It was during this critical year, a few months after the passage of the Reform Bill, that English Evangelicalism may be said to have reached its apogee. It constituted the essence of the Methodist preaching, and in their hatred of Catholics and Latitudinarians [1] the Wesleyans were drawing closer to the Church from which they were sprung. And

[1] Those who distrusted strict interpretation of the dogmas of the Christian creed.

99

within the Church the influence of the Evangelicals grew stronger every day. The number of clergymen who had given their formal adherence to the party were estimated at between two and three thousand. The parochial clergy were no longer the keen hunters and hard drinkers they had been a few years earlier. By their preaching and example the Evangelicals had enforced a stricter observance of decorum, and a more obvious regard for the dignity of their vocation. And in the last resort it is to the influence of the Evangelicals that we must attribute the moral reform which Thomas Arnold and several others were effecting at this time with enormous success in the Anglican public schools.[1] Among the aristocracy who governed the country the Evangelicals were bringing the duel into discredit.[2] Among the lower classes they were attacking the use of intoxicating liquors: the first Temperance Societies had just been founded in imitation of an American model, and the House of Commons was shortly to appoint a Committee to consider the advisability of passing legislation with the object of diminishing drunkenness. The credit of the two great humanitarian measures passed by the new parliament, the emancipation of the slaves and the protection of child labour in factories, belongs to the Evangelicals even more than to the Radicals. Sir Andrew Agnew introduced annually a Bill to prohibit Sunday work in any form whatsoever. He was always defeated, but the number of votes recorded in favour of his Sabbatarian Bill increased every year, and every year

[1] Most public schools owe their modern prosperity to some great Victorian headmaster, and in most cases these were strong Evangelicals, e.g. Pears at Repton and Welldon at Tonbridge. Such headmasters belonged to the generation following that of Dr. Arnold, whose Rugby dates were 1828–42.

[2] Castlereagh and Canning fought a duel in 1809. Wellington fought a duel in 1829, amid general disapprobation. Peel issued several challenges, but on each occasion the affair was compromised by an apology. In 1846 a friend dissuaded him from sending a challenge by threatening to inform the police—his own Bobbies! The friend was a nobleman of old family, Lord Lincoln.

the habits of the people, steeped in Evangelical piety, rendered more superfluous the legal enactment of a rule which everybody freely obeyed.

'Men of letters disliked the Evangelicals for their narrow Puritanism, men of science for their intellectual feebleness. Nevertheless during the nineteenth century Evangelical religion was the moral cement of English society. It was the influence of the Evangelicals which invested the British aristocracy with an almost Stoic dignity, restrained the plutocrats newly risen from the masses from vulgar ostentation and debauchery, and placed over the proletariat a select body of workmen enamoured of virtue and capable of self-restraint.' [1] Evangelicalism was a greater force than Benthamism. Benthamism inculcated a line of thought in the minds of thinking persons—always a minority; Evangelicalism moulded the character of the nation. Evangelicalism was the principal ingredient in the state of mind which to-day we describe, contemptuously perhaps, as 'Victorianism'. We have now emerged from the Victorian atmosphere. Its defects are so obvious to us that we need waste no time in analysing them, especially as we shall come across them when we consider some of the great Victorian critics. M. Halévy does not dismiss 'Victorianism' with contempt.

One of the marks of the dominance of Evangelicalism was the appetite of the mid-nineteenth century Englishman for sermons. Not only were sermons much longer; vast numbers of them were collected and published in book form, and commanded large sales. To-day novels form by far the largest class in the annual census of books; they constitute one-seventh of the whole. Popular opinion probably imagines that they bulk still larger, and no doubt if the census were of copies sold and not of books published, the share of fiction in the total would be greater. In the first half of the nineteenth century volumes of sermons occupied the pride of place now enjoyed by novels. To-day there

---

[1] Halévy, *op. cit.*, Vol. III, p. 165.

are very few preachers whose sermons are welcomed in publishers' offices.

Utilitarian *laissez-faire* in politics and Evangelical piety in religion were contemporaries in their rise, their climax, and their decline, and this fact naturally suggests an inquiry whether they had any points in common. Their origins certainly lay far apart; it is difficult to imagine two men with fewer points of contact than Wesley, the ardent and active missionary, preaching the gospel of righteousness, temperance, and judgement to come, and Bentham, the sedentary rationalist, testing the laws of England in his crucible of utility. Yet both of them were supporters of Wilberforce in his crusade against the slave-trade. Both movements were in fact affected by the new humanitarian sentiment which was something deeper and more universal than either of them. The Benthamites fought against all forms of cruelty because they stood for 'the greatest happiness of the greatest number'; the Evangelicals fought the same battle because good works were practical religion, and the relief of the victims of cruelty was the most obvious and necessary of all good works. We may go further. The Benthamites, advocating the elimination of abuses and scandalous privileges by means of legal reform, strongly supported the measures taken by parliament shortly after the Reform Bill for the Reform of the Church. Plurality, i.e. the holding of more than one living, and non-residence of clergy in their parishes were made illegal, and a better distribution of the revenues of the Church was secured by the establishment of a permanent body of Ecclesiastical Commissioners, of whom half were laymen. The Evangelicals also supported these reforms. They desired to eliminate abuses from the Church and, like the Protestant Reformers of the sixteenth century, they regarded the State as the proper authority to reform the Church.

Such agreement between Benthamites and Evangelicals in support of special causes may however be regarded as purely accidental. Is it possible to go further, and show that the two movements had certain fundamental points in common? Professor Dicey holds that they had.[1]

Benthamism was a form of political individualism. It reposed great, in fact excessive, confidence in the capacity of individuals to 'work out their own salvation', as we say, so far as their social and economic welfare in this world was concerned. Its view of society has been called 'atomistic'. The human community was viewed as a concourse of atoms, each going its own way and minding its own business. The function of government is essentially that of an umpire, laying down and enforcing rules to prevent the atoms jostling and inflicting avoidable injuries on one another. But Evangelicalism was also a form of individualism—individualism in religion. Its care was the salvation of the individual human soul. It was uninterested in the conception of a single Divine Church, and indifferent to problems of ecclesiastical organization. It was acceptable to episcopalians and nonconformists alike, and drew them together in bonds of common sympathy.

And if the movements were alike in what they asserted they were alike also in what they ignored. Both were indifferent to tradition. As the Benthamites despised the teachings of history, as set forth in the philosophy of Burke or Coleridge, so did the Evangelicals ignore, if they did not positively despise, the treasures of spiritual inspiration contained in the history and the theology of the Church. Their one authority was the Bible, which they interpreted according to the light of their own natures. The Church, once it emerged from the New Testament, quickly became 'Romish' in their eyes, and what was 'Romish' was not edifying.

Lastly the Benthamites with their pursuit of material happiness and the Evangelicals with their pursuit of spiritual salvation were both alike tempted to form a very narrow conception alike of happiness and of spiritual salvation. Both

[1] Dicey, *Law and Opinion in England*, pp. 397–404, on which the paragraphs which follow are based.

tended to become what Matthew Arnold called Philistines, so concentrated upon prosperity or piety, or both, that art, literature, and science, the pursuit of beauty and of truth for their own sakes, found no place in their lives, being in fact dismissed as 'vanities'. Bentham, we are told by John Stuart Mill, could not bear to hear pronounced in his presence the words *good* and *bad taste*, which he regarded as expressions of irrational prejudice, like the preference for poetry rather than 'pushpin'. I do not know whether any leading Evangelical expressed himself with the same positiveness on this subject, but many of them may well have done so.

The year 1833, which Halévy takes as marking the high tide of Evangelicalism, was also the birth year of a very different religious movement, the Oxford Movement, which is the principal source of modern Anglo-Catholicism.

The Oxford Movement was provoked by a false alarm. The Act of 1829 had emancipated the Roman Catholics, the Reform Bill of 1832 had created a new electorate containing a large body of Dissenters, and in 1833 a Bill was introduced for the suppression of ten of the twenty-two sees of the Irish Protestant Church, then regarded by churchmen as an integral part of the Church of England.[1] The Elizabethan Settlement had assumed that the Established Church would be the Church of the whole nation. That assumption had been falsified, but the Church had continued to be the Church of the governing classes. Power was now passing to its enemies, and what would be the result? The cry was raised that the Church was in danger. From the pulpit of St. Mary's, Oxford, John Keble, a Fellow of Oriel College, already known to a wide circle as the author of a book of religious verse called *The Christian Year*, denounced the Irish Church Bill as a 'direct disavowal of the sovereignty of God'

---

[1] The Irish Established Church ministered to the needs of only a very small fraction of the Irish population, and its revenues were grossly excessive. It was disestablished and partially disendowed by Gladstone in 1869.

and an act of 'national apostasy'. In the next year Keble and John Henry Newman, another Fellow of the same college, began to publish a series of *Tracts for the Times*, and in the first of these Newman warned the clergy that disestablishment, disendowment, and perhaps actual persecution might lie ahead of them. Of the bishops he drily remarked, 'we could not wish them a more blessed termination of their course then the spoiling of their goods, and martyrdom,' but for the clergy, more particularly the young clergy whom he sought to influence, he had more practical counsel. Let them remember that theirs was the gift of the Spirit of the Apostles, received in ordination; the State had not given it and the State could not take it away. His advice to them was, 'Magnify your office'.

The Church was not in danger. The Evangelicals, who welcomed reform, would have stoutly and effectively opposed anything remotely resembling spoliation. The enemies of the Church were a mere handful, and had no programme to offer. The only 'dangers' ahead of the Church were the abolition of pluralities and the establishment of the Ecclesiastical Commission. None the less the Oxford Movement survived its original negative purpose, for it gave expression to grand conceptions, not new but long neglected in Protestant England. It took as its text an almost forgotten clause of the creed, 'I believe in the Holy Catholic Church'. 'I have ever kept before me', wrote Newman, 'that there was something greater than the Established Church, and that was the Church Catholic and Apostolic, set up from the beginning, of which she was but the local presence and organ.' The Church in fact was not a department of the State, as the High-and-dry party had been content to regard it, nor a convenience provided for the salvation of the individual, as the Evangelicals seemed to think; it was a Divine— *the* Divine—institution, the Body of Christ. The appeal of the *Tracts* was not general but professional. They were addressed to the clergy, and their purpose was to kindle what, in a secular institution, we should call *esprit de corps*.

The Oxford leaders were not as yet, and most of them never became, admirers of the Church of Rome, yet they were certainly not Protestants. Some of the more headstrong adherents of the Movement made insulting remarks about the Protestant martyrs, and many plain Englishmen were unable to understand how an anti-Protestant could be anything but a Papist in sheep's clothing. Less than fifty years had elapsed since the Gordon Riots; many were still sore about the emancipation of the Catholics; in fact the young theologians of Oxford rapidly achieved a scandalous notoriety which they did not at all regret, in old-fashioned circles. It was a theological age, when sermons were as popular as novels are to-day. Excitement reached its climax when Newman published the ninetieth and last of the *Tracts* in 1841. It is a long pamphlet, designed to prove that the Thirty-nine Articles, though 'the offspring of an uncatholic age, are, through God's good providence, to say the least, not uncatholic, and may be subscribed by those who aim at being Catholic in heart and doctrine'. It does not sound like a 'best-seller', but Newman tells us that 'in every part of the country and every class of society, through every organ and occasion of opinion, in newspapers, in periodicals, at meetings, in pulpits, at dinner-tables, in coffee-rooms, in railway carriages, I was denounced as a traitor who had laid his train and was detected in the very act of firing it against the time-honoured establishment'. Edition after edition was issued, and the author was enabled to buy a large and valuable library out of the proceeds. When four years later Newman fulfilled the forecast of his enemies by going over to Rome, the event created almost as much stir as Sir Robert Peel's conversion to Corn Law Repeal a few months afterwards.

It is difficult to imagine the Oxford Movement without Newman. Perhaps it would have run much the same course and achieved the same results, for it supplied a real need; but it would lack the greater part of its attraction for posterity. Newman was a man of extraordinary personal charm, a really great preacher, and one of the acknowledged masters of English prose. Long after he left the Church of England his Anglican sermons, in book form, brought to many of a younger generation, dissatisfied with the narrow outlook and stuffy pieties of nonconformist or Evangelical homes, the revelation of a grander, a more romantic, conception of the Church of Christ. Poets and literary men who find theological controversy the most wearisome of mental activities have often regretted that Newman gave to religion gifts that might have been devoted to pure literature. The greatest of his books would not have been written but for an accident. In 1863, eighteen years after Newman's secession to Rome, Charles Kingsley, the robust and admirable 'muscular Christian', casually remarked in the course of a magazine article that 'Truth for its own sake has never been a virtue with the Roman clergy. Father Newman informs us that it need not, and on the whole ought not to be.' Newman was roused to reply, and, after demolishing Kingsley in a piece of writing that will always rank as a masterpiece in its own class, proceeded to tell at length the story of the development of his religious opinions. The *Apologia pro Vita sua* at once restored Newman to his rightful place as one of the greatest men of religion our country has produced. It also, there can be little doubt, helped Englishmen of all creeds to form a juster and more kindly opinion of the Church of Rome.

Newman lived to extreme old age, the most completely isolated of all the great Englishmen of his day. After his death in 1890, R. H. Hutton of the *Spectator* wrote of him: 'In a century in which physical discovery and material wellbeing have usurped and almost absorbed the admiration of mankind, such a life as that of Cardinal Newman stands out in strange and almost majestic, though singularly graceful and unpretending contrast to the eager and agitated turmoil of confused passions, hesitating ideals, tentative virtues, and groping philanthropies, amidst which it has been lived.' [1]

[1] Hutton, *Cardinal Newman*, p. 251.

He had been hardly more at ease in the Church of his choice than in the Church of his birth; his true spiritual home, it has been said, was with St. Ambrose and St. Augustine in the fourth century.

After Newman's secession the Movement rapidly ceased to agitate with its controversies the quadrangles of Oxford. Its romance was over, but its work was only beginning. It gradually penetrated the vicarages and transformed the ordering of the services. Black gowns disappeared from the pulpits, choirs began to wear surplices and to turn to the east for the Creed; candles and crucifixes appeared on altars. More important, the Communion Service was more frequently celebrated and began to resume its position as the essential act of Christian devotion. 'High Churchmen' of the Oxford school were raised to the episcopate, and established new standards of episcopal activity. Prominent among such was Samuel Wilberforce, son of the great Evangelical layman, a man admirable alike in piety and in society and the close friend both of Gladstone and, for a time, of Disraeli. He might have become Archbishop of Canterbury had not three of his brothers and his two brothers-in-law all gone over to Rome.

Yet 'Puseyism', as it was often called from the name of one of the Oxford leaders, was a powerful rather than a popular movement. Its original appeal was to the vocational pride of the clergy, and its principal adherents have always been found among the clergy and what are conveniently called the clerically-minded laity. It created a powerful, well-organized, and sharply defined party within the Church; it never succeeded, like Evangelicalism, in pervading the mind of the nation. It was in fact intensely self-conscious and denominational, whereas Evangelicalism had been the opposite. One could become in all essentials an Evangelical without being aware of the fact; to become a 'Puseyite' was an act of deliberate volition.

In the latter part of the century the ritualistic practices of the extremer adherents of the party, overstepping as they did the law of the Church of England, excited growing irritation. Queen Victoria always disapproved of 'Pusey-ites', and it was largely to please his Queen that Disraeli in 1875 supported a Bill to 'put down ritualism',—practices which Disraeli described as 'mass in masquerade'. The Bill passed, in face of Gladstone's vehement opposition, but it did not achieve its purpose. Ritualism was not to be suppressed by any legal devices, and the leaders of the Church were ultimately convinced that the law of the Church had better be altered since it could not be enforced. That decision was the beginning of the long story that has led up to the Revised Prayer Book of 1927–8. The contrast between the powerful majorities that accepted that Book in the Church Assembly and the resolute and successful opposition of a large section of the House of Commons illustrates the fact that the Anglo-Catholic movement, though it dominates the Church, has not overcome the traditional Protestantism of the nation. The positive enthusiasms of Evangelicalism have, in large part, evaporated, but its negative residuum of resistance to anything supposedly 'Popish' still remains.

We have discovered points of similarity between the Benthamite and the Evangelical view of life. It is even easier to indicate the contrasts between the Benthamites and the Victorian Anglo-Catholics. The emphasis of Anglo-Catholic thought was all on the corporate body, the Church; the individual found salvation only as a member of it. If we are to seek the secular analogy to Anglo-Catholicism, we should find it in those political philosophies which exalt the State as the secular providence of the individual—either in the economic ideal of the Socialists or in the militarist and despotic ideal of pre-war Prussia.

Again, Evangelical religion, like Benthamism, can fairly be accused of indifference to art and scholarship. Anglo-Catholicism was cradled in scholarship, and became, when grown to maturity, a patron of the arts. It is no accident that the greatest of the Oxford leaders was a master of English prose and, occasionally, a considerable poet, whereas Evangelicalism produced almost nothing that will be read for its purely literary value. The early leaders of the Oxford Movement, Keble, Newman, Pusey and others as well, were profoundly versed in ecclesiastical history. Keble was at one time Professor of Poetry at Oxford, and his lectures have been praised by a great modern authority, George Saintsbury; Newman acknowledged Cicero as his master in style; Pusey studied the German theologians. All of them studied the early Christian Fathers. As the movement developed the emphasis shifted from scholarship to art; cynics have remarked that the wearing of vestments and the adornment of altars are easier pursuits than the study of the Latin and Greek theologians. Pusey was no ritualist, but Puseyism came to be identical with ritualism. Care for the adornment of priest and altar naturally begat interest in the fabric of the Church. 'Restoration' in the architectural sense, well-intentioned and generally disastrous in its results, became a favourite outlet for Anglo-Catholic energies. It is obvious that Anglo-Catholicism had affinities with other lines of thought which were rediscovering the values of the Middle Ages.

Finally, the Evangelicals were philanthropists, and, as such, allies of the Benthamites on many, though not all, reformist programmes. It would be absurd to deny the virtue of philanthropy to individual Anglo-Catholics; the devoted labours of scores, nay hundreds, of Anglo-Catholic priests in slum parishes would refute the charge; but Anglo-Catholicism as such was unconcerned with social conditions. The Church was concerned with nothing but religion; philanthropy might be excellent but it was not religion. Christ had not sought to abolish poverty, and the great Catholic teachers of the Middle Ages had not encouraged the idea that the world could be made a less painful place by intelligent legislation. 'Progress' in fact was a modern superstition. Belief in the possibilities of unlimited improvement in the conditions of this world had grown up with the decline of the belief in the reality of an Eternal Life, compared with which the pursuit of happiness in this life was mere frivolity. The purpose of the Church was to preach Eternal Life; it had nothing to do with 'Progress'.

Quite near the end of his life Newman declared that he 'had never considered social questions in their relation to faith, and had always looked upon the poor as objects for compassion and benevolence.' The position of the Evangelicals differed in this alone, that they supplemented personal benevolence with benevolent legislation. It was however inevitable, as we can see in retrospect, that the religious energies of the first half of the nineteenth century should sooner or later produce a body of thought which challenged, on religious grounds, the whole organization of industrial society, and denied, in the name of the Gospels, the principles of orthodox economics, *laissez-faire* and competitive marketing.

In 1848 a small group of men proclaimed themselves 'Christian Socialists'. It was a provocative title, for Socialism to the Englishman of 1848 suggested little except the fiasco of the National Workshops in Paris, which had just been suppressed after four days of street fighting in which 10,000 lives were said to have been lost. Those with longer memories recollected the Socialism of Robert Owen, and recollected also that Owen was an atheist and an advocate of freedom of divorce. Croker, the old 'Die-hard' of the *Quarterly*, wrote: 'Incredible as it may appear, there is, it seems, a clique of educated and clever but wayward-minded men—the most prominent among them two *clergymen of the Church of England*—who from a morbid craving for notoriety or a crazy straining after paradox, have taken up the unnatural and unhallowed task of preaching . . . not indeed such open and undisguised *Jacobinism and Jacquerie* as we have just been quoting, but, under the name of *Christian Socialism*, the same doctrines in a form not less dangerous for being less honest.' [1]

[1] The 'doctrines' Croker had 'just been quoting' were murder, spoliation, free-love, and anarchism. This passage helps one to understand

The two clergymen were Frederick Denison Maurice, Professor of Divinity at King's College, London, and Charles Kingsley, not yet famous as a novelist; among their lay allies was Thomas Hughes, barrister and Old Rugbeian. Their purpose was to rescue Socialism from its ill-repute, and to show that properly understood it meant simply the application of Christian principles to industrial organization. The keynote of Christianity was Love; the keynote of Socialism was co-operation in place of competition: co-operation was the application of the spirit of Love to the organization of industry. They started a weekly paper entitled *Politics for the People*, and in its first leading article declared that 'Politics have too long been separated from Christianity; religious men have supposed that their only business is with the world to come; political men have declared that the present world is governed on principles entirely different from that. . . . But Politics for the People cannot be separated from Religion.'

For six years the Christian Socialists promoted and supervised a variety of experiments in co-operative production. Managers were elected by, and profits devoted to the welfare of, the workers. The experiments failed, and the 'Movement' ended, its leading members each going their several ways, some of them helping to establish the Working Men's College in North London. Yet the Christian Socialists had lit a candle which has not been put out. Ever since their failure there have been more and more professed Churchmen who, whether they call themselves Socialists or not, have realized that Christianity and politics cannot be kept in separate compartments of the mind, and that it is part of the work of the churches to protest against social injustices, and to work for the establishment of a social order in which all will get a fair share of the really good things this world has to offer.

why his contemporaries regarded Croker as an unscrupulous controversialist! I owe the quotation from Croker to Mrs. Courtney's *English Freethinkers of the Nineteenth Century*, p. 37.

Hughes subsequently entered parliament and actively supported, both inside the House and outside it, the claim of Trade Unions to legal protection and privilege; it is, however, as the author of *Tom Brown's Schooldays*, published in 1857, that he will always be remembered. 'Tom Brown' has probably ceased to be popular with schoolboys; they observe that it is not 'true to life', and assume, perhaps, that it never was; they resent the fact that the author is quite obviously bent on improving them. The book remains, however, exceedingly interesting to the student of nineteenth-century opinion; it is a first-class Victorian 'document'.

When Dr. Arnold was appointed to Rugby in 1828 it was said of him that he would 'change the face of education' throughout England. Arnold was not exactly an Evangelical; he was devoted to Coleridge's fantastic scheme for making the Church once again co-extensive with the nation by the comprehension of all Christian sects, and he held liberal views on doctrine and Biblical criticism which shocked the average Evangelical. None the less it may be said in a general sense that with him Evangelicalism began its conquest of the public schools. Those 'nurseries of vice', as Mr. Bowdler had called them, were to become schools of earnest endeavour and Christian manliness. 'What we must look for', said Arnold, 'is first, religious and moral principle; secondly, gentlemanly conduct; thirdly, intellectual ability.' The originality of Arnold's methods has been exaggerated, but the fact is unimportant. He was the greatest, if not the first, of the 'great headmasters', and his reforms had an importance even he can hardly have foreseen, for the growth of wealth and the development of railway transport were to multiply many times over the fraction of the population that sent its sons to boarding schools. The public schools have been, in fact, one of the principal agents in breaking down the social division between the gentry and the enriched middle classes.

Since Arnold's time the public schools have suffered a development not unlike that which has befallen the politics of the nation. The Benthamites, of whom Gladstone [1] was in many ways the last great representative, ultimately handed over the control of parliament to the working classes, and the working classes have used their power to further anti-Benthamite ends. Arnold entrusted the government of the schools to the senior boys, and the senior boys have added a fourth item to Arnold's trio of ideals, placing it perhaps first on the list—namely, athletic proficiency, secured through compulsory organized games. The immense vogue of outdoor games (if this digression may be carried one stage further) has been one of the salient features of modern England, and has expanded far beyond the limits of the schools in which it began. It deserves attention, for devotion to athletics is as much an element in 'opinion' as devotion to any school of political or religious thought. It is not fanciful to see in it a natural reaction from the increasing urbanization of modern life. So long as men live and work in the country all nature is at their disposal for purposes of fresh air and wholesome exercise. What the countryman takes as nature bestows it, the townsman can only secure in an artificial tabloid form. With only a few acres of grass available, he needs a ball, be it of leather or india-rubber, with or without a bat or a racquet as well, if he is to amuse himself within so confined a space. If the reader is disposed to reject this explanation, he must find some other reason why our ancestors for the most part did not need games after emerging from the nursery, whereas we obviously do.

Charles Kingsley was one of the most robust and attractive of the mid-Victorians. He was not a public schoolboy, but the 'muscular Christianity' of which he was the embodiment was essentially of the public-school type. In the days of Christian Socialism he had written a pamphlet called *Cheap Clothes and Nasty* which is as effective an onslaught on sweated labour as has ever been penned. He was not ashamed of defying clerical conventions, and was accused

---

[1] Gladstone was a Benthamite in politics and a 'Puseyite' in religion: a very uncommon combination.

of being 'avowedly associated (and paraded on a placard) with several notorious infidels', one of whom appears to have delivered a funeral oration 'over an infidel adulteress, in which he speaks of the "distorted memory of *our own* Paine"'. This undesirable friend seems to have been Holyoake, an atheist and a leader of the Rochdale co-operative movement. But Kingsley was in no danger of atheism, which he disliked as much as he disliked the Church of Rome. His exceedingly happy married life provoked in him an intense distaste for professional celibacy. His poetic drama *A Saint's Tragedy* is a tract upon the subject, and his duel with Newman on Romanism and truthfulness has already been mentioned. Kingsley in his anti-Romanism as in his Socialism displayed a cast of mind the reverse of mediaeval. 'What', he asks impatiently, 'is the use of preaching about heaven to hungry paupers?' Such a question would have been incomprehensible to a mediaeval Christian, and indeed deeply shocking to William Wilberforce.

His novels cover a wide field. *Alton Locke* was an expansion (and dilution) of *Cheap Clothes and Nasty*; *Yeast* attacks the landlords and the game laws; *Two Years Ago* depicts the horrors, as he had himself seen them, of the cholera epidemic of 1849; and *The Water Babies* was perhaps the greatest of tales written expressly for the nursery until the publication of *Alice in Wonderland*. In *Westward Ho!* he achieved a historical novel worthy to rank with the Waverleys. He wrote some excellent songs, and his *Ode to the North East Wind* is a singular glorification of the English ideal of the strenuous life. It is amusing to compare it with that greater Ode in which Shelley glorified a wind blowing from the opposite direction. Kingsley's wind blows in briefer and more spasmodic gusts. Still, it is the wind that has apparently made England what she is; it is the wind that brought the Vikings; it is the 'wind of God'—the God of the Old Testament presumably. Kingsley, with his love of Vikings and Elizabethan seamen, is to be regarded as a forerunner, on its sentimental side, of the

Imperialist movement that dominated the politics of the latter end of the century.

With Frederick Denison Maurice we return to issues more strictly religious than those raised by the work of Hughes and Kingsley. We enter upon that region of the Church which was neither 'High' (Anglo-Catholic) nor 'Low' (Evangelical), but 'Broad'. Broad Churchmanship included a great diversity of opinions, of which we can only take a few representative samples.

Maurice was the son of a Unitarian minister who was yet so incompletely Unitarian that he baptized the children of his congregation 'in the name of the Father, the Son, and the Holy Ghost', thereby incurring the rebuke that he baptized in the name of 'an abstraction, a man, and a metaphor'. Maurice's life illustrates the all-pervasiveness of religious controversy in his generation. His childhood was passed amidst the religious discords of his parents and sisters, and theological conflict dogged him to the end of his days. He was a profound thinker, a saintly man, but an unskilful controversialist; for he did not like it, and skilled controversialists are normally those who enjoy the exercise, however much they may protest that they do not do so.

To Maurice more than to any other single man is due the liberation of the English churches from the incubus of Hell-fire, and what that incubus meant I imagine that only those who have made a wide study (as I have not) of the sermons of a hundred years ago, can fully realize. The evil consequences of the belief that God condemns the wicked, or all but the good, to perpetual torture are obvious enough to-day. It involved a libel upon the character of God— a libel readily exploited by the enemies of religion; and it corrupted Christian ethics by suggesting that the motive of good conduct was the avoidance of the penalties of a Divine criminal code. In fact it imparted to Christian moral teaching an element that may be called 'inverted Benthamism'. The Benthamites were denounced on moral grounds for holding that the test of goodness was simply its capacity for producing happiness, but they might have retorted that much orthodox Christian theology appeared to teach that the ultimate aim of the virtuous Christian was the avoidance of Hell. For proclaiming his disbelief in Everlasting Damnation Maurice was, in 1853, deprived of his professorship at King's College, London. Differences on subjects akin to this had involved him in controversy with Pusey, and Pusey had declared that he and Maurice 'worshipped different Gods'. It was true, and it is the God of Maurice that has survived.

Maurice was equally opposed to the extreme Sabbatarianism of the Evangelicals. He was rebuked for organizing Sunday excursions in connexion with the Working Men's College, even though he read prayers in the course of the excursion! He was quite agreed that the Working Men's College must oppose the Secularists; but, he added, 'to do this effectively it must also be in direct opposition to the Religionists—that is to say it must assert the principle that God is to be sought and honoured in every pursuit, not merely in something technically called religion'.

It should also be said in praise of Maurice that he was, with John Stuart Mill, one of the most active promoters of the movement for the improved education of women. Here 'the saint of rationalism' and the most tender-hearted and sensitive of the theologians met on common ground. Another man, very unlike both of them, had raised his voice in the same cause a generation earlier. Sydney Smith wrote: 'Can anything be more perfectly absurd than to suppose that the solicitude a mother feels for her children depends on her ignorance of Greek and Mathematics; and that she would desert an infant for a quadratic equation?' This sentence obviously expects the answer 'Nothing!' Yet is it 'absurd' to reply that though a mother will not desert a baby for an equation, a female mathematician may be inoculated by mathematics against matrimony? Maurice was not troubled by the possibilities of rivalry between mathematics and matrimony. His religion persuaded him of the equal rights of the sexes and of the right of women to a free choice among the variety of good things that life has to offer.

Yet to his own generation Maurice appeared ineffective. Mill says, 'There was more intellectual power wasted in Maurice than in any other of my contemporaries. Few of them certainly have had so much to waste.' Matthew Arnold says, 'He passed his life beating the bush with deep emotion and never starting the hare.' Maurice himself might have agreed, for he was an almost painfully self-distrustful man. But in retrospect he can be recognized as a 'seminal mind'. His books are no longer readable, but mainly because their practical effectiveness has reduced their contentions to truisms.

The most popular and conspicuous figure among the Broad Churchmen was Arthur Stanley, Dean of Westminster, a pupil of Dr. Arnold, whose *Life* he wrote, and a great favourite with Queen Victoria. His *History of the Jewish Church*, at once scholarly and picturesque, reached a wide public and familiarized its readers with liberal views of Old Testament History. It was said of him that he preferred lay to ecclesiastical virtues, and he was continually engaged in defending not only those whom he agreed with but all sections of the Church, High or Low, which were at any time in danger of exclusion. In fact he held, like Coleridge and Arnold, that it was the business of a national Church to include diversities, to be indeed neither High nor Low, but Broad. He championed no dogma but the relaxation of all dogmas. He was an admirable man but not a profound thinker. There are some people, it has been said, whose minds are so 'open' that they cannot hold anything. Critics of Stanley might regard him as one of these, and one wonders whether he reflected, and with what results, on Disraeli's famous remark to him, 'Remember, Mr. Dean; no dogma, no dean!'

The leaders of 'High' and 'Low' were by no means prepared to reciprocate the anti-dogmatic generosity of the Broad Church Dean. In 1860 there was published a volume called *Essays and Reviews*, by various writers, among them Temple, a future Archbishop of Canterbury, and Jowett, a future Master of Balliol. The aim of the book was to provoke free discussion among those who were united in a common Christianity, but the result was somewhat different. Frederic Harrison, who was not a Christian at all, welcomed the book as showing that its authors had already gone half way along the road from Christianity to infidelity, and invited them to step out boldly and complete the journey. Thereupon Samuel Wilberforce, the most conspicuous of Puseyite Bishops, and Lord Shaftesbury, the greatest of Evangelical laymen, denounced heresy. The bishops met at Fulham, and issued an official circular to the clergy condemning the book and hinting that some of the essays were inconsistent with the Thirty-nine Articles.

Two years later Bishop Colenso of Natal published a book called *The Pentateuch and the Book of Joshua critically examined*. Much of Colenso's criticism was minute, arithmetical, and a trifle absurd, but it certainly demonstrated the fact that, tried by modern standards of accurate statement, the first six books of the Old Testament were lamentably deficient. The book incurred fierce resentment among the official leaders of the Church, and one cannot help supposing that with most of them their resentment was due to the fact that Colenso had broadcasted information which well educated clergy preferred to conceal from their congregations. Most of what Colenso said is now accepted as obviously true, and the educated clergy of to-day, far from deploring the spread of such knowledge, are more inclined to deplore the fact that large sections of the nominally religious laity take so little intelligent interest in their Bibles that they are apt to be shocked when they happen to come across facts which are the commonplaces of Biblical scholarship.

Colenso's book could be condemned as merely negative and destructive. Nothing of the kind could be urged against *Ecce Homo*, issued anonymously a few years later. Its author was J. R. Seeley, a Cambridge historian whom we shall meet again as a contributor to the development of Imperialism. *Ecce Homo* was a reverent and scholarly essay upon the teaching of Christ, and his method and purpose in founding the Church. It expressly excludes all consideration of Christ's claim to be the Son of God. It isolates, for purposes of study, the human aspect of One who, if he was God, was also Man. None the less, the book was furiously abused by both Pusey and Shaftesbury. Shaftesbury declared it to be 'the most pestilential volume ever vomited forth from the jaws of Hell'.

It was perhaps natural that among Broad Churchmen there should have been some so Broad that their Churchmanship was visible to very few except themselves. Among such was Matthew Arnold, son of Arnold of Rugby, whose *Literature and Dogma* was published in 1873. Arnold was profoundly convinced of the value of the Bible, its moral teaching and its literary splendour, as an element making for stability and dignity in the life of the nation. He observed with pain and regret the assaults of the rationalists, reinforced in recent years by the dogmatic materialism popularly associated with the truths of physical and biological science, and he felt that the professional defenders of the Bible were conducting their defence in a manner that was bound to ensure their defeat. Free thought must be accepted. 'The freethinking of one generation is the common-sense of the next.' 'Miracles do not happen.' The attribution of Personality to God is mere poetry and metaphor. Religion, in fact, is nothing but 'morality touched with emotion'. The Bible is to be regarded as 'Literature', not 'Dogma'.

Matthew Arnold would have cordially agreed with Samuel Butler when he said that 'the men of religion tell a lot of little lies for the sake of one big truth, and the men of science tell a lot of little truths for the sake of one big lie'. He wanted the 'men of religion' to abandon their 'little lies', on the ground that the 'big truth', the 'secret of Jesus' as he calls it, would stand better without them. Unfortunately it is very hard to decide what is little and what big in this sphere; also, what is truth and what lie. The attraction of the Roman Church for many resides in the fact that for her the little and the big are all equally subjects not of argument but of faith. Browning has an excellent poem [1] in which a highly intelligent bishop of the Roman Church defends himself against the criticisms of a freethinker. I am, says the bishop, *on the whole* a believer, and therefore I accept everything. For if I am to pick and choose, where should I stop?

> To such a process I discern no end.
> Clearing off one excrescence to see two,
> There's ever a next in size, now grown as big,
> That meets the knife: I cut and cut again!
> First cut the Liquefaction, what comes last
> But Fichte's clever cut at God himself? [2]

On the outermost frontiers of Broad Churchmanship, may be placed those who had lost their faith, but could not be content to be without it; who retained, as it were, a fervent faith that faith was possible and necessary for men and might yet again be possible for them. Of such was Arthur Hugh Clough,[3] reputed the most brilliant of Arnold's Rugby pupils. Walter Bagehot, who knew Clough well, found in him an example of one who learnt too much from Dr. Arnold, learnt to take life too seriously, to dwell overmuch on its mysteries. The American critic, Lowell, the admired friend of many Victorian men of letters, held that a later generation would find in Clough's poetry 'the truest expression in verse of the moral and intellectual tendencies, the doubt and struggle towards settled convictions,

---

[1] *Bishop Blougram's Apology.*

[2] The Liquefaction, a peculiarly crude 'miracle' annually performed in the cathedral at Naples; Fichte, a German philosopher.

[3] Clough has been unmercifully and most misleadingly guyed by Mr. Lytton Strachey in certain passages in *Eminent Victorians;* a corrective may be found in the Essay in Bagehot's *Literary Studies.* Having said this, I should like to add that I am a profound admirer of most of Mr. Strachey's work.

of the period in which he lived'. Clough's poetry is so completely neglected to-day that a couple of quotations may provoke some reader to look for more. The first speaks for itself:

> O Thou, in that mysterious shrine
> Enthroned, as I must say, divine!
> I will not frame one thought of what
> Thou mayest either be or not.
> I will not prate of 'thus' and 'so',
> And be profane with 'yes' and 'no';
> Enough that in our soul and heart
> Thou, whatso'er Thou mayst be, art.

But Clough was by no means incapable of humour. The following couplet is a condensed criticism of a line of argument still often on the lips of defenders of the faith:

> 'Action will furnish belief'; but will that belief be the true one?
> That is the point, you know; however, it doesn't much matter.

But to Clough it mattered profoundly.

III

THE THEORY OF EVOLUTION

IN 1847 Disraeli published a novel called *Tancred*. The hero, who is the son of a Duke, has occasion to call upon a young lady of his acquaintance and the following conversation occurs:

After making herself very agreeable Lady Constance took up a book which was at hand, and said, 'Do you know this?' And Tancred, opening the volume, which he had never seen, and then turning to its title-page, found it was *The Revelations of Chaos*, a startling work just published, and of which a rumour had reached him.

'No,' he replied, 'I have not seen it.'

'I will lend it you, if you like; it is one of those books one must read. It explains everything, and is written in a very agreeable style.'

'It explains everything!' said Tancred; 'it must indeed be a very remarkable book!'

'I think it will just suit you,' said Lady Constance.

'To judge from its title, the subject is rather obscure,' said Tancred.

'No longer so,' said Lady Constance. 'It is treated scientifically; everything is explained by geology and astronomy, and in that way. It shows you exactly how a star is formed; nothing can be so pretty! A cluster of vapour, the cream of the milky way, a sort of celestial cheese, churned into light. You must read it; 'tis charming.'

'Nobody ever saw a star formed,' said Tancred.

'Perhaps not. But you must read the "Revelations";

123

it is all explained. But what is most interesting is the way in which man has developed. You know, all is development. The principle is perpetually going on. First there was nothing, then there was something; then, I forget the next, I think there were shells, then fishes; then we came. Let me see, did we come next? Never mind that; we came at last. And the next stage will be something very superior to us; something with wings. Ah! that's it: we were fishes, and I believe we shall be crows. But you must read it.'

'I do not believe I was ever a fish,' said Tancred.

'Oh! but it's all proved! By geology, you know. You see exactly how everything is made: how many worlds there have been; how long they lasted; what went before, and what comes next. We are a link in the chain, as inferior animals were that preceded us; we in turn shall be inferior; all that remains of us will be some relics in a new red sandstone. This is development. We had fins: we may have wings.'

Thus they talked, if we may believe Disraeli, in the politest circles, after the publication in 1844 of *Vestiges of Creation*. This was an anonymous work, attributed to a variety of persons from Sir Charles Lyell, the eminent geologist, to Prince Albert, but actually written by Robert Chambers, a Scottish scientist and publisher; he was an indefatigable popularizer of knowledge, whose name is still preserved in 'Chambers' *Encyclopædia*'. Science had become deeply interesting to a public that had never entered a laboratory. Harriet Martineau, writing of the 'forties, says, no doubt with some exaggeration, that 'the general middle-class public purchased five copies of an expensive work on geology to one of the most popular novels of the time'—the time of Dickens! All this was a good dozen years before the appearance of Darwin's *Origin of Species*.

The history of the theory of evolution is itself an example of 'evolution' in the looser sense of the word. The theory was given to the world in instalments; first one department of science and then another was conquered by the new school of thought. An attempt to trace the theory to its beginnings and to elaborate, however briefly, its technical aspects would be entirely outside the scope of this book, and also beyond the capacity of its author. Our concern is with the influence of the theory of evolution upon a general public who were not professional scientists, and for this purpose a very general sketch of the achievements of the professional scientists will suffice.

A hundred years before the nineteenth century began Sir Isaac Newton and other great mathematical thinkers, working on the discoveries of the astronomers, had expounded the laws which govern the motions of the heavenly bodies that compose the solar system. It was an achievement satisfyingly complete. The solar system, they held, illustrated the reign of law; it had always done so, and would always do so. Some have seen in the Newtonian theory the type of eighteenth-century thought, as illustrated for example by the French *philosophes*, the thought of an age which exalted reason but ignored development. Such bold generalizations are always rather risky; none the less, there is some truth in the epigram which affirms that, though the eighteenth and the nineteenth centuries were both self-satisfied, the eighteenth century was satisfied with what it was, and the nineteenth with what it was becoming. Paley's theology was coloured by the Newtonian theory. When he wanted a simile to express the relation between the Creator and His world, he used that of a Divine Watchmaker and his watch. The world, like the watch, was a mechanism, wound up once for all and 'going' till the Day of Judgement. What the Evolutionists did was to scrutinize the works, and the result of their scrutiny was fatal to Paley's simile. They found reason to think that the world as we know it had not been specially created; that its present condition was but a transitional stage in a process of development from unimaginably different beginnings to an unknown and unforeseeable end. The 'watch', they found reason to

think, had once been a very different sort of watch, perhaps not a watch in any recognizable sense at all.

We may begin with the Frenchman Laplace, whose
Treatise on Celestial Mechanics was published in 1799.
Newton, who was a devoutly religious man, held that God
made the solar system in a moment of time. Laplace,
working upon ideas already suggested, put forward what is
called the nebular hypothesis. Where is now the solar
system was originally a mass of whirling gases. As the
mass cooled, the centre condensed into the revolving sun,
and the outer parts became revolving rings which in turn
condensed into planets, each revolving on its own axis and
circling round the sun. The planets cooled faster than the
sun because they were smaller. Ultimately all will cool
to a point at which life is impossible. However, a collision
with another star would reduce the solar system to nebula
afresh, and the process would begin again. When asked by
Napoleon where God came in, Laplace answered (according
to the story), 'Sire, I have no need of that hypothesis.'

At the same time geologists were at work, patiently
classifying the substances composing the earth's surface and
examining its fossils. The results of their labours were
vividly presented to the British public by Lyell's *Principles
of Geology* in 1830. The working of uniform and unchang-
ing laws, he held, had transformed and was still transforming
the character of the surface of the globe. The history of
the world was recorded in its rocks, and enough had been
read of the record to prove that the length of that history
must be reckoned in millions of years.

The work of the geologists gave the evolutionary biologists
the scope they needed. Linnaeus, a Swede, the last great
biologist of the old school, had said in the middle of the
eighteenth century, 'We reckon as many species as issued
in pairs from the hands of the Creator', but this view was
already being disputed.[1] It was attractive to suppose that

[1] A Scottish judge, Lord Monboddo, had suggested that man had
originally been a monkey, in a work published about 1780. Coleridge

126

all the animal forms had developed from a few forms, or even a single form of life; the difficulty was to suggest causes to account for the diversity of development. Lamarck, working in Paris, suggested (1815) that new forms resulted from new needs produced by change of environment, the new organs being strengthened by use and handed on in a strengthened form to the offspring. The giraffe elongates its neck by trying to reach the high foliage; fleetness of foot develops in the hare by reason of its flight from its pursuers; horns develop on the heads of animals which, having weak jaws, practise butting.

Such was, roughly speaking, the state of evolutionary theory in its various departments when Lady Constance recommended Tancred to read *The Revelations of Chaos*. Charles Darwin had long been studying the subject. Lyell's book, he tells us, 'altered the whole tone of his mind', but the theory of natural selection, which is 'Darwinism' in the proper sense of that word, occurred to him after reading Malthus's *Essay on Population*. Malthus had shown that living creatures tend to 'multiply', that is, to increase in a geometrical progression, whereas the means of life increase, if at all, much more slowly. From these facts Malthus deduced what we may call (though he does not) the law of natural poverty—poverty only avoidable for the human race in general in so far as mankind restrict the increase of their numbers. Darwin saw in these facts the explanation of evolution. Living creatures are produced in vast numbers, the bulk of which cannot possibly 'survive', i.e., grow to maturity and produce offspring. There is a struggle for existence, in which the fittest survive, the fittest being simply those most capable of survival. That some are more 'fit' than others is due to the observed and obvious fact of variation; within any 'family' in any species some will be, be it only infinitesimally, better specimens than others. 'Fitness' will be of various kinds—speed, strength, protective

was probably alluding to Monboddo when he spoke contemptuously of 'orang-outang theology'.

colouring, etc. Thus the survival of the fittest will lead to specialization, in fact to the origin of new species. Nature has performed for countless ages, throughout the animal and vegetable world, the part played by breeders of varieties of pigeons or of dogs, and farmers' live stock. The human breeder selects the variations fittest for his purpose, breeds from them, and leaves the rest sterile; Nature does the same. Such, illustrated with an unprecedented wealth of examples, was the teaching of *The Origin of Species*, published in 1859.[1] In 1871 Darwin extended the scope of his argument by publishing *The Descent of Man*.

The effect of 'Darwinism' upon the non-scientific world in England was immediate and profound. Darwin had not, of course, discovered evolution, but he had elaborated an ingenious theory of the method of evolution which made the theory of evolution itself seem much more convincing. He compelled many who had distastefully shirked the subject to face it. Post-Darwinian speculation among scientists has neither added nor subtracted much from the effect of Darwin's work on the mind of the general non-scientific public. None the less, something may here be said about post-Darwinian theory before we turn to the 'Darwinism of the market-place'—and the pulpit.

By one of those coincidences which are fairly common in the history of scientific discovery, another biologist, Alfred Russel Wallace, had worked out the theory of natural selection at the same time as Darwin. In later years he suggested some of the difficulties that the Darwinian hypothesis had to meet. The theory depends upon the transmission to offspring of slight variations, and the survival of those variations owing to superior fitness. But, however useful a new organ—say, wings—might be, the slight beginnings of wings would be useless, and would have no

---

[1] 1759 is famous for its battles; 1859 might well be equally famous for its books. Besides *The Origin of Species*, the year saw the publication of Mill's *Essay on Liberty*, FitzGerald's *Omar Khayyam*, Smiles's *Self-Help* and the first big novels of George Eliot and George Meredith.

survival value. Also, it is difficult to suppose that some of the characteristics of species have any survival value even in their fully developed forms. How then were they evolved? Before the end of the century many biologists were following the lead of De Vries who, abandoning Darwinism, held that inheritable variations must be large and sudden, must in fact be complete 'jumps' or 'mutations'; but evidence for the actual occurrence of such mutations is very slight.

Again, are characteristics acquired during the lifetime of an organism transmitted to its offspring? Such transmission was the basis of Lamarck's theory. Darwin did not actually deny the possibility, but his theory did not depend on it, and neo-Darwinians have denied it. The great German biologist, Weismann, showed that the germ plasm, the seed of the future offspring, is so shut off from the rest of the body that it is hard to see how any adventures of the body can affect the germ which was alone inherited and is alone transmitted. We are beads upon a string. 'Evolution' of the string will affect the subsequent beads, but accidents to one bead will not affect the next one. On the other hand, many evolutionists are not neo-Darwinians but neo-Lamarckians and believe that acquired characters can under certain circumstances be inherited. In fact, Evolution is generally accepted but Darwinism widely rejected. The causes of the differentiation of species are still unknown.

Laplace, it will be remembered, had no need for 'the hypothesis' of God. For many it was a simple, though an entirely illogical, step in argument to say that if natural science had no need for God, then God was non-existent. There arose, in fact, that long Victorian conflict, discreditable on the whole to both parties concerned, called the conflict between science and religion. It is better, though more cumbersome, to call it a conflict between some scientists and some religionists. There were scientists, intoxicated by the achievements of science, who asserted that nothing existed outside matter and force. There were religionists who asserted that every statement contained in the Bible was true, and that every discovery of science that contradicted a statement in the Bible was therefore false.[1] At the same time there were many scientists who realized that science being the discovery of the facts and laws of the material universe, religion is outside its province; and there were many religious men who realized that science is master in its own sphere and that those passages of the Bible which contain primitive speculations on scientific subjects are of no validity against the proven results of scientific research. None the less, the more combative men of science joined battle, very properly, with the improper claims made by religionists on behalf of religion, and the more combative men of religion joined battle, very properly, with the improper claims made by scientists on behalf of science, and in the result there was the delusive appearance of conflict between 'religion' and 'science' all along the line.

Atheism, secularism, or whatever term is preferred to denote a disbelief in the possibility of any knowledge as to the existence of a God, is, of course, much older than evolution. It was widespread among the more thoughtful classes in the world of Classical Greece and Rome, and it revived with the Renaissance. Some dogmatically denied the existence of God; others more reasonably asserted that we know nothing and can know nothing about the matter, one way or another. There had been a small and uninfluential tradition of atheist opinion in England since the eighteenth century, and Charles Bradlaugh, the most conspicuous and assertive atheist of the latter part of the nine-

---

[1] It would be easy to give examples of the obstinate denial of scientific achievements by outraged 'bibliolaters'. Perhaps a case in which scientific discovery was approved for Biblical reasons is more interesting. It appears that certain religious persons reconciled themselves to the use of chloroform on account of *Genesis* ii. 21, where we are told that God put Adam into a deep sleep before extracting a rib for the creation of Eve. See Murray, *Science and Scientists of the Nineteenth Century*, p. 33.

teenth century, owed nothing of his creed to the discoveries of science. His atheism derives from Tom Paine (who, however, called himself a Deist—a non-Christian Deist, or course), and the persecuted disciples of Paine.

If anyone can claim credit for making Bradlaugh an atheist it surely is the vicar of St. Peter's, Hackney Road. Young Bradlaugh, the son of a solicitor's clerk, was, at the age of fourteen, a teacher in the Sunday school attached to that church. Study of the New Testament suggested to him that the Gospels were not on all points in agreement with one another. He applied for advice to the vicar, who not only dismissed him from the Sunday school, but secured his dismissal as an 'atheist' from the clerkship whereby he earned his living during the week. Bradlaugh grew up to be a very honest and aggressive opponent of the religion accepted, at any rate passively, by the vast majority of his fellow-countrymen, and the story of his career exhibits at its worst that intolerance which was the principal defect of Victorian piety. The story of his struggle to retain, though an avowed atheist, his seat in the House of Commons belongs to the latter end of the century. When, on the occasion of his death in 1891, Gladstone asked whether anyone could believe that the efforts to exclude Bradlaugh had been 'beneficial to the Christian religion', there was little doubt of the answer. He lies off the main line of our subject in the chapter. We have introduced him here only to illustrate the fact that there was already an anti-Christian tradition of thought in England, unconnected with the advances of science. None the less, it remains true that, in the middle of the nineteenth century, the men of science were envisaged as the principal enemies of Christianity, and the cause of 'rationalism', as its supporters termed it, became identified in popular opinion with the cause of evolutionary biology.

The outstanding figure on the side of the evolutionists was 'Darwin's bulldog', Thomas Henry Huxley. As a contributor to scientific research he was only in the second rank among the scientists of his day, but he was an admirable writer for the general public.[1] He had many interests outside the laboratory, and served on a variety of Royal Commissions, especially in connexion with public education. Huxley made no secret of his dislike of the clergy as a professional body, nor of his 'untiring opposition to that ecclesiastical spirit, that clericalism which in England, as everywhere else, and to whatever denomination it may belong, is the deadly enemy of science'. If this seems narrowminded, one should remember that, for example, the religious periodical called *The Witness* described the Darwinian theory in 1862 as 'antiscriptural and most debasing . . . in blasphemous contradiction to Biblical narrative . . . the vilest and beastliest paradox ever invented in ancient or modern times'.

Huxley was the inventor of the term 'agnostic', which quickly came into general use. Unlike 'atheist', it was free from the suggestion of dogmatic denial inappropriate to those who were themselves opposing theological dogma; an agnostic was simply one who denied that knowledge of God was possible to man. Agnostics had no use for theology, but Huxley would never allow that they were enemies of religion. 'Teach a child what is wise, that is morality. Teach him what is wise and beautiful, that is religion!' This is the creedless religion, the 'morality touched with emotion' of Matthew Arnold, and Huxley, like Matthew Arnold, was a lover of the Bible and a strong supporter of its use in schools, as literature, as folk-lore, and as a moral tonic—as everything, in fact, except what churchmen claimed that it was, the revelation of God. 'I have a great respect', he writes, 'for the Nazarenism of Jesus— very little for later Christianity. But the only religion that appeals to me is prophetic Judaism.'

As for the Homeric controversies between Huxley and

[1] As a writer one of his maxims is worth recording. 'It is', he says, 'an excellent rule always to erase anything that strikes one as particularly smart when writing it.'

the theologians, from the day in 1860 when he routed
Bishop Wilberforce at Oxford to the days thirty years later
when he fought with Canon Wace and Mr. Gladstone
the battle of the Gadarene swine in the pages of the monthly
magazine—of these things not much need be said. The
incident at the Oxford meeting of the British Association [1]
is well known : On the one side the fashionable bishop
laughing evolution out of court in the best Oxford manner
and asking Huxley whether he claimed descent from a
monkey on his grandfather's or his grandmother's side;
on the other the austere toiler after truth in laboratories
declaring that he would rather have a monkey for his
ancestor than 'a man who used great gifts to obscure the
truth'. That is the well-known part of the story; what is
sometimes forgotten is that Wilberforce had been coached
for his anti-evolutionary speech by the great biologist
Richard Owen, and that on the following Sunday Frederick
Temple, afterwards Archbishop of Canterbury, preached
a sermon to the members of the British Association, in
which he gave a learned and friendly exposition of the
Darwinian theory. Not all the scientists were on the right
side nor all the parsons on the wrong one.

The articles on the credibility of the miracle of the
Gadarene swine belong to the latter end of the century,
but they are, in fact, the last echoes of a mid-Victorian
controversy. Both Huxley and Gladstone start from the
assumption that, in Huxley's words, 'the authority of the
teachings of the Synoptic Gospels touching the nature of
the spiritual world turns on the acceptance or rejection of

[1] The annual congress of men of Science called the British Association
had been founded in 1830. In its early days it had been somewhat
derided. Keble called it 'a hodge-podge of philosophers' and Dickens
parodied its proceedings. When the Anti-Corn Law League summoned
a Convention of seven hundred Nonconformist ministers, *The Times*
(August 21, 1841) described this assemblage as a 'freak' and a 'drollery'
no less absurd than 'the British Association for the Advancement of
Science'. By 1860, however, the 'British Association' had already
attained celebrity and prestige.

the Gadarene and like stories'. They discuss such problems as whether the keeper of the swine was a Jew or a Gentile, whether Jews, though forbidden to eat, were allowed by their law to keep and sell swine for Gentile consumption. On the answers to these questions depends the solution of the further problem whether the destruction of the swine was a wanton and uncompensated destruction of legitimate property and, in consequence, discreditable to its author. If anyone reads Huxley's articles on this subject to-day, he will read because it is amusing to follow the methods of redoubtable controversialists, but certainly not for any other reason. The upshot of such a controversy no longer interests us.

Midway in date between Huxley's encounter with Wilberforce and his controversy with Gladstone, the physicist John Tyndall had delivered a Presidential Address to the British Association at Belfast in 1874 which was accepted by friend and foe as an authoritative statement of the case for Science against Religion. Darwin, having traced evolution back to the earliest form of life, had expressed himself as ready to admit, at that stage, a Divine Creator. To Tyndall this seemed unnecessary and unreasonable. He preferred to affirm, with the Roman poet Lucretius, that 'nature is seen to do all things spontaneously of herself, without the intermeddling of the gods'. 'Believing as I do', said Tyndall, 'in the continuity of Nature, I cannot stop where our microscopes cease to be of use. Here the vision of the mind authoritatively supplements the vision of the eye. By an intellectual necessity I cross the boundary of the experimental evidence, and discern in that Matter which we, in our ignorance of its latent powers, and notwithstanding our professed reverence for its Creator, have hitherto covered with opprobrium, the promise and potency of all terrestrial life.'

Much was said in those days of the 'dry light' of science, but this passage is a reminder that the scientists coloured their advocacy of agnosticism with a good deal of excellent rhetoric. It was easy to retort upon Tyndall that his 'vision of the mind' and his 'intellectual necessity' were acts of faith and not achievements of scientific analysis. To Tyndall, no doubt, the faith was irresistible, but so are all faiths to those who are unable to resist them.

For Tyndall 'religion' was in instinct, indestructible and also admirable. 'To yield this sentiment reasonable satisfaction is', he quaintly says, 'the problem of problems at the present hour. And grotesque in relation to scientific culture as many of the religions of the world have been and are . . . it will be wise to recognize them as forms of a force, mischievous if permitted to intrude upon the region of *knowledge*, over which it holds no command, but capable of being guided to noble issues in the region of *emotion*, which is its proper and elevated sphere.'

Tyndall was accused of 'patting religion on the back'. He replied that 'the facts of religious feeling are to me as certain as the facts of physics. But the world, I hold, will have to distinguish between the feeling and its forms, and to vary the latter in accordance with the intellectual condition of the age'. It would appear that only a very honourable courtesy prevented him from saying quite plainly that religion was a necessary 'make-believe', a sort of mental drug, and that each generation will need a different prescription according to the nature of its mental complaints.

Most of the scientific agnostics were not philosophers. They set themselves to destroy the temple of theological pretensions, but they were not concerned to build an alternative temple with the bricks of natural science. An interesting example of such an attempt is to be found in the essays of William Kingdon Clifford, a brilliant Cambridge mathematician, who died in the prime of early manhood in 1878. He was, says Hutton of the *Spectator*, 'a meteoric sort of moral phenomenon . . . a man of rare wit and rare powers of fascination, of extraordinary courage and extraordinary agility—both physical and mental—very great kindliness and very great audacity, enthusiastic disinterestedness and almost measureless irreverence.[1] He detested the Christian religion, calling it 'an awful plague that has destroyed two civilizations'. His religion is the religion of the Prometheus legend and of Wagner's *Ring*: he exalts Man against God. 'From the dim dawn of history', he writes, 'and from the inmost depth of every soul, the face of our father Man looks out upon us with the fire of eternal youth in his eyes, and says "Before Jehovah was, I am." '

The purpose of Clifford's philosophy is to describe the facts of life in terms which involve nothing outside the possibilities of biological evolution. The fact of self-consciousness is explained as a natural product of 'mind-stuff', which is a rarified form of matter. Ideas of right and wrong are products of evolution. Primitive man lives in tribes; 'right' is what benefits the tribe, and 'wrong' is what injures it. The tribe kills off those who think wrong, so that thinking right has survival value. Conscience, in fact, works through illusion; those who think they are following the dictates of conscience, even in opposition to the will of the actual community, are really acting in accord with what they unconsciously hold to be the tribal will. As for the religious instinct in man, that is 'cosmic emotion'; it has long diverted itself with fables, and had better return to the contemplation of the majesty of the material world, and draw its inspiration from the majestic advance of evolution.

Clifford died young, leaving a dozen brilliantly provocative essays; Herbert Spencer, a more famous evolutionary philosopher, lived to a great age and issued more than a dozen large volumes, including a ten-volume *Synthetic Philosophy*. Of all the great reputations of the Victorian Age that of Herbert Spencer has become the most mysterious to-day. I cannot do justice to his philosophy, because I

[1] I have quoted Hutton more than once. His two volumes of *Criticisms on Contemporary Thought and Thinkers* are extremely valuable to the student of mid-Victorian thought on moral and religious questions; *op. cit.*, Vol. I, p. 258.

have never been able to understand it, owing to defects of patience and intelligence on my own part. He seems to have identified evolution with progress, and 'fittest' with best, an error which Darwin and Huxley both emphatically condemned. Evolution, he held, proceeded from simple to complex, and its goal was individualism. Progress was not an accident but a necessity. Unlike Clifford he recognized the existence of the Unknowable, consigning to that department the problems he could not solve, and writing at great length about its frontiers. It seems as if most of Herbert Spencer's philosophy has itself crossed those frontiers now. The fact that so portentous a writer was widely studied, not in universities where he was always despised, but by the general public, is perhaps the most convincing evidence that can be adduced, of the intellectual energy of the Victorian Age.

It need hardly be said that the scientific assault upon religion was a cause of misery to many. Many, like Clough, lost their faith and could hardly endure the loss; 'thousands of minds', as Hutton finely says, 'anxious for faith, and yet unable to secure anything that could be said to be more than a tremulous hope'. There were many, too, who, whether or not they regretted loss of faith, were confronted by difficult problems of conduct. To avow infidelity would pain those dearest to them, and involve, in many cases, the sacrifice of cherished ambitions and careers of usefulness in, for example, the teaching profession. Many, too, held with Bishop Blougram [1] a certain 'hell-deep instinct' that there was truth in their religion, however untrue the human formulation of it, and preferred, in Samuel Butler's phrase, to 'tell a lot of little lies for the sake of one big truth'. To such in the early 'seventies John Morley, an ardent agnostic and afterwards a conspicuous Liberal statesman, addressed his *Essay on Compromise*.

The text of Morley's essay is: 'It makes all the difference in the world whether we put truth in the first place or the

[1] The Browning character already quoted, p. 121.

second', and he sets himself to consider 'the limits that are set by sound reason and positive duty to the practice of the various arts of' conformity or compromise. These limits he finds to be very narrow indeed. Erroneous belief can never be useful. To protect it for sentimental reasons is to protect stupidity, and to encourage stupidity in one sphere of thought will tend to preserve, if not actually to propagate, stupidity in other spheres of thought also. He advocates intellectual ruthlessness, and asserts that the intellectual pioneers of the past whom the world honours to-day, had not economized the expression of their own convictions even when to express them hurt the feelings of others. It is an austere essay on the discharge of unpleasant duties. The Victorian agnostics, though they rejected God, were in no doubt about the imperative claims of morality.

It was inevitable that evolutionary ideas should leave their mark upon the treatment of human history. Buckle's *History of Civilization*, published three years before *The Origin of Species*, was an attempt to make the science of human society as stable and as certain as the physical sciences. Needless to say he failed in this undertaking, but he developed some curious lines of thought. He traces the influence of climate on social organization, following up therein an idea suggested by Montesquieu more than a hundred years before. In hot climates little food is needed; where little food is needed population multiplies rapidly; where population multiplies rapidly, the distribution of wealth is unfavourable to the labourer and his wages low. It would be easy to pick holes in this argument. Again, physical nature influences the production and distribution of thought; where nature is grand, thought is stifled, and superstition encouraged; rationalism, on the contrary, is a product of the plains. Yet one would have thought that nature was 'grand' in the environs of ancient Athens, and rationalism has never flourished conspicuously in the plains of the Ganges valley.

Briefer, less ambitious, and more successful was an essay

along the same lines of thought by Walter Bagehot. Bagehot touched many subjects and touched none without adorning it. He was a shrewd and lively literary and biographical critic, he wrote the classic treatise of his day on the English Constitution and the classic treatise of his day on the money market. In the last years of his life he wrote a book called *Physics and Politics: Thoughts on the Application of the Principles of Natural Selection and Inheritance to Political Society.*

If a primitive tribe is to survive, he argues, it must hold itself firmly together. The 'survival virtue' is conformity; the successful tribe will, by 'hereditary drill', develop a 'cake of custom', a 'legal fibre'. The quality of the law is unimportant; what matters is the habit of discipline. The Jews survived because they revered their law, and even when they improved it they attributed their successive reforms to Moses, dead hundreds of years before, and thus secured for their reforms the sanctity pertaining to the unreformed tradition. Mediaeval legislators often claimed that they were merely re-establishing ancient custom. All the races of mankind that have survived have done so because they succeeded in forming a 'cake of custom'. But the cake of custom, though it ensures stability, does not ensure progress. Long after you have made your cake it becomes necessary to break it. The Greeks succeeded in breaking their cake and inaugurating the 'age of discussion', when intelligence takes over the helm from instinct. Western Europe, thanks to the Greeks, entered upon this second stage, and the Oriental races did not. Consequently, they lie at the mercy of the heirs of Greece. If Bagehot could write a final chapter to his book to-day he might describe the plight of those Oriental races whose cake has been forcibly broken by their Western invaders. They have been forced by external pressure into the 'age of discussion', and their discussions are consequently somewhat incoherent.

We shall not return to the subject of Darwinism in the final chapter of this book. Something therefore must be said here of further and wider applications of the Darwinian idea, even though these developments belong in the main to the last quarter of the century. Some of these developments deserve no better name than pseudo-Darwinian, for they are misapplications rather than applications of Darwinism. They are based upon the fatal confusion between evolution and progress, between 'fittest' and best. Against this fatal confusion Huxley made vigorous protest in the address on *Evolution and Ethics*, delivered little more than a year before his death. Progress, he says, does not consist in 'imitating the cosmic process, still less in running away from it, but in combating it'. Progress would not come through the survival of the fittest but through education and through social reform.

In the light of such a doctrine it is hardly necessary to demonstrate the falsity of the commercial pseudo-Darwinism that justified *laissez-faire* and unlimited competition, not by Benthamite arguments, but by the argument that the fittest competitors would survive; as though society had no duty to the economically weak, and as though proficiency in money-making were the same thing as excellence. Nor need we criticize the military pseudo-Darwinism popular in Prussia before the Great War. The God of battles, said writers of this school, holds his assizes and awards victory to those who deserve it: a queer amalgam of pseudo-Darwinism and primitive Old Testament religion. But we should delude ourselves if we found military pseudo-Darwinism in Prussia alone. Every nation that has seen in its military successes the proof of its moral virtue has succumbed in a greater or less degree to the same error.

The most interesting modern application of Darwinian theory has been the science of Eugenics. It stands at the opposite pole of thought from the pseudo-Darwinism of commercial *laissez-faire*, and is in fact the Darwinian counterpart of Socialism. Social reform and medical science, says the eugenist, have made possible the survival and propagation of the unfit who formerly went to the wall.

At the same time, the fittest have been taking the advice of Malthus and raising their standard of comfort by restricting their families. Thus in modern society the processes of evolution are reversed and the new generation is bred preponderantly not from the 'fit' but from the 'unfit'. What is to be done about it? That is an unsolved problem, and anti-eugenists deny that there is any problem to solve. We may dismiss, as outside practical politics, fantastic projects for 'breeding the superman'. Whether it is desirable or possible to restrict the breeding of inferior stocks of society, whether poverty or disease or crime are marks of 'inferiority' in a biological sense and transmitted to the off-spring of their victims, whether there are any ascertainable tests of 'fitness' and 'unfitness' among human beings—these are problems of the twentieth century.

IV

SOME VICTORIAN MEN OF LETTERS

SAMUEL BUTLER, exercising the pleasant art which he calls quoting from memory, says 'A country is not without honour save in its own prophets'. Certainly Thomas Carlyle found little worthy of honour in mid-nineteenth-century England. We have already surveyed the leading features of the period—industrial and commercial enterprise, the growth of democracy, Benthamite legislation, Evangelical piety and philanthropy, the new Anglo-Catholicism of the Oxford Movement, the popularizing of scientific theories of evolution; and Carlyle despised and derided every one of these things. The quest of material wealth he called the Gospel of Mammon: political economy was 'the dismal science'; the House of Commons was a 'talking-shop' unfit to govern; democracy was absurd in a community 'mostly fools'; the religion of Bentham he compared, greatly to its disadvantage, with the religion of Mahomet; negroes were better enslaved than free; Evangelical piety clothed itself in 'Hebrew old clothes' better discarded as long worn out; 'spectral Puseyisms' were 'very lamentable', and, as for the idea that men were descended from monkeys—only monkeys would have allowed such an idea to enter their heads. Carlyle was essentially a prophet, a preacher; he was too passionate and impatient to be a thinker. If he attained the truth, he attained it by impulse and by instinct, not by argument. He was a great writer because he had an intensely vivid personality and because, through the medium of his queer, humorous, volcanic style, he could get his personality into his books.[1]

Carlyle was the son of Scottish peasants living near the Border. They were members of one of those strange little sects that had seceded from the Scottish Kirk in the eighteenth century, because the Kirk was no longer sufficiently strict for them. Carlyle early lost his faith in Christian doctrine, but he never ceased to be essentially a Puritan—a Puritan without a creed; he never lost the Puritan's contempt for 'Vanity Fair', its standards, and its customers; he never ceased to maintain that moral values were the only values, and that morality was something quite other than expediency or 'happiness', something God-given from another world; though what God and his other world were, was wrapped in a cloud of Carlylean rhetoric. His endless reiterations of the claims of 'Duty' are found wearisome to our own generation which, even when it does its duty, is quickly tired of talking about it, but in his own age it was far otherwise. That burning and effusive zeal for moral values secured a respectful hearing for the most extravagant political and religious heresies. The Evangelical world accepted Carlyle as an ally, and ignored or forgave his religious improprieties.

Carlyle was one of those to whom the loss of faith is extremely painful, and he found some consolation in the German philosophers with their theory of Appearance and Reality. The external world known to our senses and explored by our sciences is mere Appearance: Reality is its divine, unseen counterpart, standing to Appearance as Soul stands to Body. Thus he came to occupy a position distinct alike from the orthodox and religious on the one hand, and the Benthamite rationalists and the scientists on the other. He first made his mark as an exponent or translator of the Germans (like Coleridge whom he characteristically derides, though engaged upon the same task),

[1] A long and very typical example of Carlylic style will be found on pages 65–6.

and in his first important original work he uses an imaginary German Professor Teufelsdrochk (Devilsdung) as his mouth-piece. This book is the still famous and readable *Sartor Resartus* (1833), expounding the Philosophy of Clothes. It is, like *Gulliver's Travels*, written just over a hundred years before, a satire upon things in general. 'Clothes', in their innumerable manifestations, from coronation robes to fig-leaves, are the conventions upon which civilization is built. Strip them off, and what remains? The book abounds in whimsicality and mystification, and was not appreciated till Carlyle had made a reputation in other fields.

Sartor abounds in quotable paragraphs upon every subject under the sun, from the mysteries of Time and Eternity to the shooting of partridges. One of the most notable is that in which the Professor observes that the British nation is dividing itself into two rival sects, the Dandies and the Drudges, i.e. the rich and the poor. 'In numbers and even in individual strength, the Poor-Slaves or Drudges, it would seem, are hourly increasing. The Dandiacal, again, is by nature no proselytising Sect, but it boasts of great hereditary resources, and is strong in union; whereas the Drudges, split into parties, have as yet no rallying point. If, indeed, there were to arise a *Communion of Drudges*, as there is already a Communion of Saints, what strangest effects would follow therefrom! Dandyism, as yet, affects to look-down on Drudgism; but perhaps the hour of trial, when it will practically be seen which ought to look down and which up, is not so distant. To me it seems probable that the two sects will one day part England between them; each recruiting itself from the intermediate ranks, till there be none left to enlist on either side. Those Dandiacal Manichaeans, with the whole host of Dandyising Christians, will form one body; the Drudges, gathering round them whatsoever is Drudgical . . . sweeping up all manner of Utilitarians, Radicals . . . will form the other . . . and then!'

Disraeli had this passage in his mind when, twelve years

later (1845), he published the most fundamentally serious of his novels, *Sybil, or The Two Nations*.[1] By the date of Disraeli's novel the 'Drudges' had already manifested themselves as the Chartists. Chartism, as we have seen, was due to fail, and throughout the long mid-Victorian prosperity Carlyle's forecast must have seemed fantastic pessimism; to-day it has again become significant. Disraeli's remedy was Tory-Democracy, an alliance between the old English gentry, dear to Burke and Scott, and the 'commons of England', dear to Cobbett, against the Whigs, Benthamites, manufacturers, and middle-classes. In was in this faith that Disraeli overthrew Peel, a faith thoroughly congenial to Carlyle and Ruskin. Tory Democracy never quite materialized in the middle Third of the century, but Disraeli's *Sybil* is still, according to Mr. Baldwin, one of the accepted scriptures of the Conservative party.

'History', says Carlyle, 'is not only the fittest study, but the only study and includes all others. It is the true epic poem and universal divine scripture.' In 1838 Carlyle published his *French Revolution*, an epoch-making book in many ways. 'It delivered the English mind', said Lord Acton, himself a great historian, 'from the thraldom of Burke.' Hitherto it had been orthodox to regard the French Revolution as an unmitigated evil, an orthodoxy not less firmly cherished because a few English 'Jacobins' still worshipped at its shrines. Carlyle called upon his readers neither to approve nor to condemn, but to marvel at an epic story, an astonishing explosion of human passions. Since Carlyle's day the French Revolution has ceased to be for us—what Burke and Paine made it—a shibboleth of our own party politics; it has become instead the most popular of historical events. Most Englishmen who read history at all have probably read more books about the French Revolution than about any event in the history of their own country previous to the Great War.

[1] By calling one of the characters in the novel Devilsdust, Disraeli seems to make an oblique acknowledgement of his debt to Carlyle.

Carlyle's philosophy of history comes straight out of the Old Testament. The people are sheep, and God (or Providence or whatever one likes to call it) provides them with shepherds. When kings really govern, all is well. When the titular king is, like the Bourbons, a sham king, a real king or 'hero' must be found elsewhere. Democracy is mere absence of leadership, and revolution is simply a game of hunt for the hero. Shall he be Mirabeau?— no: Danton?—no: Bonaparte?—yes! The Revolution is over. But how is Bonaparte chosen?—by reason of the fact that he blew the mob to pieces with a whiff of grapeshot. Carlyle thinks this a better method than the ballot box.

Carlyle's next important book was *Past and Present* (1843). 'Past' is a mediaeval monastery: 'Present' a modern factory. Needless to say the argument is all in favour of the former. Carlyle never drew a more charming portrait than that of Abbot Samson of Bury St. Edmunds, the hero of his historical sketch, and *Past and Present* has its place in that revival of respect for the Middle Ages to which so many diverse influences contributed—Scott, the Oxford Movement, Coleridge, Carlyle, and many after them down to Mr. Chesterton and Mr. Belloc among our contemporaries.

In idealizing the Middle Ages Carlyle was contributing to a movement already begun; his discovery of the hero in Cromwell was all his own work. For close on two hundred years Cromwell had been left to languish with Guy Fawkes and Titus Oates in the historical chamber of horrors. To Tories he was a rebel and a regicide, to Whigs a traitor who destroyed the parliament which had given him his commission, to all a fanatic, a hypocrite and a tyrant. Carlyle, as counsel for the defence, put his client into the witness box; published, in fact, all he could find of Cromwell's letters and speeches, together with his own commentary. The result was a conversion of the public such as historians rarely secure. Carlyle was mistaken on certain points; and on these points he has been corrected by Gardiner and

Firth, the scientific historians who have since worked over the ground with a skill and patience beyond Carlyle's capacity. Carlyle, however, established the fact that Cromwell was a great man, and one of the most honest men that ever played a hand in a revolution.

As the subject of his last and biggest book, Carlyle took Frederick the Great of Prussia, the 'last real king'. It was hard to make a hero of Frederick, but he suited Carlyle's purpose in that he was the greatest representative of the most notable dynasty of despots then surviving in Europe. It was a sound instinct for contrasts that turned the bitterest critic of English institutions and ideals to a study of the greatest of the Hohenzollerns. When the last of the five stout volumes was published Bismarck had already entered upon his policy of 'blood and iron'; Carlyle had given the new German Empire his blessing in advance.

Carlyle spoke of himself as 'a radical and an absolutist'. He approved Cromwell because he had been radical enough to overthrow an unworthy despotism and absolutist enough to establish a far more ruthless hero-despotism in its place. He was one with the Chartists in so far as their ultimate aim was to deliver the poor from poverty. 'The progress of human society', he wrote, 'consists in the better and better apportioning of wages to work.' But with their political programme he had no sympathy whatever. One of his last outbursts was provoked by the enactment of the second Reform Bill. This pamphlet, entitled *Shooting Niagara*, contains a fantastic scheme for the salvation of our already well-nigh ruined country. In its remoteness alike from democratic ideals and practical politics it has been compared,[1] with the constitution outlined in Plato's *Republic*. 'The few wise' are to 'take command of the innumerable foolish.' The scheme is a modernized variety of the feudal system.

Carlyle was regarded by many good judges, even among

[1] Ernest Barker, *Political Thought from Spencer to the Present Day*, p. 186.

those who disagreed with him, as the foremost writer of his time. The influence of his phrases and his favourite quotations is to be found broadcast in the literature of his day—from the novels of Disraeli to the popular lectures of eminent scientists such as Tyndall. Merely as a man of letters, as a humorist, and as a picturesque historian, he was a unique and eminent figure. How far his view of life influenced his generation is a difficult question to answer. He had, of course, his immediate disciples, of whom the most eminent were Ruskin and Froude. Kingsley, Hughes and the Christian Scientists claimed that they owed much to his inspiration. Most of his readers, one must suppose, took his preachings as the less earnest among us have always taken the eloquence of the pulpit. They enjoyed a fine performance, experienced a vague and transitory moral exaltation, and went their ways. Victorian optimism, Victorian faith in commerce, in parliamentary institutions, in church and chapel or in popular science, was much too solidly founded to be shaken by the eloquence of any prophet of pessimism. The country could afford to enjoy its prophets even though it got no honour from them. It was not afraid of them.

The greatest disciple of Carlyle among the historians was James Anthony Froude. In his youth he had been caught by the Oxford Movement, from which he emerged with the loss of his religious faith and an intense prejudice against the Church of Rome. With Carlyle's encouragement he wrote a history of England from the beginning of the Reformation to the defeat of the Armada, in twelve volumes. His style was as brilliant and easy as Macaulay's, and his work was very widely read. His heroes are Henry VIII, John Knox, and the Elizabethan seamen. Henry and Knox are heroes after Carlyle's own heart, and an early article of Froude's on the Elizabethan seamen inspired his friend Kingsley to write *Westward Ho!* It is possible that Froude did something to prolong the life of the 'no-popery' prejudice, which is an ancient inheritance of Englishmen. It is more certain that, with Kingsley, he may be reckoned one of the forerunners of the romantic Imperialism of a later day which found its most gifted exponent in Rudyard Kipling.

Three nineteenth-century historians, Macaulay, Carlyle and Froude, enjoyed a vogue with the general public unequalled by their successors to-day,[1] unless we include among historians one or two writers of epigrammatic biography. Judged by the standard of modern University professors, all of them, even Macaulay, were brilliant amateurs in the arts of research; but if they were something less than scientific historians, they were also something more. They addressed themselves not to the students in their own department, but to the public at large; they wrote history not only to tell the story of the past but, indirectly, to interpret the present.

Another notably popular historian of the day was John Richard Green, whose *Short History of the English People* was published in 1874. It was the first book of moderate compass and popular style to present as an organic whole the development of the nation from its beginnings down to Waterloo. The teaching of English History in schools was just beginning to be seriously considered, and Green's book made it possible for teachers to give their pupils something better than dated lists of kings and battles.

John Ruskin claimed, in the latter part of his career, to be a disciple of Carlyle, and indeed he shared to the full Carlyle's contempt for Benthamite liberty, political economy, and material progress; but he was much more than a disciple and his best work lay quite outside the range of Carlyle's interests. Ruskin was, like Wordsworth, intoxicated with the beauty of Nature. At the age of twenty-four he published the first volume of that immense and passionately eloquent miscellany which he called *Modern Painters*, and in it he praises the moderns, especially Turner, at the expense

[1] The nearest approach to an exception to this statement is furnished by Macaulay's great-nephew, Mr. G. M. Trevelyan.

of their predecessors, because they had emancipated themselves from conventions of the studio, and devoted themselves to the reverent and truthful interpretation of Nature.

Soon he was opening up wider visions. There are, it is agreed, three ultimate 'goods' in life, each good in itself and for its own sake—moral excellence, truth, and beauty. The first and second of these had no lack of advocates in an age dominated by moralists and scientists, by Evangelicals, Benthamites, and Evolutionists. Ruskin made himself the champion of the claims of beauty, but in no narrow sense. For him art and beauty were no idle superfluities, 'extras' which a busy and earnest generation could dispense with from lack of spare time; they were indispensable to the healthy development of the spirit of man. 'He saw', says Mr. Clutton-Brock,[1] 'that the prevailing ugliness was not caused merely by the loss of one particular faculty, that the artistic powers of men were not isolated from their other powers. He was the first to judge works of art as if they were human actions, having moral and intellectual qualities as well as aesthetic; and he saw their total effect as the result of all those qualities and of the condition of the society in which they were produced. So his criticism gave a new importance to works of art as being the clearest expression of men's minds which they can leave to future ages; and in particular it gave a new importance to architecture and all the applied arts, since, being produced by co-operation and for purposes of use, they express the general state of mind better than those arts such as painting which are altogether the work of individual artists . . . Art was not a mere superfluity that men could take or leave as they chose; it was a quality of all things made by men, which must be good or bad, and which expressed some goodness or badness in them.'

[1] Clutton-Brock, *William Morris*, p. 13. The passage refers in its original context, as here, to Ruskin, though much of it is, of course, equally applicable to Morris.

Ruskin was a rash and wilful writer. The objects of his admiration and his dislike were not always, we are compelled to think, well chosen. His theory that great art is always the product of a morally sound society and bad art always the mark of social corruption, is hard to sustain in face of the sober records of history. None the less he triumphantly and unforgettably established his main point, that art is not a bye-way to which only artists and connoisseurs need seek admittance, but a matter of urgent public concern. We do not admire the Venetian Gothic style which Ruskin tried to force upon us;[1] but if, on the whole, we build more beautiful houses, for rich and poor alike, to-day than we built in 1860, if at least we feel that the beauty of our buildings is a matter of serious public importance, Ruskin has not laboured in vain.

It is convenient to treat Ruskin's career in two divisions. Up to about 1860 he was engaged on long treatises upon subjects of art; after 1860 he is a lecturer and a pamphleteer on social problems, he becomes the acknowledged disciple of Carlyle, he makes a terrific onslaught upon Mill's *Political Economy*, he writes 'open letters' to working-men on the conduct of their daily lives. This division of Ruskin's career is obvious and convenient, but it should not be allowed to conceal the fact that the prophet of Art and Life was shifting his ground rather than changing his aim. Only a sound society could produce good art; to preach good art to an unsound society was, as it were, to seek to cure the disease by attacking its symptoms. Society was all astray in its ideals. The industrial revolution and the lust for wealth were transforming the craftsmen, on whom national

[1] The Ruskinian buildings in Oxford and elsewhere are now generally condemned. The Victorian Gothic movement was not, indeed, admired even by all Victorians. Leslie Stephen wrote, in the 'eighties: 'What will posterity think of our masquerading in old clothes? Will they want a new Cromwell to sweep away nineteenth-century shams or will they be content to let our pretentious rubbish find its natural road to ruin? One thing is pretty certain . . . no one will ever want to "revive" the nineteenth century.'

the well-meant but disastrous activities of the Victorian 'restorer'.

In his writings he harked back to the Middle Ages, the golden age of craftsmanship, and even further afield. Like Kingsley he delighted in the healthy barbarism of the Vikings, and he composed spirited verse translations of some of the old Icelandic sagas. Heroic action delighted him, for he was before all else a man of action. In this spirit he plunged into the midst of the British socialist movement in its early days, and devoted himself to the thankless tasks of street-corner oratory and the debating-society politics. But his Socialism had little grounding in economic doctrine; he was a socialist because—in sharp contrast here with Carlyle and Ruskin—he was an ardent democrat, and Socialism was the cry of a working-class beginning to realize the possibilities of a good life hitherto denied to it. There was in Morris, alone of the great Victorians, a touch of the revolutionism of Rousseau, but it was as a preacher and a practiser of craftsmanship, not as a forerunner of the 'class-war', that his valuable work was done.

Carlyle and Ruskin were leaders of opposition to the dominant ideas of what Ibsen, their Norwegian contemporary, called 'the damned compact liberal majority'. Another leader along a rather different line of attack was Matthew Arnold. Carlyle and Ruskin wear the mantle of the prophet; they denounce their generation as altogether given over to evil; they are hot with a righteous indignation, and like Jonah they think that they do well to be angry. Arnold claimed to be no more than a critic—and no less, for he held that criticism rather than prophecy was the need of his age. He surveyed a scene of earnest bustling energy, but of energy, alas, so misdirected, so stupid. He appealed to his generation to pause and think; he sought to lower rather than to raise the social temperature.

But long before he entered on the task of social criticism Arnold had made his name as a poet. He was by turns a poet, a literary critic, a social critic, and a religious critic, and all the while a Government inspector of schools. He touched the thought of his age at many points. At one of them, religion, we have already encountered him.

Two themes run through Arnold's poetry: the Greek ideal of serenity, as seen for example in his favourite Sophocles 'who saw life steadily and saw it whole'; and a profound and melancholy conviction that such serenity is impossible to one who is truly alive to the facts of modern life:

> . . . This strange disease of modern life
> With its sick hurry and divided aims,
> Its heads o'ertaxed, its palsied hearts. . . .

Arnold the poet was a young man, and his poetry has the romantic but entirely sincere melancholy of youth, such as one finds, for example, in the best lyrics of Shelley. But Arnold had none of Shelley's faith in Utopias; he had been too well brought up for that, and in fact Shelley was one of the few great poets whom he disliked.

If Arnold found his ideal among the Greeks he also found it symbolized by that Oxford with which, more closely than any other great Victorian except Newman, he will always be associated,—the Oxford of *The Scholar Gypsy* and *Thyrsis*, the Oxford that was 'the home of lost causes, and forsaken beliefs, and unpopular names, and impossible loyalties'. His best poems are the cry of one who has gone out from the quiet cloisters of Oxford into the deserts where the elementary school inspector travels to and fro. A man less finely sympathetic would have felt the contrast less deeply. In one of his strongest poems, *Self-dependence*, the poet interprets the message of the stars:

> Wouldst thou be as these are? Live as they.
> Unaffrighted by the silence round them,
> Undistracted by the sights they see,
> These demand not that the things without them
> Yield them love, amusement, sympathy.

Sainte-Beuve and Joubert, in the philosophic journal
Amiel, in Tolstoy.

'A schoolmaster's prescription!' one may say, and it
to be remembered that Arnold was by profession an inspecto
of schools. His father had been the great headmaste
his brother-in-law, W. E. Forster, piloted the Educatio
Act of 1870 through the House of Commons, and Arnol
himself did perhaps as much for education, even in th
narrower sense, as either of them. He was always a stron
advocate of State supported and controlled secondary educa
tion, and the Education Act of 1902, establishing long afte
his death the present County school system, may fairl
be regarded as the posthumous climax of his labours. Ther
is something—it must be admitted even though it be t
his discredit—a trifle schoolmasterish about Arnold's literar
methods. He is infinitely patient in his method of exposi
tion, repeating the points he wishes to be remembered, a
all schoolmasters are bound to do. His humour is th
analytical humour of the philosophic spectator, quietl
recording the singular antics of his fellow-creatures. 'H
kept', says Mr. Chesterton, 'a smile of heart-broken for
bearance, as of a teacher in an idiot school.' It was th
trick of his trade, for all schools are unhappily idiot school
in a greater or less degree. And certainly he succeeded u
to a point, for he has given us more quotable and stil
quoted phrases and catchwords than any other moder
English writer of prose.

Arnold's England was dominated by its middle classes
and he called them Philistines, because they were the dogge
and inveterate enemies of the 'children of light', or culture
The gospel of the Philistines was the gospel of 'getting-on'
in this world and the next, both forms of getting-on being
summarizable under the term respectability. Its exempla
was 'Mr. Bottles', who 'has certainly made an immense
fortune', but ever since he left school has, 'with a sturdy
self-reliance thoroughly English, left his mind wholly to
itself, his daily newspaper, and his Particular Baptist minister'.

In fact, Mr. Bottles is a typical Benthamite-Evangelical. Six days of his week are devoted to the making of money, and the seventh to the securing of 'salvation' as understood among the Particular Baptists. Needless to say he is a firm believer in progress, and supports all the measures advocated by *The Daily Telegraph* [1] and the Liberal Party.

Arnold had a strong prejudice against the Dissenters. He felt that they, even more than the majority of members of the Established Church, obstinately set themselves against the application of a 'free play of the mind' (a favourite phrase of his) to religious questions; that they were, in fact, the most bigoted of 'bibliolaters'. He felt also that their very organization was narrowing to the mind; they had cut themselves off from the great historic ecclesiastical tradition, and Arnold's ideal Church would have been at once undogmatic and catholic. He was a freethinker who none the less earnestly desired to maintain both Church and Bible as cardinal elements in the spiritual life of the nation. He saw in Dissent an enemy of the Church and a very dangerous, because misguided, friend of the Bible. Only 'culture' could understand the Bible, and a Bible misunderstood and treated as 'verbally inspired' would sooner or later be a Bible rejected.

All this mistaken religion he attributes to an overdose of 'Hebraism'; Puritanism, still dominant in the bulk of the middle classes, he calls 'a Hebraizing backwater', out of the main stream of life. To Hebraism he opposed Hellenism. Hebraism says: 'Follow the best light that you have'; Hellenism says: 'Be sure that your light is not darkness'. Hebraism is strictness of conscience, Hellenism spontaneity of consciousness. Both are necessary to the well-balanced life, and indeed Hebraism is the primary need. But in the England of his day he held that the

---

[1] *The Daily Telegraph* had been established in 1855 as the first penny London paper, and occupied a position roughly similar to that of *The Daily Mail* at the end of the century.

The poem was annotated by clergymen, and analysed an quoted from a hundred pulpits.

In his preoccupation with evolution Tennyson gave a ne turn to the literary treatment of Nature. To the theoris of the eighteenth century Nature had been 'Reason' an Utopia; to Wordsworth Nature was the mother of Man, th source of physical health and spiritual wisdom; to Tennyso she is already the Nature of the evolutionists, Nature 're in tooth and claw', as august as the Nature of Wordswort but much less benign. 'Tennyson', says Dr. Andrew Brac ley,[1] 'is the only one of our great poets whose attitude towar the sciences of Nature was what a modern poet's attitud ought to be; the only one to whose habitual way of seeing imagining, or thinking, it makes any real difference tha Laplace, or for that matter Copernicus, ever lived.'

Tennyson was the first great poet since Dryden who wa also a great poet laureate; he was not merely a national poe as Wordsworth had been in some of his greatest sonnet He was a court poet, and his success in this very difficu line of business is a tribute alike to the poet and to the cou he celebrated. For what poet but Tennyson addressir what queen but Victoria in a *Dedication* like that of 185 (now printed at the opening of the Poetical Works) cou fail to stumble over the frontier that separates and protec the sublime from the ridiculous? Perhaps Albert the Goc with his 'white flower of a blameless life' no longer appea to us; he did not indeed appeal very strongly to his Englis men contemporaries. But Tennyson set him beside h own *Arthur*, and that was no doubtful compliment in 186 whatever it may seem to be to-day.

There can, I think, be no doubt that Tennyson made quite perceptible contribution to that revival of royali sentiment which was one of the notable features of politic thought in the nineteenth century. It is a far cry fro Shelley's

[1] The author of *Shakespearean Tragedy*. The quotation is from lecture on Tennyson published by the English Association.

TENNYSON

An old, mad, blind, despised, and dying king,
Princes, the dregs of their dull race, who flow
Through public scorn, mud from a muddy spring.

to

Her court was pure: her life serene;
    God gave her peace: her land reposed;
    A thousand claims to reverence closed
In her as Mother, Wife, and Queen.

But Shelley, it will be said, was a revolutionist. Perhaps: then let us quote from *The Times* article on the death of George IV:

The truth is—and it speaks volumes about the man—that there never was an individual less regretted by his fellow-countrymen than this deceased King. What eye has wept for him? What heart has heaved one throb of unmercenary sorrow? etc.

All that was changed by 1851 and it was to change far more in the half-century that followed. The change was of course in the main the work of the royal couple themselves, for Albert, though himself unpopular, was in large part the architect of his wife's popularity; the change had begun before Tennyson ever introduced his sovereign's name into his verse. But as (if the simile may, with apologies, be allowed) the best goods gain by advertisement, so the Queen owed something to the dexterous compliments of her Poet Laureate.

Tennyson had expressed himself on questions of the day before he became laureate, and his office was an invitation to further utterance on the same theme. He was an exponent rather than a critic of the orthodoxy of his day. The well-known passage in *Locksley Hall* chants the praises of illimitable progress.

Yet I doubt not through the ages one increasing purpose runs
And the thoughts of men are widened with the process of the suns . . .
For I dipt into the future, far as human eye could see,
Saw the vision of the world and all the wonder that would be;
Saw the heavens filled with commerce, argosies of magic sails,
Pilots of the purple twilight, dropping down with magic bales;
Till the war-drum throbbed no longer, and the battle flags were furled,
In the Parliament of Man, the Federation of the World.

It is perhaps significant that in Tennyson's prophecy the coming of the 'pilots of the purple twilight' precedes the coming of the Federation of the World.

A somewhat similar forecast of progress has already been quoted from Macaulay, the optimist historian. Another could be quoted from Herbert Spencer, the optimist philosopher of evolution. 'Progress', wrote Spencer, 'is not an accident but a necessity. What we call evil and immorality must disappear. It is certain that man must become perfect. The ultimate development of the ideal man is certain—as certain as any conclusion in which we place implicit faith; for instance, that all men will die. . . . Always towards perfection is the mighty movement—towards a complete development and a more unmixed good.' [1]

Tennyson might, in exalted moments, envisage a future of international federation. For the present, however, he remained a very hearty, a very insular patriot. He had all John Bull's traditional contempt for the French with their 'red fool-fury of the Seine', and the lines on Napoleon III's coup d'état, entitled *The Third of February, 1852*, will repay study as perhaps the finest flower of our national arrogance. Two years later came the Crimean War, and the opening stanzas of his *Maud* voiced the vigorous bellicosity of the national mood; exactly the same sentiments were to be expressed in the outpourings of lesser bards fifty years later when the South African War began. As he grew old, however, Tennyson found that he did not like democracy, and in 1881 he lamented 'the new Dark Ages of the popular press'. It is not, of course, for these topical sentiments that Tennyson will be always read with delight and remembered with honour. The student of English poetry may do well to ignore them; but they have a place in a study of popular opinion.

Tennyson had secured his position as the great poet of

---

[1] Quoted from J. H. Randall, *The Background of the Modern Mind* (a very useful American book).

his age by the middle of the century. But after *In Memoriam* (1850) he produced no work of equal power and significance, and the interest and admiration of eager minds was transferred little by little from Tennyson to Browning. Endless were the discussions of their respective merits. Browning was uncouth; he was easily parodied; but his range and variety were immense, and his poetry appealed to all those who like being made to use their brains.

Robert Browning was a singularly detached figure, living much abroad and intervening not at all in the popular controversies of his day. There is almost nothing in his poetry bearing upon modern English political and social questions, though much that bears on the significance of the Italian Renaissance. He certainly held that the proper study of mankind was man, but his concern was with the mystery of the individual soul and his method of approach psychological. In an untechnical sense of the word he was far the greatest of English psychologists, surpassing all the novelists within what might be regarded as their own province.

As a student of the individual soul he was strongly drawn to the fundamental problems of religion, and it was as a religious 'teacher' that he influenced the thought of his age. Bishop Westcott, one of the most eminent of Victorian bishops, declared that his three principal teachers had been St. Paul, Origen,[1] and Browning. Browning attached himself to no Church, and had no 'faith' as Wilberforce or Newman or F. D. Maurice would have understood that term. He was his own *Bishop Blougram*, whom we have already quoted (p. 121). But whereas Blougram was only a man in a mitre, his creator was a great poet, and he strengthened in many readers the faith that he did not himself possess. One may ask why he did this, but to answer that question at length would be to traverse ground already covered in this book. He held, perhaps, that though religion as presented by the orthodox was faulty and incredible, yet the alternative of no religion was much further from a true philosophy.

[1] An Alexandrian Greek Christian philosopher of the second century.

The primary dogmas of Christianity—a Personal God and His love for Man, and the Immortality of the Soul—were no doubt a human attempt to express the Infinite, and as such presented an easy target to human criticism; but they were the nearest man could get to the truth, and in affirming them, even if one did not explicitly believe them, one was nearer to the truth than in denying them, and Browning's characteristic technique as a writer of 'dramatic' monologues enabled him to give expression to the religious sentiments of his fictitious characters without expressly associating himself with the sentiments expressed.

Browning's position was in fact not far removed from Arnold's position as expressed in *Literature and Dogma*. Both felt intensely the necessity of religion, and both felt also the impossibility of most of what passed under the name of religion. Arnold wrote an essay in direct advocacy of undogmatic religion. It is eloquent, ingenious, and, in places, very funny, like all Arnold's essays; and it annoyed almost all its readers. Browning chose a better way. He wrote a succession of admirable philosophic character studies in verse—*Karshish, Cleon, Saul, Christmas Eve and Easter Day*. Character studies do not claim to prove anything, and for that reason they are the more convincing.

Browning was a thorough Victorian in another respect, his robust and incorrigible optimism and his glorification of energy, of 'work'. Even his three suicides in the Paris Mortuary will not, in the long run—on the Day of Judgement—be found to have been wasted. Optimism convinces him of Heaven, but his furious energy will allow no harps and haloes there. In the Epilogue to his last volume of poems the living are bidden to greet the dead 'with a cheer':

> Bid him forward, breast and back as either should be,
> 'Strive and thrive!' cry 'Speed—fight on, fare ever
> There as here!'

Even a Benthamite utilitarian might be willing to accept a Heaven in which he could still find bustle and 'progress'.

The novel grew steadily in popularity throughout the middle years of the century, and it would be possible to interrogate all the novelists, good and bad, for evidence bearing upon our subject, for there is hardly a single writer of fiction or verse, unless it be Edward Lear, who could not be proved to be at least a reflector, if not a direct exponent, of some phase of the thought of his generation. A very few examples must suffice. For instance, the parliamentary sessions of the later 'forties were constantly occupied with the problem of controlling the hours and conditions of work in factories. It is not fanciful to connect this political activity with the contemporaneous publication of four notable novels dealing with industrial life—Disraeli's *Sybil* (1845), Mrs. Gaskell's *Mary Barton* (1848), Charlotte Brontë's *Shirley* (1849), and Kingsley's *Alton Locke* (1851).

Of all Victorian novelists Anthony Trollope has come to be recognized as the most faithful recorder of ordinary life and manners. The *Chronicles of Barsetshire* are tales of an imaginary provincial diocese. Trollope's sympathies are with the old High-and-dry school. In the first novel we see the amiable 'Warden' of the ancient almshouses ejected from his comfortable sinecure owing to the misguided agitation of a young Benthamite reformer of theoretical abuses, and the results are unfortunate for all concerned. In the second novel, *Barchester Towers*, the comfortable old bishop has died and is succeeded, not, as he should have been, by his son the Archdeacon, but by the Evangelical Dr. Proudie. Dr. Proudie is ruled by his wife, and his chaplain, Mr. Slope, who may be defined briefly as Uriah Heep in Holy Orders.

Trollope was not a clerically minded man; the career of his dreams was a seat in the House of Commons. Yet his political novels suggest that for him the House was little more than the best of clubs and debating societies. His political novels are very pleasant, but their politics is purely formal. His Prime Minister is a Duke, and his nobility (in both senses of the word) is more apparent than his statesmanship. The legislative *pièce de resistance* is usually 'an alteration in the franchise'—a reminder that at least half a dozen abortive Reform Bills were debated with academic apathy between 1850 and 1867. If Trollope has a lesson for the student of Victorian thought, it is that the period, in spite of the earnest exhortations of its protagonists, was after all, judged by modern standards, a fairly placid one.

It is no easy task to find the place of Charles Dickens in the history of English thought, yet it is a task which cannot be altogether ignored, for he was as far the greatest popular writer of the middle decades of the century as Scott had been of its earliest decades. He became, long before he died, like Lord Palmerston, a national institution, and he created more characters whose names are still household words than all the other nineteenth-century novelists put together. Scott was by temperament an aristocrat, and his novels popularized, unconsciously, the philosophy of Burke. Dickens was by temperament a democrat; though he early became rich and revelled, very unwisely, in his riches, he never abandoned the sublime paradox that there is a curse on riches and a blessing on poverty. But if Scott finds his place in our scheme as a pendant to Burke, where are we to find a place for the 'thought' of Dickens? Mr. Chesterton, in the most brilliant pages of his brilliant little book on *Victorian Literature*, places him with Newman, Carlyle, Ruskin, and Arnold, among the leaders of opposition to the Benthamite-Evangelical Victorian orthodoxy. 'That which had not been achieved by the fierce facts of Cobbett, the burning dreams of Carlyle, the white-hot proofs of Newman, was really or very nearly achieved by a crowd of impossible people. In the centre stood the citadel of atheist industrialism: and if indeed it has ever been taken, it was taken by the mob of that unreal army'—the army of the Dickens 'characters'. But is there not something fantastic about this notion? Dickens, like Scott, was first and foremost a popular entertainer; neither of them made any secret of the fact. What they found to be unpopular with their vast constituencies they took care not to repeat. How then can Dickens, any more than Scott, have been a rebel against the orthodoxies of his day?

Dickens was a man of great public spirit, wide interests, close observation, and no theories. We may contrast him with Mr. Wells. Mr. Wells is also a novelist of great public spirit, wide interests, and close observation. Like Dickens he excels in broad and humorous panoramas of contemporary life; but he is a theorist, a socialist. He not only sees what is wrong, but he has distinct and elaborate notions of how it should be righted, notions which not only dilute his novels but overflow from them in a spate of sociological essays. Dickens had none of this; he lays his finger upon one thing and another thing; he makes one thing and another thing stink in the nostrils of his public, and his task is done. What are the victims of these simple and effective methods?

In *Oliver Twist*, the new workhouses recently established under the Poor Law Amendment Act; in *Nicholas Nickleby* [1] and *David Copperfield*, the worst type of 'profiteering' private school; in both these novels and in *The Old Curiosity Shop*, industrial cruelty to children; in *Martin Chuzzlewit*, the United States of America; in *Dombey and Son*, the pomp and pride of capitalism; in *Bleak House* the 'law's delays'; in the same novel and also in *Pickwick*, the cant of the worse kind of nonconformist preacher; in *Bleak House* again, the false philanthropy of the mission-monger who neglects her own family in her preoccupation with the heathen of Borriaboula-Gha; in *Hard Times*, political economy; in *Little Dorrit*, the debtors' prison and also red-tape as symbolized by the Circumlocution office.

It would of course be quite easy with a little industrious ingenuity to weld all these and other examples together into a coherent scheme of political and social thought; but the

---

[1] Wackford Squeers was, under another name, a real person who kept a school at Richmond in Yorkshire; its iniquities had been exposed in the press. 'Squeers' was a contemporary of Dr. Arnold, and I remember seeing obituary notices of one of the last surviving pupils of each of these famous headmasters in *The Times* a few years ago.

labour would be worse than wasted, for its result would be misleading. Dickens belonged neither to the orthodox school of thought nor to the opposition; and the best evidence for this is the fact that he has been claimed by both. Mr. Chesterton claims him as the prince of anti-Benthamites; Sir Henry Maine, a great lawyer and political philosopher of his own day, claims him as an unconscious Benthamite, as being related to Bentham as Scott was related to Burke. 'It does not seem to me', wrote Maine, 'a fantastic assertion that the ideas of one of the great novelists of the last generation may be traced to Bentham', and the novelist is Dickens.[1]

Dickens was a democrat by sentiment. His sympathies were all with the poor, for he had known bitter poverty in childhood, and he deserves the title given to him by Edward FitzGerald,—the Cockney Shakespeare. In his novels he has given us an amazing panorama of what used to be called 'the lower classes' before their whole outlook and way of life was transformed by the cheap press, trade unionism, democratic politics, and, we may now add, the cinema, the wireless, and the motor-charabanc. But though a democrat by sentiment he had no interest in, and no realization of the significance of, the democratic movements of his day. He was as old-fashioned as Lord Shaftesbury, perhaps more so, for the only remedy for poverty discoverable in his novels is the Christian charity of the Cheeryble brothers. In spirit he was much nearer to Father Christmas than to Karl Marx. Only in his last completed novel, *Our Mutual Friend*, does he portray a working man of a recognizably modern type, Charlie Hexam, and he is a most displeasing person. 'This youth', wrote George Gissing in his admirable book on Dickens, 'has every fault that can attach to a half-taught cub of his particular world. He is a monstrous egotist to begin with, and "school" has merely put an edge on to the native vice. The world exists solely for his benefit; his esuriency, to use Carlyle's word, has no bounds. . . . His like may be found throughout London by anyone studying

[1] Maine, *Popular Government*, p. 153.

DICKENS

the less happy results of the board-school system.' We need
not go further, and seek to draw a moral from the fact that
Charlie's schoolmaster turns out to be a murderer! Mur-
derers were required by the exigencies of most of Dickens's
plots, and the murderer Headstone is a more attractive person
than his pupil. But if we set over against Charlie Hexam
some such idealized character as Joe Gargery, the village
blacksmith of *Great Expectations*, strong as a horse and gentle
as a woman, not only unable to read and write but well-nigh
incapable of expressing himself in articulate English, yet
every inch a gentleman by right of nature,—if we set side by
side two such figures as these, we realize the fundamental
conservatism of Dickens. It is not the conservatism of
party but the conservatism of instinct.

CHAPTER III
THE LAST THIRD OF THE CENTURY

I

IMPERIALISM

IN 1872 Disraeli, then Leader of the Opposition, outlined, in a speech at the Crystal Palace, the policy he would follow if circumstances were to make him at last, and for the first time in his long career, the head of a Government commanding a majority in the House of Commons. The part of his speech which attracted most attention was devoted to Imperial problems. 'If', he said, 'you look at the history of this country since the advent of Liberalism, forty years ago, you will find that there has been no effort so continuous, so subtle, as the attempts of Liberalism to effect the disintegration of the Empire of England.[1] It has been proved to all of us that we have lost money by our Colonies. How often has it been suggested that we should emancipate ourselves from this incubus! Well, that result was very nearly accomplished. When those subtle views were adopted under the plausible plea of granting self-government to the Colonies, I confess that I myself thought that the tie was broken. Not that I for one moment object to self-government; I cannot conceive how our distant Colonies can have their affairs administered except by self-government. But self-government, when it was conceded, ought to have been conceded as part of a great policy

---

[1] This phrase was, I think, generally used by Disraeli to designate the British Empire. I have somewhat compressed the quotation from the speech.

of Imperial consolidation. It ought to have been accompanied by an Imperial tariff, and by a military code, which should have precisely defined the means by which the Colonies should be defended, and by which, if necessary, this country should call for aid from the Colonies themselves. It ought also to have been accompanied by the institution of some representative Council in the metropolis, which would have brought the Colonies into constant and continuous relations with the Home Government. All this, however, was omitted. . . .

'Well, what has been the result of this attempt, during the reign of Liberalism, for the disintegration of the Empire? It has entirely failed. But how has it failed? Through the sympathy of the Colonies for the Mother Country. They have decided that the Empire shall not be destroyed; and in my opinion no Minister in this country will do his duty who neglects any opportunity of reconstructing as much as possible our Colonial Empire.'

'That', says Mr. Buckle, Disraeli's biographer, 'is the famous declaration from which the modern conception of the British Empire largely takes its rise.' Twenty-five years later Gladstone said, 'There was a time when some statesmen considered that when the Colonies grew in strength, importance, and numbers, they would wish to be severed from the Mother Country. We thought that nothing could be done that would prevent them doing so. But there were those who said, "No, the Colonies will not wish to sever themselves from the parent stock. . . . The more freedom they have the greater will be their love for the Mother Country, and the closer the connexion." . . . The ideals and aspirations (of these men) have been fully verified.' [1]

Disraeli's Government took office in 1874. If we take 1874 to 1901 as the period covered by this chapter, we find that Conservative Governments held office for fully eighteen

[1] Quoted from Duncan Hall, *The British Commonwealth of Nations*, an admirable book, to which I am indebted for much in the material of the next few pages.

of these twenty-seven years; and the Conservative Governments were, with varying degrees of intensity, Imperialistic in character, though their energies took the form of extending rather than consolidating the Empire—to use Disraeli's word. The Liberal Governments, on the other hand, were anti-Imperialistic, and their misfortunes were principally due to the fact that the current of public opinion was, in this matter, against them. They owed such power as they possessed to the immense prestige accumulated and, as it were, capitalized by Gladstone in the course of his earlier career; but Gladstone, the last of the Benthamites, was out of touch with the aspirations of the rising generation.

Disraeli's 1874–80 Government purchased the control of the Suez Canal, conferred on the Queen the title of Empress of India, championed the 'integrity of Turkey' against Russia on the express understanding that the integrity of Turkey was necessary to the safety of British India, established, with France, the Dual Control over Egyptian finances, annexed the Transvaal, conquered the Zulus, and attempted the conquest of Afghanistan. Gladstone's Governments of 1880–86 withdrew from Afghanistan and, after Majuba, from the Transvaal, reluctantly undertook the government of Egypt but abandoned the Sudan—and General Gordon; it also launched what Imperialists regarded as a vital blow at the Empire by proposing to establish Home Rule in Ireland. Salisbury's 1886–92 Government was not very actively Imperialistic, but it secured several new colonies in Africa. Gladstone's 1892–95 Government made a second unsuccessful attempt to enact Irish Home Rule. Salisbury's 1895–1902 Government achieved the climax of Imperialism in the reconquest of the Sudan and of the South African Boer Republics.

Such were, in brief outline, the political manifestations of the period of Imperialism announced by Disraeli's speech at the Crystal Palace. We have here to consider the general character of the thought and the sentiment underlying the Imperialist movement, and the circumstances out of which it arose. Nothing has been said in the previous chapters about public opinion regarding the Empire. It is therefore necessary to take up the subject from the beginning of the century.

The victory of George Washington meant for England something more than the loss of thirteen much-prized colonies; it involved the abandonment of our old colonial philosophy. According to that philosophy, colonies were maintained for the sake of their trade with the Mother Country, and that trade was not a 'natural' or free trade, but a regulated trade —regulated not merely by tariffs but by direct prohibitions. Colonies, for example, were forbidden to export various commodities to any destination except the ports of the Mother Country. In all matters except their commerce the colonies were left very much to their own devices. They had elective assemblies, though they also had governors appointed by the Crown.

The War of American Independence proved that centralized control of trade and elected local assemblies 'go ill together'. At the same time the economic doctrine that free trade was profitable to all concerned had begun to penetrate political circles in England; the younger Pitt spoke of himself as a pupil of Adam Smith. Then came the Revolutionary and Napoleonic wars, and for over twenty years there was little time or inclination for calm discussion of colonial problems.

After Waterloo two schools of thought about the colonies began to define themselves—schools roughly identical with the Old Toryism and with Benthamite Liberalism. The Old Tory school did not talk very much, nor perhaps think very much, about the matter, but in a general way it was determined to maintain what remained of the old empire and also the new colonies acquired as a result of the Napoleonic Wars. They served various purposes—Australia, for example, was invaluable for convicts—and the way to maintain them was to refrain from encouraging the establishment of local organs of self-government. 'Since the close of the American War', wrote Cornewall Lewis in 1841, 'it has not been the policy of England to vest any portion of the legislative power of the subordinate government of a dependency in a body elected by the inhabitants. The only partial exception is in the Canadian provinces.'

The colonies, in fact, were to be governed by a bureaucracy of modest dimensions in London. The Mother Country was 'Mr. Mother Country', an industrious and obscure official residing in one of the suburbs of London, and travelling daily to Whitehall to 'govern the Empire'. 'In some back room', wrote Charles Buller, a brilliant forerunner of modern Imperial ideas, 'you will find all the Mother Country which really exercises supremacy, and really maintains connexion with the vast and widely scattered Colonies of Britain. . . . There are rooms in the Colonial Office with old and meagre furniture, book-cases crammed with colonial gazettes and newspapers, tables covered with baize and some old and faded chairs scattered about, in which those who have personal applications to make are doomed to wait until the interview can be obtained. . . . These are men with colonial grievances. The very messengers know them, their business, and its hopelessness, and eye them with pity as they bid them wait their long and habitual period of attendance.' [1] This is a brief excerpt from a long and vividly ironical description; the reader is perhaps reminded of the Court of Chancery and 'the man from Shropshire' as described in Dickens's *Bleak House*.

The Benthamite Liberal school was in opposition, and consequently much more vocal, but Bentham himself condensed its message in the three words 'Emancipate your colonies'. Brougham in 1839 described Wolfe's capture of Quebec as a performance 'which crowned our arms with imperishable glory, and loaded our policy with a burden not yet shaken off'. Cobden a few years later wrote: 'It is customary to hear our standing army and navy defended as necessary for the protection of our colonies, as though some other nation might otherwise seize them. Where is the

[1] Quoted from Egerton, *British Colonial Policy*, p. 297.

enemy (?) that would be so good as to steal such *property*? *We* should consider it to be quite as necessary to arm in defence of our national debt.' Such sentiments seem to-day not merely mistaken but repulsive, yet Brougham and Cobden were enlightened and patriotic men, and the views they expressed were a natural reaction from the system of 'Mr. Mother Country'. Colonies had been valued for the control of their trade; the acceptance of free trade rendered them valueless. To retain them for no purpose, in a spirit of passive obstinacy, and to misgovern them was merely to provoke animosity against England in the hearts of Englishmen beyond the seas. The colonies emancipated would not cease to be English in all respects that really mattered, English in race, language, and traditions. Even Disraeli—in a casual private letter, it is true—spoke in 1852 of 'these wretched colonies which will all be independent in a few years, and are a millstone round our necks'.

There was another motive which led the Benthamite school to desire the break-up of the Empire. In 1842 Cobden wrote: 'Our Free Trade agitation and the Peace Movement are one and the same cause. . . . The Colonial system, with all its dazzling appeals to the passions of the people, can never be got rid of except by the indirect process of Free Trade, which will gradually and imperceptibly loose the bands which unite our Colonies to us by a mistaken notion of self-interest. Yet the colonial policy of Europe has been the chief cause of wars for the last hundred and fifty years.'

As a statement of historical fact Cobden's last sentence was undeniably true,—true ever since English and Dutch had 'fought for the fairest of all mistresses, trade'. It was very natural to assume that tariffs, colonies, and war were inseparable components of one evil system; if tariffs were going, colonies must go, and war would go also. It is true also, as the following pages will show, that the revival of Imperialism was in part at least a British response to the revival of militarism in Central Europe. When Cobden wrote, Great Britain alone of European Great Powers west of Russia had a great colonial empire. France had lost her colonies to England; Spain and Portugal had seen their colonies emancipate themselves. It seemed, therefore, to those who shared Cobden's view, that the emancipation of our colonies was something like a sacred duty owed by Great Britain to the cause of international civilization; moreover, the discharge of the duty involved in their opinion no sacrifice, except a sacrifice of pride.

But about 1830, ten years before Cobden wrote the words just quoted, another colonial policy had begun to make its appearance, the policy of a small but distinguished group of Radicals and Whigs who called themselves Colonial Reformers. The founder of this school of thought was Gibbon Wakefield, an indefatigable agitator who immersed himself in the details of organized emigration and settlement in Australia and New Zealand. Its most conspicuous adherents were Lord Durham, son-in-law of Lord Grey of the Reform Bill, and author of the famous Durham Report upon Canada, and Charles Buller, Durham's secretary in Canada, and author of the satire on 'Mr. Mother Country' already quoted. The Colonial Reformers had an ardent faith in the future of the Empire, which they believed could be secured by the granting of complete self-government in all that pertained to the local affairs of the various colonies. Such self-government was to be very different from the Assembly system which had prevailed in the old American colonies and survived in Canada down to the date of Durham's mission. Such assemblies did not control their executives, and an elected assembly which did not control its executive authority was, in Buller's words, like a fire without a chimney; it enjoyed, in fact, exactly the position of a House of Commons under Charles I. In Upper and Lower Canada Durham found two Assemblies, each at loggerheads with their English Governors. He proposed that the two Canadian provinces should be united, and that the government should be entrusted to ministers fully respon-

sible to the Canadian Assembly, the Governor being hence-
forth simply the representative of the Crown, governing
Canada through the ministers provided for him by the
Assembly.

The *Quarterly Review*, the organ of orthodox Toryism
to which Croker contributed his 'slashing articles', denounced
Durham's policy in 1839 as 'this new and to us incomprehensible system of colonial *connexion*; the Report calls it
connexion—to our understanding it is absolute separation'.
The author of this article had not read the Durham Report
with very much care, for it expressly excludes 'Imperial
functions' from the control of the Canadian government,
and among Imperial functions were classed not only foreign
policy, but also tariffs and even the disposal of Crown lands
situated within the colony. On all these points there was
to be 'a perfect subordination' of Canada to the British
government at home.

The principles of the Durham Report were, with some
hesitation, accepted. Peel opposed them, showing himself
in this matter almost a disciple of Lord Eldon. If the people
of Canada were discontented, he said, that was no reason
for releasing them from their allegiance. The principle
might, he said, equally be applied 'to a part of England that
expressed itself dissatisfied with the rule of England'; and he
gave as an example the Isle of Wight! Still, with the Gover-
nor-Generalship of Lord Elgin, sent out by the Whigs in
1847, complete self-government in the Durham sense of
the term began, and proved an entire success. Lord Dufferin,
who held Lord Elgin's post in the early 'seventies, pleasantly
compared his position to that of the overseer who watches
the working of some great piece of machinery, and 'walks
about with a little tin vessel of oil, and pours in a drop here
and a drop there as occasion or the creaking of a joint may
require'. Lord Dufferin's successor, appointed by Disraeli,
was the Marquis of Lorne, who had married Queen Victoria's daughter. The appointment was no doubt a part of
Disraeli's policy of exalting the position of the royal family:

it was also a recognition of the complete success of Lord Durham's proposals, for it would obviously have been undesirable that the Queen's son-in-law should be involved in political controversies. His appointment was evidence of the fact that the Governor-General's position could now be reckoned outside the sphere of political controversy.

We have described the result as a triumph of Lord Durham's policy, yet the safeguards which he deemed essential to his policy had never been enacted, and the strictures of the *Quarterly* reviewer had therefore a kind of justification. No limits to the sovereignty of the Canadian government had ever been laid down, a most fortunate result attributable partly to the difficulty of drawing the line between Imperial and local functions, but mainly to the lethargy and indifference of the House of Commons. It was a fortunate omission. When, in 1859, Canada desired to impose tariffs on imports, from Britain as from elsewhere, no Act of the British parliament stood in her way. By this date the Australian colonies had received the same privileges as Canada. Cape Colony, Natal, and New Zealand were to follow.

By a curious stroke of fate the leading Colonial Reformers all died young. They might have lived to share in the revival of Imperialism, led by Disraeli in the 'seventies. Instead, they were all dead by 1855, having achieved colonial self-government untempered by any measure of imperial control. Old Toryism had disappeared; Benthamite *laissez-faire* was in power, and its attitude to colonial problems has been defined as 'pessimism'. It was no longer necessary to agitate for the emancipation of the colonies and the abolition of Mr. Mother Country. Mr. Mother Country had gone, and the colonies were, to all intents and purposes, emancipated. The attitude of the 'sixties might be expressed in the phrase—'Why prolong the farce of an imperial connexion from which all reality has departed?' This attitude was by no means confined to Liberals in the party sense of the word, though its most articulate spokesmen were Cobden and Bright. It was the attitude of the principal officials of the Colonial

Office. 'I go very far with you', wrote one Colonial Office civil servant to another, 'in the desire to shake off all responsibly governed colonies.' He goes on to speak of Canada as 'a colony which is no good to us and has no real care for us'.[1] And again, 'I have always believed that the destiny of our colonies is independence; and that in this point of view the function of the Colonial Office is to secure that our connexion, while it lasts, shall be as profitable to both parties, and our separation, when it comes, as amicable as possible.' The writer of these words was, from 1860 to 1871, the head of the Office under the Colonial Secretary.

And then, with curious suddenness, came the beginnings of that utterly different school of thought we call Imperialism. It was visible before Disraeli's famous speech of 1872, for Disraeli, if he was a philosopher, was also a politician and as such a professional vote-catcher. He saw Imperialism coming, and for that reason he bade it come and offered it a welcome in the Tory party.

Many causes can be suggested for the change of view, and many no doubt co-operated. Even such a local trifle as the discovery of diamonds at Kimberley in 1869 may have played a part. More important by far was the revival of military imperialism in Bismarck's Germany. The 'Little Englander' philosophy of Cobden had tacitly assumed the universal adoption of free trade, the triumph of nationalism on the Continent by means of civilian revolutions, the development of a multiplicity of small nations on the lines of Belgium and Greece, and the disappearance of war from civilized life. The Crimean War had been the first shock to this optimism. There had followed in rapid succession the war of Napoleon III against Austria and the three wars of Bismarckian Prussia. And with the growth of militarism had come the decline of the free-trade movement, which had reached its climax on the Continent in 1860. People began to say —how mistakenly the events of our own time have shown —that 'the day of small nations was past'. The future

[1] Duncan Hall, *op. cit.*, p. 50.

seemed to lie with the great aggregations of organized military power, and how was England to be a leader among such aggregations, unless she drew tighter the as yet unsnapped links with her colonies, and operated upon the international stage as a world-wide yet coherent Empire?

But there was another and quite different cause contributing to the Imperialistic movement. The colonies themselves, once the irritant of 'Mr. Mother Country' was removed, were determined to maintain an outward and visible connexion with the homeland from which they had sprung, and the British working classes were entirely in sympathy with them. Indifference to the colonies was an aspect of Benthamite Liberalism, and that Liberalism had been mainly a middle-class creed. It was the working classes whose brothers and cousins had emigrated to the colonies, who knew that, if bad trade returned, emigration might be their lot also. These men liked to think of their emigrant brothers and cousins as fellow-citizens within the same 'Greater Britain'; they liked to think that, if it should be their own lot to leave their homes, they need not also say good-bye to the British flag. Thus the Reform Act of 1867, which created a new body of working-class electors equal in numbers to the whole of the old upper and middle class electorate, opened the way to Imperialism as it also opened the way for the introduction of the semi-socialistic policies to be discussed in the next section of this chapter. Both Imperialism and Collectivism (or Socialism) are reactions from Benthamite Liberalism. Of the two, Imperialism rose to power the earlier, perhaps because it was definitely backed, from the first, by a statesman of genius, who was the leader of a great party.

There was a popular kind of Imperialistic sentiment which no doubt found complete satisfaction in the various projects for 'painting the map red' which were carried out in the last quarter of the century. Yet Disraeli's 'Crystal Palace' ideal had been not extension but 'consolidation'. What was consolidation, and how could it be achieved? In 1884 an

Imperial Federation League was founded, for the study of this problem.

The problem bristled with difficulties. Assuming that ties of loyalty and sentiment were not enough, what more could be added to them? The genuine Federationists recommended the adoption of an imperial constitution with an imperial parliament and an imperial Cabinet for imperial affairs, which would presumably include foreign policy, armaments and the revenue required for these purposes. Within such a scheme, each of the colonies and also Great Britain would occupy the position of subordinate self-governing bodies. There would be, presumably, two Prime Ministers, two Cabinets, and two parliaments in London. London would perform the functions both of Washington and of New York. The Prime Minister of the Empire would stand to the Prime Minister of Great Britain as the President of the United States stands to the Governor of New York State. Such schemes were amusing exercises in the art of drafting constitutions, but they had no importance, for they were utterly unacceptable both in Great Britain and in the colonies.

Others suggested the creation of an 'Imperial *Zollverein*' or customs union, like that which had preceded and laid foundations for the establishment of the German Empire. Such a scheme, however, involved the surrender by Great Britain of her cherished tradition of free trade, since it was impossible to grant a preference to trade with the colonies unless there was first a duty on imports from outside the Empire. The scheme also involved the surrender by the colonies of their control of their own tariffs. Mr. Chamberlain proposed a scheme of Imperial Preference with a view to strengthening the bonds of empire, in the opening years of the new century, but his party was decisively defeated in the General Election of 1906.

One of the notable books inspired by the Imperialist movement was Sir John Seeley's *Expansion of England* (1883). Seeley was one of the greatest University teachers of his generation, and the book is admirable as an historical sketch of the development of the Empire; but when the argument passes, in accordance with the author's avowed intention, 'from history to politics', it becomes curiously inadequate. The wrongness of Seeley's conception of the Empire is indicated in his title. The Empire was not merely an 'expansion of England'; the colonies were emphatically not what Seeley so quaintly called them—'so many Kents and Cornwalls'. The greater colonies were rapidly becoming nations; a Kentishman is also an Englishman, but that is just what the Canadian was not. Indeed the national sentiment of the colonies was to defeat the constructive schemes of the Imperialists as decisively as the imperial loyalty of the colonies had falsified the expectations of the 'Pessimists'.

Seeley made no constructive constitutional proposals. His object was to rouse interest and he was eminently successful. Indeed the foundation of the Imperial Federation League in the next year was largely the result of his book. The League dissolved ten years later owing to the divergency of the views of its members, and in 1899 Lord Rosebery, once a speculator in 'Federalism' and a President of the League, declared that 'Imperial Federation in any form is an impossible dream'. Yet the 'dream' was re-dreamt in the decade before the war, and once again a historical essay may be held to have given the impetus. F. S. Oliver's *Alexander Hamilton* (1904) is a work of the same class as Seeley's *Expansion of England*. As a biography of the great statesman who was the principal architect of the American Union it is entirely admirable, but its explicit aim is to convince the reader that what Hamilton did for the thirteen ex-colonies could and should now be done for the Dominions of the British Empire. In 1910 a brilliant group of writers founded a quarterly periodical called *The Round Table*, for the study of Imperial politics and the advocacy of Imperial Federation. The periodical has survived but now serves only the first of these purposes.

Meanwhile accident had led to the establishment of a

better, because less ambitious, method of Imperial co-operation. In 1887 Queen Victoria celebrated her Jubilee, and
the presence of all the Colonial Premiers in London suggested to the Colonial Secretary the holding of a somewhat
informal Colonial Conference. In 1897 the Queen celebrated a second Jubilee, and there was a second Conference;
in 1902 King Edward celebrated his coronation, and there
was a third Conference. The regular recurrence of such
royal pageants could hardly be premised, and the Conference
of 1902 arranged for future meetings every four years.

But we have been dwelling too much, perhaps, upon merely
political considerations, for the Imperialism of the late
Victorian period went deeper than any political action or
political theory. Its greatest exponent was not Sir John
Seeley, nor even Joseph Chamberlain, most notable of
Colonial Secretaries. Imperialism was a sentiment rather
than a policy; its foundations were moral rather than intellectual; its greatest exponent was Rudyard Kipling.

Kipling's first book, *Plain Tales from the Hills*, was published in the year of the Queen's first Jubilee; *Soldiers Three*
followed in the next year. Here was a brilliant teller of
tales who found his heroes neither in the streets of London,
nor in the villages of Wessex, nor among the aristocracy of
the country houses, but among the officers and men of the
British Army. To a whole world of readers Kipling introduced the honourable and lovable figure of Tommy Atkins,
and the world in which he lived. The philosophy of that
world was a simple philosophy—loyalty, discipline, duty;
'don't talk, but get on with the job.' The celebrated *Jungle
Books*, published in the 'nineties, may fairly be regarded as
an allegorical treatment of the same theme. The great
beasts of the Jungle fulfil themselves in obedience to the law
of their being—all except the monkeys, detestable alike to
Mr. Kipling and to the old bear Baloo. The monkeys have
no chiefs. They boast and chatter and pretend, but the
fall of a nut suffices to distract them. In fact they are rather
like Radical politicians! In 1899 Mr. Kipling published

his school story, *Stalky and Co.* It is, as explicitly as *Tom Brown's Schooldays*, a tract, but the moral is somewhat different. It sufficed for Arnold and Tom Hughes that the school should turn out Christians and gentlemen. For Kipling the school is a nursery of soldiers and Empire-builders. 'Just imagine', says the Beetle, 'Stalky let loose on the south side of Europe with a sufficiency of Sikhs and a reasonable prospect of loot.' To which the Infant replies: 'You're too much of an optimist, Beetle.'

In 1897, on the morrow of the second Jubilee, *The Times* published Kipling's *Recessional*. That poem, alike in its instinctive national pride and its prayer for national humility, was the perfect expression of all that was best in that climax of Imperialism of which the second Jubilee was the symbol.

> If, drunk with sight of power, we loose
> Wild tongues that have not Thee in awe—
> Such boastings as the Gentiles use
> Or lesser breeds without the law—

Some wild tongues had indeed been loosed, and perhaps the allusion to 'lesser breeds' was itself a symptom of patriotic intoxication.[1] But to commit a fault in the very moment of praying to be delivered from committing it is neither ludicrous nor contemptible. It is only very human. The unlucky metaphor is a reminder that Kipling's thought, like Carlyle's (and in many respects Kipling might be accounted a disciple of Carlyle), is soaked in the Old Testament. Many great writers of English prose are full of Biblical phraseology and Biblical quotation. Kipling comes very near the adopting the Old Testament philosophy of history.

---

[1] Mr. Chesterton's parody is well known:

> Though drunk with sight of power and blind,
> Even as you bowed your head in awe
> You kicked up both your heels behind
> At lesser breeds without the law.

His British are God's chosen people, chosen not so much for privilege as for service. Indeed the privilege and the service are but different names for the same thing. The privilege is to rule a quarter of the globe, the service is to bear 'the white man's burden'.

It would not be altogether fanciful to connect indirectly with Imperialist sentiment other less didactic novelists of the last twenty years of the century. There was romance in the thought that some of the strangest peoples of the earth were numbered among the subjects of 'the Great White Queen'. Kipling himself has many fascinating and some horrifying tales of native Indian life. Rider Haggard had been private secretary of the Governor of Natal at the time of the first annexation of the Transvaal and the Zulu war; he afterwards used his South African knowledge in *King Solomon's Mines* and its sequels. Stevenson's South Sea tales belong to the same period; in fact the Equator became more popular in fiction than it had ever been before. At the same time the indefatigable Henty was providing a generation of schoolboys less sophisticated than their successors with an endless series of historical romances, many of them illustrative of the remoter exploits of the British Army. Again, it is an easy transition from historical fiction to popular military history. One of the 'best sellers' of the second Jubilee year was Fitchett's *Deeds that won the Empire*. It was followed by *Fights for the Flag* and *How England saved Europe* (i.e. from Napoleon). Another writer produced, in obvious rivalry with Fitchett's 'Deeds', a book of the same calibre called *Men who made the Empire*, a set of seven popular biographies, concluding with Cecil Rhodes. Mr. Fitchett was an Australian Wesleyan minister, and when he died, in 1928, a contributor to *The Times* stated that the sale of his books had far exceeded that of any other Australian writer.

Imperialism in the later 'nineties had become a genuinely popular emotion, and like all such emotions it occasionally expressed itself with vulgarity. There was some excuse for

JUBILEE SENTIMENT

We don't want to fight, but, by Jingo, if we do,
We've got the ships, we've got the men, and we've got the money too

for that ditty dated from 1877, when the country seemed on the verge of war with Russia. But what are we to say of the production, amid the profound peace of the second Jubilee, of such a song as *The Soldiers of the Queen*? The chorus ran as follows:

> The soldiers of the Queen, my boys,
> Who've been, my boys, who've seen, my boys,
> In the fight for England's glory, boys,
>   When we've had to show them what we mean.
> And when we say we've always won,
> And when they ask us how it's done,
> We'll proudly point to every one
>   Of England's soldiers of the Queen.

These words speak for themselves, but no mere words can do justice to the combination of sentimentality and bumptiousness exuded by the music.

What was good in the Imperialist movement, its sober sense of the unity of what we now call the British Commonwealth of Nations, and the interdependence of its members, has survived. The romantic and bombastic elements in the movement withered away as suddenly as the movement itself had arisen. What had happened? In the first place, the 'Black Week' of December, 1899, with its three humiliating defeats in South Africa. The war had opened in a vainglorious mood. Pride had gone before a fall, and pride was consequently discredited. There was an old saying attributed to the Duke of Wellington to the effect that 'the battle of Waterloo was won on the playing-fields of Eton'. Some cynic now remarked that the battle of Colenso had been lost on those same fields. Kipling soon afterwards published an almost savage satire on the 'Wellingtonian' theory, in which he derided 'the flannelled fool at the wicket, the muddied oaf in the goal'. Sportsmanship was not patriotism, and it was no substitute for efficiency.

189

In the following May the relief of Mafeking was followed by an orgy of hysterical jubilation, which, when it was over, seemed to many to be as discreditable in a different way as the inefficiency that had culminated in 'Black Week'. The nation whose destiny was to rule the lesser breeds, seemed to have little power of ruling its own emotions. The verb 'to maffick' enjoyed a temporary vogue, and its sense was anything but complimentary.

In a different way again the long-drawn-out conclusion of the war wearied the nation of its imperial activities. If that stage of the war had any hero it was the elusive De Wet.

Then came Chamberlain's political crusade for Imperial Preference. Beginning as a plea for Imperial solidarity on a commercial basis, the movement was rapidly entangled in arguments for the protection of home industries. And if the principal imports from the colonies were to enjoy a preference in the British market, what about the inevitable tax on non-imperial corn. 'Your food will cost you more', said the free-traders. Liberal cartoons depicted the big loaf and the little loaf, and the little loaf was the loaf offered by the Imperialists.

Then in 1904 came the importation of rigidly controlled Chinese labour to work in the gold mines of the conquered Transvaal. Had we, it was asked, conquered the Transvaal in order to introduce 'Chinese slavery' into the country? There had always been an undercurrent of feeling that British soldiers had fought and bled for the sake of a crowd of cosmopolitan millionaires, and that feeling was now fanned into flame. At the General Election of 1906 the most effective Liberal poster was a hideous yellow Chinese face. Whether this poster won votes for Liberalism because we hated Chinamen or because we hated the enslavement of Chinamen, is far from clear; but in that hideous yellow face the voter somehow recognized the symbol of a now discredited Imperialism.

Ever since the retirement of Gladstone, Chamberlain

had stood alone as the great political spell-binder. But against this Goliath of Imperialism the Liberals could now confidently pit their David Lloyd George. Mr. Lloyd George, himself the champion of a small nation, had ardently championed the cause of the Boers. That offence no longer needed forgiveness.

II

COLLECTIVISM AND SOCIALISM

IN the year 1865 Walter Bagehot published his admirable—and incidentally most amusing—treatise on *The English Constitution*. It has something of the significance that attaches to certain family photographs, the last family group, let us say, taken before the father died, the eldest son emigrated, and the eldest daughter married. The group was taken just in time; there you had the family whole and complete: the thing could never be done again. Bagehot's sketch was made in the last year of the life of the old political England of the first Reform Bill. Almost before it was published Lord Palmerston had died; then Lord Derby died and Lord Russell retired. The last three aristocratic leaders of the old generation were gone. Gladstone and Disraeli leapt to the front of the stage, and wrestled there. The populace became interested, and smashed the railings of Hyde Park. In response, a part of this same populace was enfranchised by the second Reform Bill, and its children given schooling by the Education Act. Abraham Lincoln proved that democracy was a winning and not a losing cause in the United States. Bismarck made the modern German Empire. In 1872 Bagehot issued a new edition of his book with a seventy-page *Introduction* demonstrating how much had changed in seven years.

In his book as originally published Bagehot found that the secret of the success of our parliamentary system lay in the fact that we were 'a *deferential* nation'. The lower classes were content to be voteless, and to leave the franchise to their betters; the middle-class voters were content to elect upper-class members, and upper-class members to accept an aristocratic Cabinet. The masses, in fact, were hypnotized by 'what we may call the theatrical show of society. . . . Their imagination is bowed down; they feel they are not equal to the life that is revealed to them. . . . This imaginative sentiment is supported by a sensation of political satisfaction. . . . If a political agitator were to lecture to the peasants of Dorsetshire and try to excite political dissatisfaction, it is much more likely that he would be pelted than that he would succeed. Of parliament these miserable creatures know scarcely anything; of the Cabinet they have never heard. But they would say that, "for all they have heard, the Queen is very good", and rebelling against the structure of Society is to their minds rebelling against the Queen.' [1]

It was Bagehot's way to exaggerate this 'deference', for he always liked to emphasize the smallness of the part that reason plays in human affairs. But there was an element of truth in the picture he drew; the novels of Trollope confirm it. He realized, too, that this state of 'deference' was already endangered; it would be swept away by a popular franchise, popular semi-education, and a cheap Press. When he wrote again in 1872 he noted that the change had already begun, and he frankly deplored it. Statesmen, as he saw it, were now confronted with a great temptation, and consequently a great responsibility. 'If they raise questions which will excite the lower orders of mankind; if they raise questions on which those orders are likely to be wrong; if they raise questions on which the interest of those orders is not identical with, or is antagonistic to, the whole interest of the State, they will have done the greatest harm they can do. . . . They will have suggested topics that will bind the poor as a class together; topics which will excite them against the rich; topics the discussion of which in the only form in which that discussion reaches their ear will be to make them think

[1] Bagehot, *The English Constitution*, pp. 265–69.

that some new law can make them comfortable—that it is the present law which makes them uncomfortable—that Government has at its disposal an inexhaustible fund out of which it can give to those who now want. . . . If the first work of the new voters is to try and create a "poor man's paradise", as poor men are apt to fancy that paradise, the great political trial now beginning will simply fail.' [1]

We have seen Lord Liverpool complaining (p. 56) that the Press had begun to represent public opinion; here is a Conservative of fifty years later dreading lest parliament should really represent the new electorate. We have seen Burke, with his superb foresight, demonstrating that there was no permanent abiding place between the Old Toryism and complete democracy; here was another political philosopher born thirty years after Burke's death, finding that Burke had spoken only too truly.

It need hardly be said that things fell out as Bagehot had feared. The statesmen sought to attract the votes of the new electorate (further enlarged by the third Reform Bill of 1885), and the new electorate, thus encouraged, began to discover its political aspirations. But the transformation of our politics came about more slowly than might have been expected, owing, in the main, to the longevity of our statesmen and to the mysterious prestige commanded in politics by old age. Disraeli, in his last ministry, was more interested in the empire than in social questions. Gladstone always remained a Benthamite of the school of Peel, and most of his energies were occupied in undoing the work of Disraeli or in attending to Ireland. Both of these were born before Waterloo. Even Salisbury, whose premiership lasted over the end of the century, was born in 1830 and was chiefly interested in foreign affairs. Chamberlain and Lloyd George were the first statesmen of the front rank to deserve the full weight of Bagehot's censure. But signs of the new school of thought were apparent in practical politics as early

[1] Bagehot, *op. cit.*, *Introduction*, p. xviii.

as the 'seventies. Some call it Collectivism and others Socialism; but the two terms are best kept apart and used for different purposes.

Collectivism is a term used to denote the tendency of political thought to abandon the ideal of Benthamite individualism. The school of Bentham believed in individual liberty; it held that the duty of legislation was, so far as possible, to give free scope to the energy and intelligence of the individual. Its works have already been illustrated at length. In the last third of the century, however, it was becoming apparent that this was not enough. Individual liberty, as secured by legislation, was an illusion for all but a fortunate minority, and the untrammelled energies of that minority tended to cramp the lives of all the rest. Capitalists might have the best intentions, but 'capitalism' uncontrolled was a tyrant. Legislation must, in the interests of all, undertake tasks of social control and social organization. Collectivism was hardly a 'school of thought', and it had no acknowledged exponent of the calibre of Bentham. It was rather a general term that can be used in retrospect to cover a large body of practical legislation.

Socialism, on the other hand, is a complete system of political and economic thought. It looks forward to a new organization of society, an organization in which there will be no private 'capitalism', and the means of production will be owned by the State. Yet most British socialists, accepting what has been called 'the inevitability of gradualism', have accepted a programme of 'socialism by instalments'. They have been content, that is to say, to promote a number of quite modest reforms, looking forward to the establishment of the socialist state as the final result of a long series of measures. Thus all socialists support collectivist measures, and all supporters of collectivist measures are held by socialists to be contributing unintentionally to the ultimate triumph of socialism.

The distinction may be illustrated from current politics. In 1928 both the Liberal party and the Labour party published detailed statements of their policy, in view of the next General Election. A weekly paper compared these programmes in the following terms:[1] 'The immediate proposals of the two opposition parties present, at many points, a striking similarity. But the idea behind them is essentially different. The Liberals still think in terms of a fundamentally capitalist economy, based on individual saving and private enterprise, but subjected perforce to a greatly increased amount of State regulation and centralized control. The Labour party thinks in terms of a collectivist order of society, arising out of the capitalist order by a gradual taking of one thing after another into the hands of the democratic community and its agents. To a large extent . . . they propose the same immediate measures; but to the two parties the same or similar measures mean quite different things. The Liberal report means, by way of salutary reform, to strengthen the capitalist order against the threat of dissolution. The Socialist programme means to bring order out of a dissolution it regards as inevitable, by a drastic, albeit gradual, change in the basis of social organization.'

These sentences could not be bettered as a statement of the difference between the collectivist tendency and the socialist policy, both of which were active side by side in the last years of the nineteenth century. In a study of legislation they might be treated as one and the same; for a study of thought or opinion they are quite distinct, and must be treated separately.

Collectivism had no Bentham as its acknowledged exponent, but all the great writers of the middle period of the century who attacked the orthodoxy of *laissez-faire* were prophets of collectivism. Their influence was less marked in the sphere of legislation than Bentham's had been, simply because they were essentially artists and men of letters, whereas Bentham had been an inventor of practical legislative expedients. We have already seen Carlyle deriding the results of unrestricted competition and idolizing the enlightened despot; Ruskin assaulting the economists and advocating

[1] *The New Statesman*, July 14, 1928, p. 444.

a sort of socialism administered by an aristocracy; Matthew Arnold dismissing liberty as 'mere machinery' and exalting the State as the organ of 'the right reason of the community'; the Christian Socialists upholding co-operation against competition, and condemning the latter as a negation of the Christian religion. Lord Shaftesbury, again, had no political theories outside an old-fashioned conventional Toryism; he abhorred 'socialism' and had never heard of 'collectivism'; none the less, he was the principal author of the first important group of collectivist laws, the Factory Acts.

There is an excellent story—it seems almost too good to be true—that Lord Melbourne introduced Lord Ashley (i.e. the future Lord Shaftesbury) to Queen Victoria as 'the greatest Jacobin in your Majesty's dominions'. The remark must have mystified both the Queen and the philanthropist, but, if Jacobinism is to be taken to mean collectivism, John Morley found it to be true forty years later. Writing in 1881 he says: 'Cobden was fully justified in describing the tendencies of this legislation (i.e. the Factory Acts) as socialistic. It was an exertion of the power of the State in its strongest form, definitely limiting in the interest of the labourer the administration of capital. In the thirty years that followed (the Factory Act of 1847) the principle has been extended with astonishing perseverance. We have to-day a complete, minute, and voluminous code for the protection of labour; buildings must be kept pure of effluvia; dangerous machinery must be fenced; . . . (a long list of similar provisions is given). . . . We find the rather amazing result that in the country where socialism has been less talked about than any other country in Europe, its principles have been most extensively applied.' [1]

Besides the literary men we have mentioned, and the Christian Socialists, and the great unconscious collectivist, Lord Shaftesbury, another school of thought had arisen in the 'sixties and 'seventies, which provided a philosophical basis for collectivism, namely the Oxford school of philosophy,

[1] Morley, *Life of Cobden*, quoted in Dicey, *Law and Opinion*, p. 287.

in which T. H. Green was the greatest teacher. These Oxford philosophers wrote very difficult books and made no attempt to reach the general public. But when we consider that Green was accounted the most influential teacher in Oxford since Newman, and that a considerable number of the most influential public men of the next generation passed through his hands, it is obvious that one cannot measure his importance by the extent of the sale of his books. Green's philosophy was based upon the system of ideas elaborated first by the ancient Greeks, Plato and Aristotle, and afterwards by the Germans of the end of the eighteenth and the beginning of the nineteenth century, particularly Kant and Hegel. Coleridge and Carlyle had studied these Germans, but Coleridge had not the mental energy nor Carlyle the patience required of a philosopher.

Green held that the life of the individual was absolutely dependent upon the life of the community, and that a scheme of thought which regarded the liberty of the individual as something distinct from the welfare of the society, was entirely false. The individual depends on the community for all that makes life worth living; the community must therefore secure for the individual all the conditions necessary for his full spiritual development. As Aristotle said, the State exists to secure 'a *good* life' for its members, not merely to prevent them from suffering concrete injuries. Liberty is not the absence of restraint, but 'a positive power of doing and enjoying something worth doing and enjoying'. The only really free man is the good man, the man whose will is set on being what a man is meant to be. The man whose will is enslaved by the ignorance and wickedness within him is no more truly 'free' than the man who is enslaved by poverty; and the man who is enslaved by poverty is no more truly 'free' than the man who is locked up in a prison. The true function of statesmanship is to produce a community in which all the individuals shall, so far as is possible, be capable of living, and free to live, a good life.

From these profound and exalted reflections we pass to

the collectivist legislation of the last third of the century. The connexion between the two is admittedly somewhat remote, for our collectivist legislation was, from first to last, a haphazard affair. Each measure was designed to remedy an evil rather than to advance a cause. Yet the writers and lecturers who were exposing the defects of Individualism in the sphere of pure theory no doubt helped to smooth the way for collectivist legislation.

It is impossible to fix a date for the beginning of collectivist legislation. Not only were the Factory Acts of the philanthropists strictly collectivist in character, but there was an element of collectivism in a part of the legislation advocated by the most orthodox Benthamites. Free Trade and religious equality were obviously purely individualistic policies, but the New Poor Law and the Board of Health (see p. 84) both involved an increase of State control. From the Benthamite standpoint the aim of both of them was to set free the competent from an incubus imposed upon them by the poverty or the insanitary habits of the incompetent; but they were also measures for the control and improvement of the incompetent, and as such they were collectivist measures. The great Education Act of 1870 again bears a character part Benthamite and part collectivist, as has already been shown.

The most characteristic group of purely collectivist measures in the latter part of the nineteenth century and the beginning of the twentieth were those imposing a liability on employers to compensate workmen who suffered injury in the course of their work, and, later, imposing upon employers and employees alike a share of the cost of compulsory insurance against sickness and unemployment. Here was a clear case of the curtailment of liberty in the interests of welfare. These laws only applied to wage-earners or to persons with less than a certain minimum income, and the cost of the insurance was borne either wholly or in part by others than the insured person. They came to include insurance against accidents, against sickness, against unem-

ployment, and against old age. The problem of the employers'
liability to compensate workmen for accidents arising in the
course of their employment, even though the accident was
not the fault of the employer, even though, indeed, the accident was the fault of the workman involved, was a special
interest of Joseph Chamberlain. He carried his first Act
dealing with the subject in 1880 when a Liberal in Gladstone's Cabinet and his last in 1897 when a Conservative in
Lord Salisbury's Cabinet. This last Act practically compelled the employer to insure his workmen against risk of
accident, and forbade the workman to enter into a contract
excluding this insurance. The modern system of compulsory
insurance against sickness and, in certain trades, against
unemployment was established by Lloyd George's Insurance
Acts of 1911. The cost is shared between the employer,
the employee, and the State, that is to say, of course, the
general body of taxpayers. Old Age Pensions had been
introduced three years earlier, at the cost of the taxpayer.

Collectivism took far too many forms to be enumerated
here. Many of them have little or nothing in common with
one another except for the fact that they all extended the
sphere of public enterprise or public control at the expense
of the old freedom of individual enterprise. One of the
most important was the extension of municipal trading, i.e.
the undertaking of public services such as the supply of gas
or tramways by elected organs of local government. In 1880
Liverpool made the first successful experiment in appealing
for funds to the general body of the investing public instead
of borrowing from the central government. The Municipal
Corporations Act of 1882 swept away all restrictions upon
the services that municipal bodies could undertake.

Local government is exceedingly important, and most
people find it very dull. Except where gross mismanagement
has occurred it excites little controversy, and what controversy arises is concerned with practical details rather than
general principles. It was possible, therefore, for what
socialists called 'municipal socialism' to attain surprising

dimensions without those who believed themselves to be opponents of 'socialism' becoming in any way alarmed. Mr. Sidney Webb, a leading Socialist, has an amusing description of the position of municipal affairs at the end of the century. 'The practical man, oblivious or contemptuous of any theory of the social organism or general principles of social organization, has been forced, by the necessities of the time, into an ever-deepening collectivist channel. Socialism, of course, he still rejects and despises. The individualist town councillor will walk along the municipal pavement, lit by municipal light and cleansed by municipal brooms with municipal water, and seeing, by the municipal clock in the municipal market, that he is too early to meet his children coming from the municipal school, hard by the county lunatic asylum and the municipal hospital, will use the national telegraph system to tell them not to walk through the municipal park, but to come by the municipal tramway, to meet him in the municipal reading-room, by the municipal museum, art-gallery, and library, where he intends to consult some of the national publications in order to prepare his next speech in the municipal town hall in favour of the nationalization of canals and the increase of Government control over the railway system. "Socialism, sir," he will say, "don't waste the time of a practical man by your fantastic absurdities. Self-help, Sir, individual self-help, that's what has made our city what it is." ' [1]

The quotation illustrates one of the characteristics of the growth of collectivism, its way of escaping the attention of the observer. Other kinds of collectivism, however, especially the kind of which national insurance and old age pensions are the type, have had on certain minds a very marked effect. They have encouraged the notion that governments can set everything right, and are to blame for everything that goes wrong. Professor Dicey quotes in illustration of this tendency a curious letter from an Ulster working man,

---

[1] Quoted from Dicey, *Law and Opinion*, p. 287.

published in *The Times* of July 7, 1903. The writer states that workmen are better off in America than in the United Kingdom, and proceeds: 'Now there is something wrong here. You will, no doubt, agree that it should be the object of every statesman and of every Government to promote the welfare of the people and improve their conditions. How is it then, that the British Government has not succeeded in placing us working men in anything like the splendid position that the American Government has placed its workmen in? Britishers should, I submit, be second to none. Our workmen are, without doubt, the finest and most intelligent in the world; they should therefore receive the highest wages, and no Government, in my opinion, ought to experience any difficulty in securing the highest remuneration for such men; yet the British Government has been unable to do it, and I for one would like to know the reason why.' [1]

This man was obviously not a socialist, or he would not have expressed surprise at the shortcomings of a Conservative Government. But he held that faith in the omnicompetence of Government which is the principal article of the socialist faith, and any socialist missionary would have found in him an easy convert.

Nothing was said of socialism in the first two chapters of this book, for British socialism was an affair of very small sects in the first forty years of the century, and may be said to have been extinct during the forty years that followed. John Morley has already been quoted as saying in 1881 that in no country had socialism been so little discussed as in England. When socialism returned in the 'eighties, it drew its doctrines from the Continental socialists of the middle period of the century, and in particular from the German Jew, Karl Marx. It is, however, worth remembering that Marx had done most of his literary work as an exile in London, and that he had studied the works of the early British socialists. This early British socialism is therefore the grandparent rather than the parent of the British socialism

[1] Dicey, *op. cit.*, p. 445.

which, beginning in the 'eighties, has a continuous history until our own day.

Thomas Spence may be reckoned the first of the British socialists. He was, like so many of the more famous men who have figured in this book, a southwards-moving Scotsman. Born at Aberdeen, he migrated to Newcastle, where he was a schoolmaster, and afterward to London where he was a hawking bookseller. He began to write in 1776, the same year as Bentham, and was thus, like Bentham, independent of the influence of the French Revolution. His doctrine was the confiscation of all property in land. The unit of common ownership was not, however, to be the nation but the parish, and rent paid to the parish was to be the only tax. The Governments of his day were sufficiently aware of his existence to prosecute and imprison him on two occasions for writings deemed seditious. Shortly before his death, which occurred in 1814, his disciples formed themselves in the Society of Spencean Philanthropists. They were a minute body, but as they definitely advocated the confiscation of property they were a source of alarm to the Old Tory Government during the troubled years that followed Waterloo. In 1817 they organized a procession in the streets of London; there was a small riot and a great deal of alarm. The Habeas Corpus Act was suspended. Four Spenceans were tried for high treason. One was acquitted and the others released. One of the four was afterwards the leader of the assassination plot known as the Cato Street conspiracy. After that little was heard of the Spenceans.

The next leader of British socialism was a much more significant figure. Robert Owen was unquestionably a man of genius in his own way, and one of the most disinterested men that ever lived. The son of poor Welsh parents, he was a successful mill-owner in Manchester when little over twenty, and in 1800, at the age of twenty-nine, became part owner and sole manager of the cotton mills of New Lanark, near Glasgow. Here he reversed the practice of the ordinary employers of his day, and made the welfare of his workpeople his first concern. Good housing and schooling for the children were provided out of the profits of the industry, which none the less prospered exceedingly. Owen showed, in fact, that it was the employer's interest as well as his duty to do his best for his workpeople, and New Lanark was the pioneer of such vast and successful modern undertakings as Bournville and Port Sunlight. But this was not enough for Owen. He could have gone to his grave as a model employer; he preferred the career—a more glorious career, perhaps—of an eccentric and entirely unsuccessful prophet of revolution.

Why should not all industrial England be covered with New Lanarks? Leaving his industry in 1817, he turned to the governing classes, and at first interested many important persons in his schemes, including the Duke of Kent, who was the father of Queen Victoria. But these great persons listened, agreed, and went their ways. Owen then turned to the workers, with a scheme for the establishment of 'villages of co-operation'. He went to America, and established a 'village of co-operation' called New Harmony —with disappointing results. His opportunity came in the years immediately after the passage of the Reform Bill. Trade was bad, and the results of the famous Bill invisible, so far as the welfare of the workers was concerned. A wave of Owenite revolutionism swept over the country, amazing, unsubstantial, and transitory. A Grand National Consolidated Trades Union was formed. There was no subscription, only an oath of allegiance. The G.N.C.T.U. would achieve a 'General Strike' of all workers. The governing classes would be cowed into submission, and Owen would establish a socialistic Utopia. It appears that over half a million joined the G.N.C.T.U. in 1833–34. Then the Government took action. Six unfortunate labourers were prosecuted for administering an illegal oath, and sentenced to seven years' transportation. This ferocious sentence dealt a death-blow to the tottering scheme. Owen was already an apostle of other unpopular causes besides the social revolution; he was an ardent advocate of atheism and freedom of divorce. He lived to extreme old age, and became a spiritualist. He was, as Mr. and Mrs. Webb remark in their *History of Trade Unionism,* an 'extravagantly bad' leader of a working-class movement, for he had almost nothing in common with his followers.

Chartism succeeded to the place left vacant by Owenism. It was not a socialist movement, and has been described elsewhere in this book. Chartism died in the 'forties, killed by the outbreak of thirty years of unprecedented economic prosperity. In such a generation individual 'self-help' might well seem sufficient. Conversely, the fundamental cause of the return of socialism was the great industrial depression which, beginning in the middle 'seventies, lasted with only slight intermissions until near the end of the 'eighties. Prosperity returned in the 'nineties, but by that time socialism had taken root. The returned prosperity was, after all, for the great mass of the nation, a very qualified and comparative prosperity, a poor thing judged by standards of what might be. Its shortcomings were scrutinized as the shortcomings of the mid-Victorian prosperity had never been. The theory of democracy had been accepted in the sphere of politics; why then should such glaring inequalities be tolerated in the distribution of wealth? Equality in the exercise of the vote was a mere mockery unless it was an instrument for securing equality in the things that really mattered every day. Moreover, a new generation was arising in which all could read. The kind of working man Bagehot had depicted with so much satisfaction was becoming scarcer. Books and pamphlets proved that the existing distribution of wealth was a man-made accident:

> Ah, Love! could you and I with Fate conspire
> To grasp this sorry Scheme of Things entire,
>   Would we not shatter it to bits, and then
> Remould it nearer to the Heart's Desire.

Such a 'conspiracy with fate' began to appear to many to be

by no means the impossibility it had seemed to Omar Khayyám.

Moreover, quite apart from the alternations of prosperity and depression, the whole structure of industrial society had been steadily changing since the early days of the century. So long as the factory system was in its experimental stage, when factories were small, and the normal type of business was a 'one-man show', every able and enterprising workman had a chance of becoming a master. Most of the first generation of employers were self-made men. We have just mentioned Owen; the reader may remember Daniel Gooch (p. 89). As late as 1859 Smiles could still convince his thousands of readers with his picture of the virtuous employee, whose virtues transform him into an employer. Those days were now passed. The industrial structure had stiffened; its organization had become infinitely complicated. The normal type of business was coming to be the vast limited company, owned by thousands of shareholders, and directed by economic supermen. A capitalist *class* and a working *class* stood over against one another, and there seemed to be an unbridgeable gulf between them.

The Liberal individualist of the first half of the century had been content that there was a natural 'ladder' whereby the enterprising could climb into the upper regions of the industrial and social system. He was prepared to demand that this natural 'ladder' should be broadened by the introduction of free State-supplied elementary education. But this artificial broadening of the ladder was of somewhat illusory benefit if those who climbed it found all the seats at the top of the ladder already occupied. The Socialists rejected the philosophy of the ladder altogether. To them it seemed by no means desirable that the most gifted members of the working class should climb out of the working class. Their hero was not the Smilesian self-made employer but the working-class leader. The aim of the Socialists was to 'level up' a whole society. The ladder—if one may use the ladder metaphor at all—ought to be broad enough for all to proceed up it abreast. There were some tyrannical equalitarians who would go so far as to forbid anyone to use his natural aptitudes to proceed up the ladder any faster than the average of his fellows.

Mr. and Mrs. Webb assert, and their authority is beyond dispute, that the event which, more than any other, stimulated the revival of socialism in Great Britain was the publication of an American book, Henry George's *Progress and Poverty*, in 1879. It is a long and elaborate economic treatise, but, unlike many economic treatises, it is eminently readable. It is lucid, aggressive, and optimistic in tone, and the whole argument is made to lead up to a single and apparently simple remedy for the ills of society, namely the 'single-tax' on land. The book is not, perhaps, socialistic in the strictest sense of the term, but in England it was accepted as an argument for what was, in the 'eighties, the principal item on the programme of British socialism, namely, the nationalization of land— the programme of the long-forgotten Thomas Spence. George came over to lecture in Ireland in 1881, where the land question had reached an acute stage, the Land League being engaged in a boycott of alien English landlords. He was arrested by the Government and, with this advertisement in his favour, came to lecture in England.

In 1881 H. M. Hyndman, a wealthy man and a student of Karl Marx, the most elaborate and scientific of socialist writers, founded the Social Democratic Federation, which soon became pledged to the advocacy of revolutionary socialism of the Continental type. Hyndman was, like Owen, a leader from outside the working class, and it appears that he was known as 'the socialist in the top hat'. The most notable of his early associates was William Morris (see p. 154), but Morris and Hyndman soon quarrelled. Indeed, there was a good deal of quarrelling within the young socialist movement, as there is apt to be in any movement where the leaders are ardent and the results of their efforts disappointing. Mr. Wells, himself a socialist, recalls the 'eighties as a time when the socialists marched round and round the walls of the Jericho of capitalism 'blowing their own trumpets'—and the walls did not fall down. None the less, the movement survived the quarrels of its leaders, and it received powerful impetus from the work of some who were not socialists.

The age of statistics was beginning. Charles Booth, a member of a great Liverpool firm of shipowners, began in 1886, at his own expense, a thorough inquiry, street by street and house by house, into the actual economic conditions of the population of London. His results were published, and revealed the appalling and hitherto unrecognized fact that one-third of the population of London were living 'below the poverty line', i.e. below the line at which, with the utmost possible economy, the bare necessities of health are procurable. Forty years before, the Reports of the Factory Commissions established at the instigation of Lord Shaftesbury had created the public opinion which forced the Factory Acts of 1847–50 through parliament. The revelations of Charles Booth kept alive the socialist movement. For forty years free trade in corn had been in operation, for forty years a middle-class parliament had been tinkering at the capitalist system by means of piecemeal collectivist legislation, for fifteen years the Education Act had been in force, for ten years trade unions, still confined for the most part to the 'aristocracy' of skilled labour, had enjoyed the new legal privileges conferred on them by Disraeli in 1875 and 1876; and yet things were as Booth's survey revealed them to be. Was it not obvious that 'middle-class remedies' were played out, and that something new and altogether more drastic was required? In 1886 there was widespread unemployment, demonstrations in the streets, and a riot in Trafalgar Square. But the professional politicians were entirely absorbed in Irish Home Rule; the distress of the English poor was not a 'political question'. It was held to be 'undignified' to refer to it in the course of the annual tournament of oratory at the Lord Mayor's Banquet.[1]

[1] Gretton, *A Modern History of the English People*, Vol. I, p. 195.

It is fair to say, however, at this point that, if the politicians were indifferent, the leaders of religious thought were actively occupied with the problems of poverty. General Booth's Salvation Army had established its garrisons in the slums. Oxford men, stimulated by their Slade Professor of Art who was no other than John Ruskin, founded Toynbee Hall as a settlement for university men anxious to undertake social work in the East End. Public schools founded their 'Missions'. In 1889 the Christian Social Union was established in order to link together once again, after the manner of Maurice and Kingsley forty years before, the work of the Churches and the work of the social reformers.

Still, great though the provocation of poverty might be, English people are not attracted by the preaching of 'revolution'. Something different from the unadulterated gospel of Karl Marx was needed. In 1883 the Fabian Society was established, taking its name from the Roman general of old who was reputed to have conquered Hannibal by avoiding encounter with him in pitched battle. Fabianism stood for 'the inevitability of gradualism'. Professional politicians of both parties would soon be finding that they needed a policy of social reform. The Fabians would supply it, and the politicians would be grateful to the experts who had done their work for them. Socialism would come by instalments, through the instrumentality of guileless Liberals and Conservatives. Between 1887 and 1893 the Society circulated three-quarters of a million copies of its tracts, and in 1889 published a volume entitled *Fabian Essays in Socialism*. Few composite volumes have included work from more remarkable contributors. Two of them, Sidney Webb and Sydney Olivier, were thirty-five years later to be members of the first Labour Government; another was Mrs. Besant, long afterwards a leader of Indian nationalism; and another was Bernard Shaw.

The programme of *Fabian Essays* is little more—and nothing less—than the nationalization of land, in order that the State may for the future secure for itself those automatic increases in land values, due to growth of population and industry, which economists call unearned increment. Confiscation, however, is expressly repudiated, as unjust to the landowner and disastrous for every one else. The policy advocated is one of bit-by-bit purchase, at a fair market price, the purchase money being secured by taxation of the other landlords not for the moment expropriated. The authors foresee an immense extension of municipal activity, which is in effect municipal socialism. Many hard things are said about the bloated capitalist, but he is threatened with no very alarming punishments for his misdeeds, and all talk of a catastrophic socialist revolution is dismissed as the vapouring of socialistic adolescence. The socialistic State is regarded as inevitable; all schools of thought are unconsciously working towards it, and the socialist differs from the *soi-disant* anti-socialist not because he is the driver of the chariot of progress—at present his party is too weak to drive anything—but because he alone realizes the goal for which the chariot is making. Such being the position, the Socialist must work for the cause, but he can afford to work quietly and with patience. There are some shrewd political forecasts which underestimate rather than otherwise the rate of the advance to be expected. There will be a socialist political party, which will absorb the 'genuine' Radicals, while the remnants of the Liberalism of wealth and *laissez-faire* will take refuge in the Tory party. A socialist Prime Minister is foreseen. He will need to be 'as able as, and more conscientious than, any of the great parliamentary figures of the past. The eye expectant searches in vain for such a man now among the younger broods of the new democracy. He is probably at this moment in his cradle, or equitably sharing out toys and lollipops to his comrades in the nursery'. As a matter of fact, Mr. Ramsay MacDonald had already reached man's estate.

But it was not the publication of *Fabian Essays* that made 1889 the most important date in the early history of the modern British socialist movement. It was the year of the Dock Strike.

Hitherto the trade unions had stood aloof. The Trade Union Congress had been established in 1868 to agitate for certain reforms in the legal position of trade unions. These reforms had been secured in the course of the next eight years, and thereafter the Congress had relapsed into routine and somnolence. It was not a democratic body, for the unions comprising it were not democratic. They were organizations of skilled workmen, as intent on preserving the privileges of their skill against the unskilled mass as on bargaining for better terms from their employers. Twice in the early 'eighties the Congress rejected motions in favour of manhood suffrage for parliamentary elections, by large majorities. Certain individual trade unionists, such as John Burns, afterwards one of the first Labour members entirely independent of either of the older parties, were in active protest against the conservatism of the Congress, but they had little following.

Then came the great Dock Strike, a strike among the most hopelessly depressed body of workers in the country. This is not the place to tell the story of that strike; of how Burns and other trade unionists gave their leadership to the dockers; how the employers in their unwisdom drove all that was best in the public opinion of the whole country on to the side of the men; how eminent persons of all sorts, from the aged Cardinal Manning downwards, threw themselves into the fray. The result was a vast extension of trade unionism among the unskilled. Both trade unionism and socialism were powerfully affected. Trade unionism awoke from its slumbers and became democratic; socialism was diverted from revolutionary idealism into the practical work of inspiring a new and more ambitious trade-union policy, a policy of fighting the industrial battle by industrial methods.

From that date British socialism began to develop along the lines that have brought it where it is to-day. It was another ten years before the Trade Union Congress reconciled itself to the plan of financing a Labour Party for parliamentary purposes. The beginning was made by the Scottish socialist miner, Keir Hardie, and his Independent Labour Party. Keir Hardie showed that he could win an election in 1892; in 1895 he and his twenty-eight associates all suffered defeat. The two events taken together stimulated the Trade Union Congress, and in 1899 a Labour Representation Committee, representing the Trade Union Congress, the Independent Labour Party, the Fabian Society, and the Social Democratic Federation, was established. It was in effect the establishment of the Labour Party, and Mr. Ramsay MacDonald was the first secretary of the committee. In 1904 a judicial decision of the House of Lords in the Taff Vale Case deprived the trade unions of certain legal privileges which for thirty years every one had believed them to possess. This furnished a good election cry, and in 1906 fifty Labour members took their seats in the House of Commons.

British socialism has had its distinguished men of letters, but their work is too nearly contemporary to be summarized here. Mr. and Mrs. Webb have advanced the cause of socialism by a series of works of research into the history of our social institutions, works in which unimpeachable accuracy is combined with skilful and persistent advocacy of the socialist cause. Mr. Wells came before the public as an artist in the construction of Utopias. Mr. Shaw began the long series of his critical comedies. Mr. Shaw's plays are all dated in the standard edition, and the reader will find that the first three volumes, *Plays Pleasant and Unpleasant* and *Plays for Puritans*, all belong to the nineteenth century. One of these dates has a certain piquancy. Something was said, on an earlier page, of the ranker outbreaks of sentimental Imperialism that marked the year of the Diamond Jubilee. That year was selected by Mr. Shaw for the production of the rollicking lampoon upon the British army contained in the last Act of *The Devil's Disciple*.

III

SOME ASPECTS OF MODERNITY

A COMPARISON between the work of the great minds of the Victorian Age and the work of the great minds of our own day can hardly fail to suggest that the present is, by comparison, an age of specialists.

Macaulay and Carlyle were reckoned the leading historians of the Victorian Age, but neither of them occupied a professorial chair. Macaulay had been a Cabinet Minister and an Indian administrator, and his purpose in writing history was to give the general reader a notion of the characteristics of his country's greatness. Carlyle was first and foremost a moralist, and he wrote history because history was, in his judgement, the 'truest philosophy'. Ruskin was an art critic and Morris a practitioner in many arts, but both regarded art as a product not of specialized artists but of a whole society, and both of them, as they advanced in life, devoted themselves more to social than to aesthetic problems, because they considered that aesthetic problems, properly understood, were nothing but social problems. The religion of the Evangelicals overflowed with philanthropy, that of Maurice and Kingsley with 'Socialism'. The Oxford Movement began as a protest against a certain aspect of political liberalism. Matthew Arnold preached Culture not for the cultured but for the Philistine, because he found in it a cure for our political stupidity. The evolutionary scientists gladly engaged in the task of reforming or abolishing the Christian religion.

How different is the position to-day! History has strengthened its position in the schools and universities, but there are no Macaulays and Carlyles. The professional historian writes, in the main, for a specialized public, and those who aim at, and reach, a larger public, principally through the medium of biography, have neither the purpose nor the point of view of the typical Victorian. They are—be it said in no depreciatory sense—nearer to the novelist than the propagandist. The art of Mr. Strachey and Mr. Guedalla is to tell a true story for the story's sake alone.

A change has come over the position of science not unlike that which has come over the position of history, though the parallel is far from complete. Science, like history, has withdrawn somewhat from the arena of common interests. There were, of course, even in the Victorian Age, many departments of science, physical and mathematical, in which achievements as great as those of the evolutionists made no impression upon the current of public opinion, because public opinion was incapable of appreciating them. Yet in evolution, especially in so far as it concerned the descent of man, Victorian science had a subject of intense public interest. To-day the general principle of evolution is accepted, and the progress of science is most sensational in departments where it is least 'human' and least comprehensible. The untrained public does its best, it must be admitted, to understand 'the A B C of the Atom' and the Principle of Relativity, but these things are really beyond it. Even those who think they understand are unable to see what difference discoveries in these fields make, or should make, to their outlook upon life. They had already realized that the physical universe was very strange indeed; they now know that it is much more so. For a brief period science was more exciting than politics; it has now become more abstruse than philosophy.

In art, again—specialization. The art critics of to-day, Mr. Roger Fry and Mr. Clive Bell, are, it need hardly be said, not occupied like Ruskin and Morris, with social reforms. Indeed our conception of art, at least in the pictorial sphere, has entirely changed.

Two of the greatest of Victorian painters were Holman Hunt and G. F. Watts. The following quotations, which speak for themselves, are taken from the articles on these painters in the *Encyclopædia Britannica* (1911). 'In 1854 Holman Hunt achieved his first great success by the famous picture *The Light of the World*, an allegorical representation of Christ knocking at the door of the human soul. This work produced perhaps the greatest effect of any religious painting of the century. "For the first time in England", wrote William Bell Scott, "a picture became a subject of conversation and general interest from one end of England to the other, and indeed continued so for many years. . . ." In January, 1854, Holman Hunt left England for Syria and Palestine with the desire to revivify on canvas the facts of Scripture history, "surrounded by the very people and circumstances of the life in Judæa of old days". The first fruit of this idea, which may be said to have dominated the artist's life, was *The Scapegoat*. . . . His ambition was always "to serve as high priest and expounder of the excellence of the works of the Creator".'

Watts was a great portrait painter, and it may be that posterity will esteem him chiefly for the wonderful record of his age he has left in his portraits of his distinguished contemporaries. But, to return to the *Encyclopædia*, 'even more significant from an artistic point of view is the great collection of symbolical pictures which forms the artist's message to mankind. Believing devoutly in the high mission of didactic art, he strove ever to carry out his part of it faithfully. "My intention", he wrote, "has not been so much to paint pictures that charm the eye as to suggest great thoughts that will appeal to the imagination and the heart, and kindle all that is best and noblest in humanity"; and his tenet is that the main object of the painter should be "demanding noble aspirations, condemning in the most trenchant manner prevalent vices, and warning in deep tones against lapses from morals and duties".'

It is abundantly plain that Hunt and Watts were, quite

as much as Ruskin and Carlyle, preachers to their generation. Their pictures were so many 'tracts for the times'. The purpose of the modern painter is very different. The 'literary picture', the picture which is in effect an illustration of an incident or an allegory in paint, is now derided as a perversion of art. The picture exists for its own sake alone, a thing of beauty and nothing more nor less, a 'pattern', signifying, like a classical symphony, nothing but itself. The masters of our modern artists are not the great Victorians but their French contemporaries. The name of Cézanne must have been almost unknown in Victorian England,[1] though he was painting from 1860 onwards and died within a few years of Holman Hunt and Watts. To-day he is reckoned by many connoisseurs the greatest of modern painters. We have not to consider here whether Watts and Holman Hunt were better or worse artists than the moderns. But it is plain, and characteristic, that Watts and Holman Hunt appealed to a vast public deeply moved by religion and morality whereas the moderns appeal to a limited public of connoisseurs of art.

As in art, so in music. The Victorian Age revelled in what was called 'sacred music'. Handel's *Messiah* and Mendelssohn's *Elijah* were far more widely known and loved than any symphony of Beethoven and Schubert, and the public that accepted these great works accepted with almost equal enthusiasm sentimental music of what has been called the *eau sucrée* school, such as Stainer's *Crucifixion* or Gounod's *Nazareth*, which combines all the bad qualities of a popular hymn tune and a popular waltz. To-day the very phrase 'sacred music' has acquired a certain disrepute on account of its sentimental associations, so that one would think twice, and more than twice, before using it to describe the *St. Matthew Passion* or the *Mass* of J. S. Bach.

Of the many aspects of the Renaissance, one of the most important was the emancipation of the arts and sciences

[1] It does not appear in the 1911 *Encyclopædia Britannica*.

from the service of the Church,—the secularization of art and science. Matthew Arnold described Victorian England as given over to Puritanism, and Puritanism as a 'Hebraizing back-water' of reaction from the spirit of the Renaissance. Thus the departing of the Victorian Age has witnessed a secularizing of the arts in England like that which marked the Renaissance in Europe.

'Art for art's sake' was a favourite formula in the late Victorian period. I do not know who first put the formula into circulation, but the idea found its best and most carefully considered expression in the writings of Walter Pater, whose first volume, *The Renaissance*, was published in 1873. For Pater the appreciation of art should be an ecstasy. 'To burn always with this hard, gem-like flame, to maintain this ecstasy, is success in life. . . . Art comes to you professing frankly to give nothing but the highest quality to your moments as they pass, and simply for those moments' sake.'

Pater was, strange as it may seem, an Oxford tutor. He discharged his professional duties with the utmost conscientiousness, living also, there can be no doubt, an ecstatic interior life that was not apparent to most of his pupils. He wrote only for such as were kindred spirits. The style of his writing is almost more eloquent of his message than anything that he has to say. His prose is composed with a scrupulous care such as a poet must give to the composition of a sonnet. It is exquisite, elaborate, and, some will say, a trifle languid. Contrast him with Ruskin, William Morris, or Matthew Arnold, and we realize at once that Pater is fundamentally a specialist.

His work enjoyed a vogue which surprised and somewhat disconcerted him. He was acclaimed as a prophet by groups of young persons who called themselves, or were called, aesthetes. For these young persons art was to be the only thing that mattered in life. Their pose attracted the comic genius of W. S. Gilbert and is the subject of *Patience*, one of the most delightful of the Gilbert and

Sullivan operas. 'Twenty love-sick maidens' pursue the aesthetic poet Bunthorne, who has discovered that the value of words resides wholly in their sound and not at all in their meaning. 'Calomel' is one of his favourites, and he is, very inconsiderately, in love with a dairymaid. The opera contains the lines about the young aesthete who

> walks down Piccadilly
> With a poppy or a lily
> In his mediaeval hand.

The aesthetic craze was for most of its devotees a fairly harmless form of silliness, from which most of them rapidly recovered. It was an unfortunate accident that a movement proclaiming the all-importance of art got entangled with a movement proclaiming the unimportance of some of the elementary rules of morality.

Nothing could have been more abhorrent to Pater than laxity of any kind. A year before his death he published a series of lectures on *Plato and Platonism*, which contain a very interesting passage upon the death of Socrates. Socrates was condemned to death as a corruptor of youth. 'Those young Athenians', Pater writes, 'whom he was thought to have corrupted of set purpose, he had not only admired but really loved and understood; and as a consequence had longed to do them real good, chiefly by giving them that interest in themselves which is the first condition of any real power over others. . . . Only the very thoroughness of the sort of self-knowledge he promoted had in it something sacramental, so to speak; if it did not do them good, must do them considerable harm: could not leave them just as they were. He had not been able in all cases to expand "the better self", as people say, in those he influenced. Some of them had really become very insolent questioners of others, as also of a wholly legitimate authority within themselves.' It has been generally assumed that in writing this passage Pater was not thinking only of Socrates.

Pater was very strongly drawn towards the ritual of the Catholic Church. 'The religious, the Catholic ideal,' he writes, 'is the only mode of poetry realizable by the poor.' His longest and most elaborate work, *Marius the Epicurean*, is a study of an imaginary seeker after truth in the days of the Roman Empire. Marius finds satisfaction at last within the persecuted Christian Church, and it seems to be the ritual more than the doctrine of the Church that attracts him. 'You seem to think, Mr. Pater,' said Jowett, the Broad Church Master of Balliol, 'that religion is all idolatry.' The aesthetic movement was, it need hardly be said, entirely hostile to Puritanism; it may have contributed something to the growing power of Anglo-Catholic ritualism.

It was inevitable that in the sphere of religion 'specialization' should take a very different form, yet there also, if the same term may be used in a somewhat different sense, specialization is the mark of modernity. It is sometimes asserted that religion has for the last fifty years or so been losing its hold upon society; and it is also asserted, with equal confidence, that the churches have, during the same period, been developing new life and health and vigour. These statements seem to be in flat contradiction; but they are not, and it may well be that both are true. It may well be that the influence of the churches has declined in extent, but gained in intensity. A much higher proportion of the population never go to church at all, and do not even 'profess and call themselves Christians'. Even in country districts it is possible to be an agnostic without being accounted eccentric by one's neighbours. Yet at the same time those who are members of churches are more active and positive in their membership than of yore. If the percentage of church-goers to the total population has declined, the percentage of communicants among church-goers may well have increased. Diocesan and parochial organizations are far more elaborate and ambitious than formerly, and make more calls upon the time and thought of their members, and the time and thought for which they call is often enthusiastically given.

In fact, the nation has become less religious, but the churches have renewed their vigour as 'sectarian' bodies. In these circumstances it is not surprising that the Catholic type of religion, emphasizing the corporate unity of the Church as a body distinct from and more august than the nation, should have made a strong appeal to religious minds. It suits the facts of the time, whereas the Evangelical ideal of a nation of Christian individuals does not. Equally natural is the complete change that has come over the attitude of parties within and without the Church to the question of Disestablishment. The ideal of establishment was that the Church should be, in the fullest sense of the word, the Church of the nation. Never, from the beginning of Elizabeth's reign, was that ideal completely realized, yet for nearly three centuries the Establishment retained, in law if not always in fact, a position of political privilege. When the privileges had gone, the demand arose, especially among the mid-Victorian Benthamite Nonconformists, for the disestablishment of the Church. In the 'seventies Mr. Miall used to introduce an annual Resolution in the House of Commons in favour of Disestablishment much as Mr. Isaac Butt used to introduce an annual Resolution in favour of Irish Home Rule. Ireland has got Home Rule and something more, but the Church is not disestablished. Indeed, the position of the question has been entirely transformed. Nonconformists no longer regard the Establishment with unfriendly feelings (though some of them feel sorry for it), and the movement for disestablishment, so far as it exists, finds its support among the more ardent Anglo-Catholic clergy, who desire to free their Church from the shackles of state patronage and the control of a non-sectarian parliament.

On this subject of disestablishment, as on so many others, Disraeli and Gladstone illustrate opposing schools of thought. Disraeli was a secular statesman with a very strong feeling for the value and the charm of what Bagehot called the 'dignified parts' of the constitution. Among such he included not only the Crown but also the Church. 'Few great things are left in England', he wrote, 'and the Church is one of them. . . . By the side of the State in England there has gradually arisen a majestic corporation—proud, wealthy, and independent—with the sanctity of a long tradition, yet sympathizing with authority, and full of conciliation, even deference, to the civil power. Broadly and deeply planted in the land, mixed up with all our manners and customs . . . one of the prime securities for our common liberties, the Church of England is part of our history, part of our life, part of England itself.' Praise of this type is more exasperating to a modern Anglo-Catholic than any kind of criticism can possibly be. As for a dis-established Church, it would, said Disraeli, 'subside into a fastidious, not to say finical, congregation'. It would become, in fact, a specialized religious society, lending no support nor dignity to the State. Gladstone, on the other hand, had been a devout Churchman before ever he was a statesman, and he entered the House of Commons with the avowed purpose of defending the Church against 'the World'. Disestablishment, he had said as early as 1838, would be a blow to the State, but not to the Church. 'Her condition would be anything rather than pitiable, should she once more occupy the position she held before the reign of Constantine.' [1] Forty years later, when Disraeli, to please the Queen and the bishops, introduced the Public Worship Act 'to put down ritualism', Gladstone raised the threat of disestablishment, as it has been raised again in our own day by a section of the Anglo-Catholics after the rejection of the Revised Prayer Book of 1927–28.

But as the century approached its close, ecclesiastical questions became less and less interesting to the general public. Outside all the churches there was a great body of society, a society more 'secular' than could be found at any other time in our history. This society was not, in the

---

[1] Constantine being the first Roman Emperor to recognize the Church and give it a kind of official position within the Empire.

main, actively anti-religious. From the 'eighties onwards the so-called conflict of religion and science was dying down, though, like King Charles II, it was a long time a-dying. It is perhaps not quite dead yet. A conflict of that type persists in provincial backwaters long after it has passed out of the main currents of thought. 'Village Huxleys' withstood with dauntless breast the 'little tyrant' of the local chapel long after the successors of Bishop Wilberforce had accepted all the evolution that reasonable scientists could require of them.

In fact, as the battle died down and the evolutionists found themselves in possession of the field, some who had been truculent agnostics lost all their truculence. An outstanding example of such was John Morley, who in the 'seventies had written his uncompromising essay against *Compromise*. It used to be said of Morley that he spelt God with a small 'g' and Gladstone with a big one, but had this been so he could hardly have become one of Gladstone's inner circle of friends. In fact, Morley became one of those who love everything about the Church except her creed. His letters and *Reminiscences* show him a frequent church-goer, delighting in the 'unction' of a good sermon, and so greatly moved by the Psalms and the Epistles that he writes to an old comrade in militant agnosticism to say that it is absurd to compete with 'all that' until the religion of science has produced a literature of similar 'grandeur and passion' to replace it.

In fact, once the joy of battle with 'bibliolatry' was over, such religion as evolution and agnosticism permitted was seen to be at best a grey affair,—the truth, perhaps, but a truth over which one could hardly rejoice. Clifford's 'cosmic emotion' (see p. 136) and Spencer's 'inevitable progress' carried little conviction with a generation to whom evolution had no longer the proverbial attractions of novelty. In 1895 Mr. Arthur Balfour [1] analysed the implications

---

[1] The statesman, afterward Lord Balfour.

of scientific materialism in a paragraph that has been many times quoted:

'Man, so far as natural science by itself is able to teach, is no longer the final cause of the universe, the Heaven-descended heir of all the ages. His very existence is an accident, his story a brief and transitory episode in the life of one of the meanest of the planets. Of the combination of causes which first converted a dead organic compound into the living progenitors of humanity, science, indeed, as yet knows nothing. It is enough that from such beginnings famine, disease, and mutual slaughter, fit nurses of the future lords of creation, have gradually evolved, after infinite travail, a race with conscience enough to feel that it is vile, and intelligence enough to know that it is insignificant. We survey the past, and see that its history is of blood and tears, of helpless blundering, of wild revolt, of stupid acquiescence, of empty aspirations. We sound the future, and learn that after a period, long compared with the individual life, but short indeed compared with the divisions of time open to our investigation, the energies of our system will decay, the glory of the sun will be dimmed, and the earth, tideless and inert, will no longer tolerate the race which for a moment has disturbed its solitude. Man will go down to the pit, and all his thoughts will perish. The uneasy consciousness, which in this obscure corner has for a brief space broken the contented silence of the universe, will be at rest. Matter will know itself no longer, "Imperishable monuments" and "immortal deeds", death itself, and love stronger than death, will be as though they had never been. Nor will anything that *is* be better or be worse for all that the labour, genius, devotion and suffering of man have striven through countless ages to effect.'

These words are taken from a book entitled *The Foundations of Belief*,[1] itself a sequel to another, entitled *A Defence of Philosophic Doubt*, in which the author had turned the arguments of agnosticism against the claims of the new

[1] P. 29.

religion of science. In fact Christian orthodoxy, having failed to justify its claims by means of verbally inspired Biblical authority, was beginning to find that attack was the best defence. 'Science' had to be accepted, but 'the religion of science' was open to as many objections as the religion that had been attacked by Huxley and Clifford a generation before. Indeed, it was open to many more. It was as incapable of proof as the Christian creed, and its conclusions, unlike those of the Christian creed, were entirely depressing. Writers of the school of Mr. Chesterton grounded their defence of orthodoxy on the fact that the Christian creed was a wholesome doctrine, whereas scientific materialism was a devitalizing poison. Their defence appeals not to logic but to psychology, not to authority but to experience. 'Try it and see!' they say. 'You will find Christianity is a religion you can live by.' Such 'evidences of Christianity' would have seemed strange to Bishop Wilberforce, and stranger still to Archdeacon Paley.

But Mr. Chesterton belongs to the twentieth century. Much of the best literature of the last third of the nineteenth century is coloured by a kind of acquiescence in irreligion.

In 1859, the year of *The Origin of Species*, Edward FitzGerald published his translation of the *Rubaiyat of Omar Khayyám*, a Persian poet of the twelfth century. The volume attracted scarcely any general attention, though it was from the first admired by poets and critics. A second edition was required in 1868. FitzGerald died in 1883, and soon after his death the sales of his poem began mysteriously to grow. At the beginning of the new century, when the first edition went out of copyright, the *Rubaiyat* had become beyond question the most popular poem since Tennyson's *In Memoriam*. For several successive Christmases this 'mid-Victorian' production of a scholar twenty years dead was a favourite gift-book of the season, being bound for the purpose in a variety of limp leathers deemed artistic. It afforded—and to-day still affords— material for innumerable readily recognized quotations, misquotations, and parodies. In fact, the philosophy of this Persian Epicurus, inappropriate as a contemporary of *The Origin of Species*, exactly hit the sentiment of the generation which grew up under the shadow of Darwin's masterpiece. If man were indeed an accident and his story a brief and transitory episode in the life of one of the meanest of the planets, then—'let us eat and drink, for to-morrow we die'

> Come, fill the Cup, and in the Fire of Spring
> The winter Garment of Repentance fling;
>   The Bird of Time has but a little Way
> To fly, and lo, the Bird is on the Wing.

And then, in the last verses, the fundamental melancholy of the Epicurean philosophy asserts itself:

> Ah, Love, could you and I with Fate conspire
> To grasp this sorry Scheme of things entire,
>   Would we not shatter it to bits, and then
> Remould it nearer to the Heart's Desire!

In Memoriam was the favourite poem of a generation of believers who, though perplexed in their belief, consoled themselves with the thought that

> There is more faith in honest doubt,
> Believe me, than in half the creeds.

The Rubaiyat appealed to a generation tired of the struggle between faith and doubt:

> Why, all the Saints and Sages, who discussed
> Of the Two Worlds so learnedly, are thrust
>   Like foolish Prophets forth, their Words to Scorn
> Are scattered, and their Mouths are stopped with Dust.

Long before the *Rubaiyat* had become a possession of the people, the genius of Swinburne had flashed and faded; all that is best in his work belongs to the years 1865–78. Swinburne, like Shelley before him, was intoxicated with the free paganism of Greece. His poetry was itself a symbol of revolt—revolt not so much against this or that, but revolt for its own sake, as an admirable gesture. He gaily defies Victorian respectability as Byron had defied it fifty years before, when it was as yet unconnected with the name of Victoria. His most popular poems, though not perhaps his best, were the most defiant—*Dolores* in which he chants the praises of a kind of 'love' with which Tennyson and Browning did not sully their pages, and *The Garden of Proserpine*, an anti-Christian hymn containing one of the most perfectly constructed stanzas in the language:

> From too much love of living,
>   From hope and fear set free,
> We thank with brief thanksgiving
>   Whatever Gods may be,
> That no life lasts for ever,
> That dead men rise up never,
> That even the weariest river
>   Winds somewhere safe to sea.

Swinburne's first volume of *Poems and Ballads* (1866) was violently attacked by several reviewers on account of the alleged sensuality of some of the poems. John Morley, writing anonymously in the *Saturday Review*, spoke of Swinburne as 'an unclean fiery imp from the pit' and accused him of exhibiting 'the feverish carnality of a schoolboy'. Six years later an attack on the same lines was directed against some poems of Rossetti, in a pamphlet by Robert Buchanan entitled *The Fleshly School of Poetry*. Some of these poems might be disliked by some readers to-day on the score of literary taste, but it may be safely said that no one could be shocked by them, or regard them as 'immoral'. They are sensuous, but not sensual. Buchanan, for example, selected as objectionable the couplet:

> And as I stooped, her own lips rising there
> Bubbled with brimming kisses at my mouth.

EXPURGATION

Swinburne wrote:

> Could you hurt me, sweet lips, though I hurt you?
> Men touch them, and change in a trice
> The lilies and languors of virtue,
> For the raptures and roses of vice,

which may be silly but is unmistakably harmless. None the less, some of the poems of Swinburne and Rossetti, and the notoriety they were given by the champions of morality, open up a much wider subject on which something may conveniently be said here—the subject of literary expurgation.

It is hardly necessary to say that much of the great English literature of an earlier day, from Chaucer and Shakespeare down to the eighteenth-century novelists, Fielding and Sterne, had dealt with matters of sex in a very frank and outspoken manner. Byron was perhaps the only great writer to carry the tradition on into the nineteenth century. Then came what may be called the age of expurgation. This careful avoidance of all direct allusion to the physical side of love and of lust was unmistakably a product of that Evangelicalism which, in its unsectarian aspects, was far the biggest single fact in English nineteenth-century thought. The custom spread with the rise of Evangelicalism: it declined with its decline.

Dickens and Thackeray were quite conscious of the limitations that the prejudices or ideals (whichever one likes to call them) of their readers imposed upon them, and occasionally resented them. Thackeray, who allowed himself more freedom in the treatment of these subjects than Dickens, wrote quite frankly in the Preface to *Pendennis* (1850), telling his readers that they must not expect to find in his novel the whole truth about the life of a young man, as they would find it, for example, in Fielding's *Tom Jones*. Dickens touched upon the subject in a private letter. Some reader of French novels, it appears, had complained that the heroes of English novels were always uninteresting. 'But,

O my smooth friend', says Dickens, 'what a shining impostor you must think yourself, and what an ass you must think me, when you suppose that by putting a brazen face upon it you can blot out from my knowledge the fact that this same unnatural young gentleman (if to be decent is to be necessarily unnatural), whom you meet in those other books and in mine, *must* be presented to you in that unnatural aspect by reason of your morality, and is not to have, I will not say any of the indecencies you like, but not even any of the experiences, trials, perplexities and confusions inseparable from the making or unmaking of all men.' [1]

All that is changed to-day. We need not trace the stages of the change, nor consider its many applications. Some of them are entirely trivial—the free use, for example, of swear words. Others go deep, and raise questions upon which there is not, and never will be, general agreement. Both expurgation and lack of expurgation have their dangers. The dangers of expurgation are hypocrisy and make-believe, unreality in the treatment of important and fundamentally wholesome subjects and an artificial limitation of the scope of art. The dangers of unexpurgation are twofold. The obvious danger is that writers may, quite unintentionally in the great majority of cases, weaken the moral sense of foolish or immature readers; the less obvious but equally real danger is that, on account of the superficial excitingness of certain subjects, the service of literature may be given overmuch to what is trivial and vulgar. Art is limited by the exclusion of 'the flesh': but it may also be limited if 'the flesh' attracts too much attention and 'the spirit' too little.

The best poetry of Swinburne was not 'fleshly' at all; it was purely pagan. Paganism, but with a difference, was also the note of the novels and poems of George Meredith. His first novel, *Richard Feverel*, appeared, with so many other notable books, in 1859. When he died, half a century later, *The Times* allotted him a place only a little

[1] Quoted from Gissing's *Charles Dickens*, p. 68.

way below Shakespeare. The moderns have rejected that estimate, and Meredith is now little honoured and less read. None the less he was in one respect the first of the English moderns, for he was the first of our novelists to write deliberately 'difficult' novels. Scott, Dickens, and Thackeray had been content to wile away the idle hour. Meredith's prayer is:

'More brains, O Lord! More brains!'

and he demands brains and the use of them from his readers. In this he is the forerunner of modern psycho-analytical, symbolical, and I know not what other schools of novelists.

Meredith is pagan, but his paganism has the serenity of one who, having never had faith, has never lost it and bears no grudge against it. He has a kind of religion whose God is Mother Earth; Man must understand the Spirit of the Earth which gave him birth. Such is the essence of worldly—or Earthy—wisdom. If he fails of this worldly wisdom man will be 'comic', and Meredith's novels are nearly all of them 'comedies'. His favourite scene of action is the English country house, which he portrays in all the glories of its golden autumn, civilized and refined by the closer contact with London established through railways, and not yet overwhelmed by the collapse of agricultural rents in the 'eighties, when the old squirearchy began to make way for the *nouveaux riches*. Meredith loved the English country house as only a snob of genius can love a lord; he does not cease to love it when it makes him smile.

If Meredith is old-fashioned in his homage to the Squire, he is a modernist in the claims he makes for the equality of the sexes. 'Where the veil is over women's faces, you cannot have *society*, without which the senses are barbarous and the Comic Spirit is driven to the gutters of grossness to slake its thirst . . . There has been fun in Bagdad. But there will never be civilization where Comedy is not possible; and that comes of some degree of social equality of the sexes.'[1] Thackeray had given the world Becky Sharp and Amelia Sedley; and women, it was said, could forgive him his clever adventuress more easily than they could forgive him the stuffed waxwork of virtue they were expected to admire. Meredith created a whole gallery of adorable creatures who, while quite sufficiently endowed with virtue, had also the competence to meet the Becky Sharps on their own ground and beat them. For many Victorian Feminists Meredith's *Diana of the Crossways* was something more than a novel; it was, like Mill's *Subjection of Woman*, one of the sacred books of their Cause.

As the previous generation had paired Dickens with Thackeray, so the later Victorians paired Thomas Hardy, the 'Wessex' novelist, with Meredith. All Hardy's novels were written before the end of the nineteenth century. What Meredith did for 'the rich man in his castle' Hardy did for 'the poor man at his gate'. Both may be called pagans, but whereas Meredith is a pagan optimist, Hardy is a pessimist. Meredith held, like Wordsworth (whom in no other respect he resembles), that it is possible for man to be in tune with Nature. To Hardy man is, in Huxley's phrase, 'Nature's rebellious son'. Nature is, within her sub-human limits, perfect, but man has risen above Nature's plan without disentangling himself from her claims. Nature holds man by the chain of sex. All Hardy's novels are tragedies, and love tragedies. The only characters immune from tragic destiny in the Wessex novels are the humblest of the peasantry; they enjoy a security and a serenity which they owe to the fact that they are, strictly speaking, sub-human. They are lovable and enviable, but as a favourite dog is lovable and enviable. For Hardy as for Meredith Nature is Providence, but for Hardy it is a malign Providence, and the Christian religion, with its pretence that Providence is not malign, is supremely irritating to him. *Tess of the D'Urbervilles*, probably the greatest and certainly the most popular of the Hardy novels, is full of anti-Christian innuendo.

[1] Meredith, *Essay on Comedy.*

A bishop has described the book as 'the devil inliterate'. Hardy is the only great Victorian for whom Mr. Chesterton has no toleration; for him Hardy is 'a sort of village atheist brooding and blaspheming over the village idiot'.[1]

And yet perhaps this explicit and rebellious pessimism is not the final impression left by the Wessex novels. No English writer, not Wordsworth nor Ruskin nor William Morris, conveys a profounder sense of the overpowering beauty of the scene on which man's destiny is played out. When the worst has happened and when the worst that can be said about it has been said, one is left with the feeling that, after all, 'it is good for us to be here'.

In the early years of the new century Hardy composed an immense historical drama, *The Dynasts*, portraying the whole struggle between the British people and Napoleon, from Trafalgar to Waterloo. It has been called the greatest Epic of War since the *Iliad*. Certainly it stands nearer than anything else in English literature to the English historical plays of Shakespeare. Yet if it is almost Shakespearian in the broad humanity of some of its popular scenes, it has a 'theology' which is as far from Shakespeare as anything can be. Supernatural personages guide the course of the drama, and the human actors are supposed to be mere puppets upon their strings. The supreme power is the Immanent Will, all-powerful, unconscious, and neuter. It does everything and knows nothing that it does.

One can assert, but one cannot believe such a religion, and Hardy himself takes great liberties with his Spirits. Napoleon is made over to them, gagged and bound; the supreme War Lord is nothing but an automaton. But Hardy is far too good a patriot to subject his English soldiers to the same indignity. They are men and free men, fighting for their country, and saving it by their own strong and wholesome manhood. A drama of automata could have no hero, but *The Dynasts* most certainly has a hero, and his name is John Bull. Hardy and Kipling

[1] Chesterton, *Victorian Literature*, p. 143.

might seem to be poles asunder, but the 'Soldiers Three'
would have found themselves quite at home in the Peninsular
War scenes of *The Dynasts*.

Most of the notes struck by Hardy in his vast irregular
Epic Drama and in his long rambling novels are touched
again with exquisite precision in the minute and dexterous
lyrics of A. E. Housman's *Shropshire Lad* (1896). One
does not, perhaps, think first of patriotism and imperialism
in connexion with *The Shropshire Lad*, but the opening
poem celebrates Victoria's Jubilee, and several more com-
memorate the soldier and his death in 'the far-flung battle
line'. Housman's lyrics, like Hardy's novels, are saturated
in the beauty of an English countryside. The lyrics, like
the novels, are full, perhaps overfull, of strange and violent
tragedies, deaths by suicide or by murder. The lyrics
even more than the novels are penetrated by an aggressive
atheism, and the final impression left by both is the same.
They do not indeed tell us, like Browning's girl heroine,
that 'All's right with the world', but they leave us with
the feeling that the beauty of life is something more fundamental than all its grief and terror.

A century is an entirely artificial division of time, and
the phases of the history of thought shade into one another
as the colours of a rainbow. We have divided our nineteenth
century into three periods. Many of the leading figures
of the first period seem to belong as much to the eighteenth
century as to the nineteenth, and in studying the last period
we have come across much which seems an integral part
of the thought of our own day. It is only in the middle
period that we are unconscious of either eighteenth or
twentieth century frontiers. This is the 'Victorian' period
par excellence, and thus 'Victorian' and 'nineteenth century'
become for many of us almost interchangeable terms. In
any balanced treatment of our nineteenth-century thought

the middle period seems to dominate; the rest falls into place as a long introduction and a long conclusion. If we attempt, on the last page of this book, to suggest a few lines of comparison between the nineteenth century and our own, we must take the middle period as our standard of comparison.

The Victorians lived in an age of absolutely unprecedented development. Population was growing as it had never grown before, and, from the 'forties onward, wealth grew faster than population. Within the lifetime of a single man we passed from general illiteracy to universal education, from rotten-boroughs to democratic suffrage, from stage coaches to railways and telegraphs, from—is it necessary to extend the catalogue? It was inevitable that those who lived in such an age should be at once bewildered and exhilarated. They felt that they were living in an epoch which, whatever else might be said of it, was certainly of unique significance. The Victorian Englishman felt that he was a member of the greatest nation in the world at the most important epoch of human history, and that he must rise to the occasion. He rose; and to the detached spectator he could not but be a trifle amusing. He felt that his conspicuous men were really great, and their achievements enormously important. A Darwin and a Huxley— was not science transformed and religion shattered? If not, how immense the responsibility resting on the shoulders of the defenders of the Faith! A Carlyle, a Ruskin, a Browning—they were not merely professional men of letters, earning a living by the exercise of a craft; they were unmistakably prophets, and their messages had to be deciphered, often no easy task. A Disraeli and a Gladstone—one of them was obviously right, and it was a matter of infinite importance to discover which.

To-day, it is said, we live in an age of disillusionment. Development has continued, perhaps, at an equal or even an accelerated pace. Where the Victorians, with much turmoil, enfranchised men we have enfranchised women; if they made the elementary school, we have made the democratic secondary school and the democratic university; to their trains and telegraphs we have added the motor and the wireless; to their evolution, the analysis of the atom and the doctrine of relativity. Yet with us the more things change the less it seems to matter. We have got used to rapid development. We do not feel that the human race is appreciably nearer the goal of its efforts. We have almost ceased to wonder if there is a goal. We regard some of our contemporaries as good writers: but while many enjoy wiling away an idle hour with the works of Mr. Shaw, Mr. Wells, or Mr. Chesterton, only very small sects follow them as prophets. We vote for one or other of the parties led by Mr. Baldwin, Mr. MacDonald or Mr. Lloyd George, but few, one would think, 'follow' any of these gentlemen as the devout Gladstonian followed the Grand Old Man.

Or is all this illusion? Will our own age look more like the Victorian Age when we, or our descendants, have got a convenient distance away from it? Was the Victorian Age, for the Victorians, more like our own than we suppose? We seem compelled to negative these suppositions.

Our own age is freely abused as an age of frivolity and mere pleasure-seeking. But these are two accusations, and they must be distinguished. To the charge of pleasure-seeking one could reply that the opportunities for pleasure are now more widely distributed, and we should be thankful that they are. Fashions in pleasure change, and change on the whole for the better. The charabanc and even the cinema are improvements upon the public-house; however it may be with other vices, there is no doubt at all that the vice of drunkenness has strikingly declined.

The charge of frivolity goes deeper, and it is perhaps justified to this extent : never, perhaps, before has so large a part of the population abandoned all interest in what the wisest of all ages have regarded as the fundamental problems of life, the problems of religion. It is not only that faith has lost its hold upon the majority of modern men and women. Even where religious feeling is deep and sincere there is, outside the ranks of professional theologians, a strong sense of the futility of the discussion of religious problems. Most of the clergy devote themselves to the 'practical Christianity' of social work; sermons have long been growing shorter and shorter.

In the mundane sphere of political philosophy one may detect the same fundamental agnosticism. At the end of the nineteenth century it looked as if a great struggle between the principles of Socialism and anti-Socialism was about to be staged; but who, outside professional controversialists, cares about 'principles of Socialism' to-day? They have been relegated to the rhetoric of political journalism. All the three political parties are faced with practical problems —unemployment and the like—and would readily apply any practical remedies if they were convinced that these remedies would do more good than harm. Whether such remedies are called or not called socialistic is a matter of little interest.

Both in politics and in religion our emphasis to-day is on practical expedients at the expense of fundamental principles. But here we may claim that we are really in earnest. Never, it seems, was there an age when more persons were actively concerned in promoting, in one way or another, the general welfare of society. Such immersion in the practical may make us, by comparison with our fathers, somewhat uninteresting both to ourselves and to posterity: but it should protect us from a too sweeping accusation of frivolity.

INDEX

237

INDEX

INDEX

INDEX

INDEX

Printed in Great Britain by
Butler & Tanner Ltd.,
Frome and London